CORNISH ROAD TRANSPORT
THROUGH TIME
Ernie Warmington

AMBERLEY PUBLISHING

This book is dedicated to Rosemary, my wife for fifty years, launched on our wedding anniversary, 30 March 2013, at the Inn For All Seasons, Redruth

First published 2013

Amberley Publishing
The Hill, Stroud
Gloucestershire, GL5 4EP

www.amberley-books.com

Copyright © Ernie Warmington, 2013

The right of Ernie Warmington to be identified as the Author of this work has been asserted in accordance with the Copyrights, Designs and Patents Act 1988.

ISBN 978 1 4456 1611 7
E-BOOK ISBN 978 1 4456 1626 1

All rights reserved. No part of this book may be reprinted or reproduced or utilised in any form or by any electronic, mechanical or other means, now known or hereafter invented, including photocopying and recording, or in any information storage or retrieval system, without the permission in writing from the Publishers.

British Library Cataloguing in Publication Data.
A catalogue record for this book is available from the British Library.

Typeset in 9.5pt on 12pt Celeste.
Typesetting by Amberley Publishing.
Printed in the UK.

Introduction

My five-year apprenticeship was with the world-famous dockyard Silly Cox & Co., Falmouth, as an engineer; this was in the 1950s, when conscription was in force. I left Falmouth on 1 June 1955, aboard a British tanker named the *British Hope*, believed to have been built in 1935. After one trip, I changed to the New Zealand Shipping Co., staying with them for nearly seven years, serving on several ships and tramping all over the world, ending up as a senior watch-keeping engineer. Then I came ashore and married. After a short while I joined the GPO, staying with them for about thirty-five years. They split Postal and Engineering. I went into Engineering, taking early retirement in 1993.

My interest in old cars came when, at home, I found an old log book for a car my father once owned – it went for scrap during the war. Looking through the *Exchange & Mart*, I found an old Austin 7 for sale in north Devon for £6 10s, towing it home and fully restoring it after about two years. On selling it, I bought several other old cars; some I still have, others have moved on. The best I ever owned was a 1903 De-Dion Bouton, doing the London to Brighton in it several times. Owning old machinery, you get to know a lot of people with the same interest, and then begin to acquire a lot of knowledge about it. When the Beaulieu Autojumble first started, I was the first one through the gates the first two years; the next year, with a friend, I had a stall and have had one ever since. One year I was interviewed on *Top Gear*, so I think I know a little about my hobby.

Acknowledgements

No matter how much you may think you know your subject, there is always someone who can help if you come across a difficult question. The following people I thank very much for their help with answers and of course photographs where most are shown here in this book, the first I have attempted to write about this fascinating hobby after almost fifty years. My thanks especially go to my wife Rosemary, who has burned the midnight oil typing the whole of the script, and for a disrupted household for six months. To anyone I may have left out, have misspelt names, dates, horse power etc., I apologise. If you have any photos, postcards, etc. and would like them included in another book, please let me borrow it to copy – it must have a Cornish number.

M. Reid, J. Smith, B. Tiddy, P. Bradley, D. Thomas, T. George, S. Veal, D. Bird, E. Jose, R. Fogg, Mr and Mrs R. Crawford, C. Bolitho, K. Kneebone, M. Caddy, C. Binney, B. Treverrow, C. G. Loader, D. Dickinson, D. Filton, Tim Harding, M. Worthington-Williams, T. Seward, R. Johns, J. Wilton, T. Watson, F. Smith, B. Williamson, J. Warburton, Mr and Mrs J. Turner, M. Callaway, T. Hoskin, R. Lewis, G. St John, S. Croall, R. Bunt, J. Rhodes, A. Bowyer, R. Grimley, J. Stover, Mr and Mrs Johns, R. Smith and K. Warren.

William Murdoch was born in Scotland in 1754. Aged 23, he went to Birmingham to work for Boulton & Watt. They saw Murdoch's ability and he was promoted to the company's most important area, Cornwall. He moved into a cottage in Cross Street, Redruth, establishing his office and workshop there; he was paid 20s a week (miners earned far less). In 1785 he married Anne Paynter, a Redruth mine owner's daughter, who bore him several children. Five years later, she died giving birth. Twelve months earlier, he had invented a three-wheeled carriage which he used to go between the Cornish tin mines, the vehicle consisting of a copper boiler, a spirit lamp and a fire box with a flue. It had a double-acting cylinder, two driving wheels and a tiller steering wheel, almost like a tricycle with a bench seat. The first trial run, on a dark night in 1784, was in a long, narrow lane with high Cornish hedges leading to the rectory of Redruth parish church. Murdoch filled the boiler, lit the lamp with shaking hands and waited for the steam to rise. When the critical moment arrived, the engine shot forward, outrunning the inventor, who was left behind in the dark. Hearing cries for help, he caught up and discovered the rector, 'puffing and snorting', shouting that he had seen the 'evil eye' in person. So an age-old problem was solved, the first self-propelled vehicle had been invented and tested and there was no need for horses to be used to get about on. During his working life in Cornwall, Murdoch also invented gas lighting, which he used in his cottage. William Murdoch died in 1839 and is buried at Handsworth parish church, Birmingham. Nothing now remains of the Murdoch Flyer except a small model; however, a small, happy band of hard-working, enthusiastic engineers have constructed a full-size working replica.

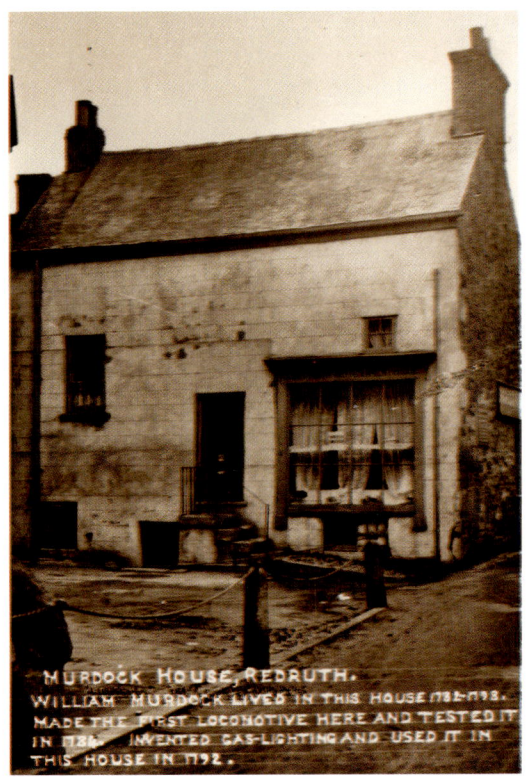

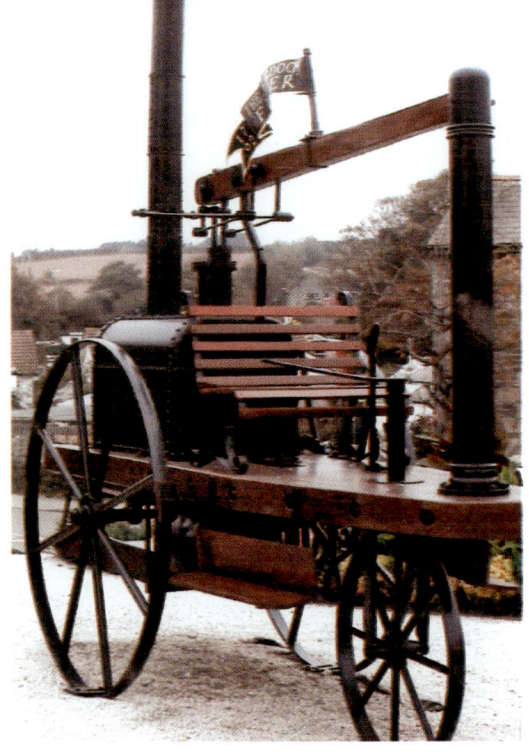

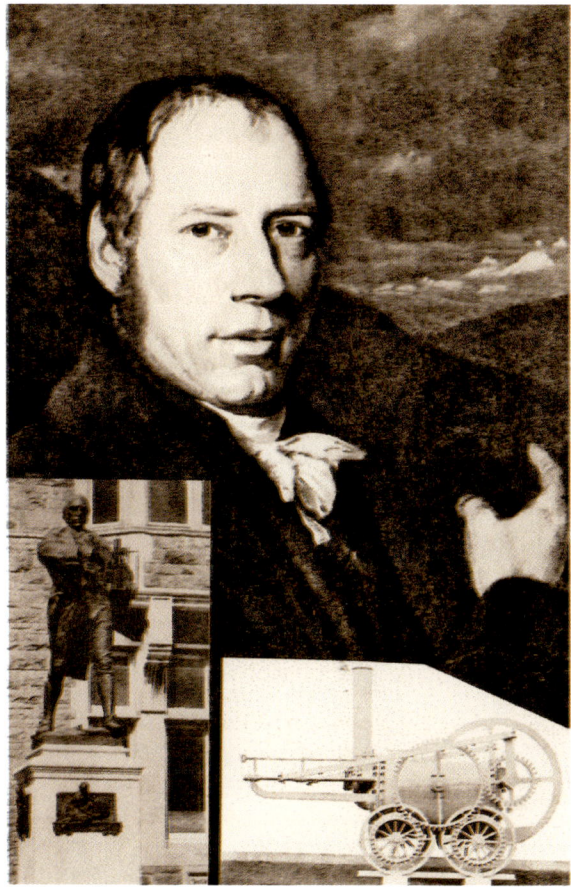

Richard Trevithick, the Cornish Pioneer, was born in 1771 at Tregajorran, the second-youngest and only son in a family of eight. His father was a mine captain, his mother a miner's daughter. At the age of 12, he would spend a considerable amount of time watching William Murdoch experimenting with the new-fangled steam-powered road locomotion. Until then, steam engines were of the low-pressure type. Richard's first job was at East Stray Park Mine; unusually for a young person, he was soon promoted to a consultant. Realising that high-pressure steam would move a piston in an engine, he set about building full-size locomotives. In 1801, he built his best one, naming it the *Puffing Devil*. On 24 December that year, he successfully carried several men up the long and steep Camborne Hill. In 1808 Trevithick built a new locomotive called *Catch Me Who Can* and ran it on a circular track in London, charging 1s for admission, including a ride. However, the response was disappointing, so he abandoned it. While recovering from bankruptcy and a bout of Typhoid Fever, he designed the Cornish Boiler. In 1812 he designed and built the Cornish Engine, the most efficient in the world at the time. Installing this high-pressure engine in a threshing machine made it cheaper to run than using horses. Trevithick died in 1833. The top image shows Trevithick with one of his engines adapted to run on rails. His statue was unveiled in 1932 by Prince George (later to become king) outside the public library in Camborne. The bottom picture shows a replica of Trevithick's road vehicle.

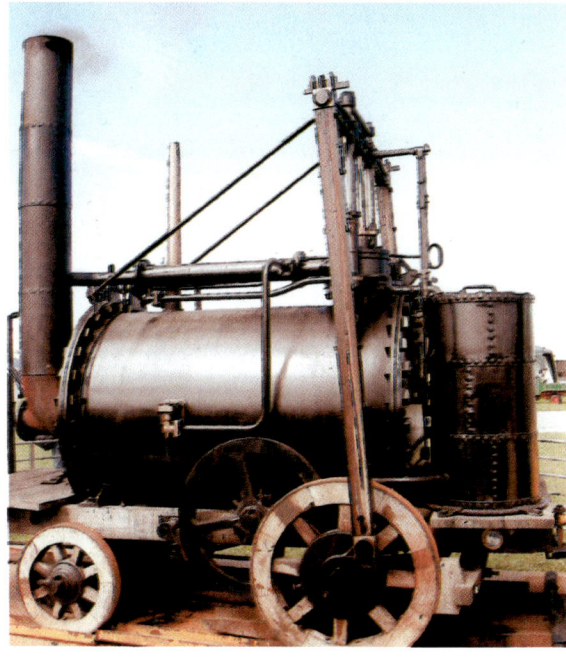

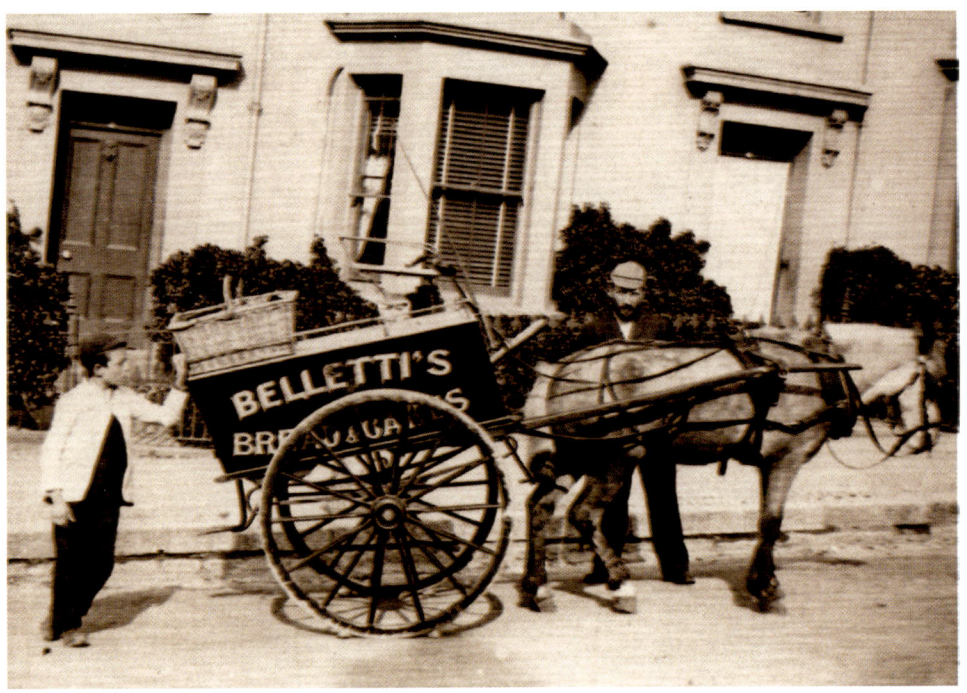

Snapped in a Falmouth street, this horse is seen having a deserved rest. Belletti's staff have stopped delivering their bread and cakes on their normal round. The cart seems to be on a funny angle; perhaps when the driver takes his seat, it may straighten up a little.

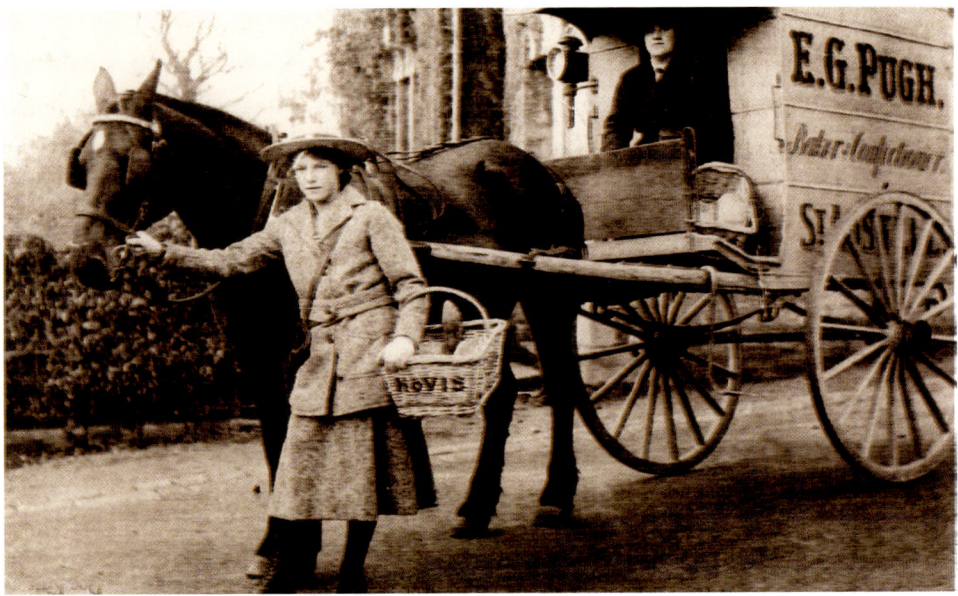

A St Austell baker and confectioner, E. G. Pugh, allowed this lady driver and young lady assistant to pause so the photographer could take this lovely photograph, an every-day early scene. Perhaps they were expected to work a long day selling the Hovis bread because the cart is equipped with candle lamps.

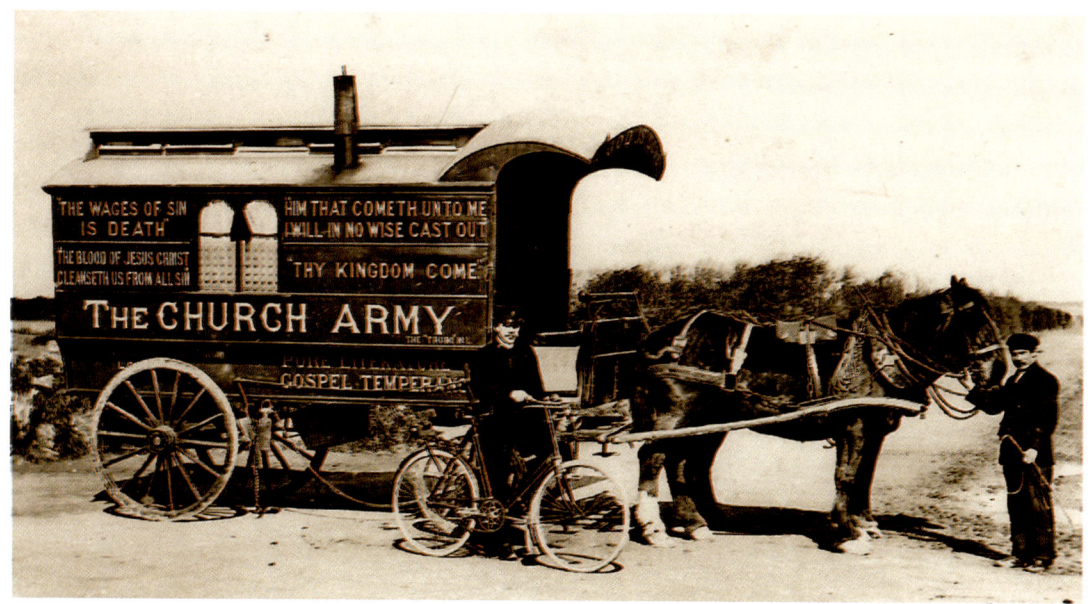

'The wages of sin is death, him that cometh unto me I will in no wise cast out, The blood of Jesus Christ cleanseth us from all our sins. "Thy Kingdom Come" Truro, No. 1 Pure literature Gospel Temperance.' So the printing says on the side of this horse-drawn religious wagon. It looks somewhat like a gypsy caravan with a wood-burning stove inside. Looking at the safety bicycle which the lady is holding helps to date this postcard to about 1910. On the back of the postcard, it says the photograph was taken near Sithney, Helston.

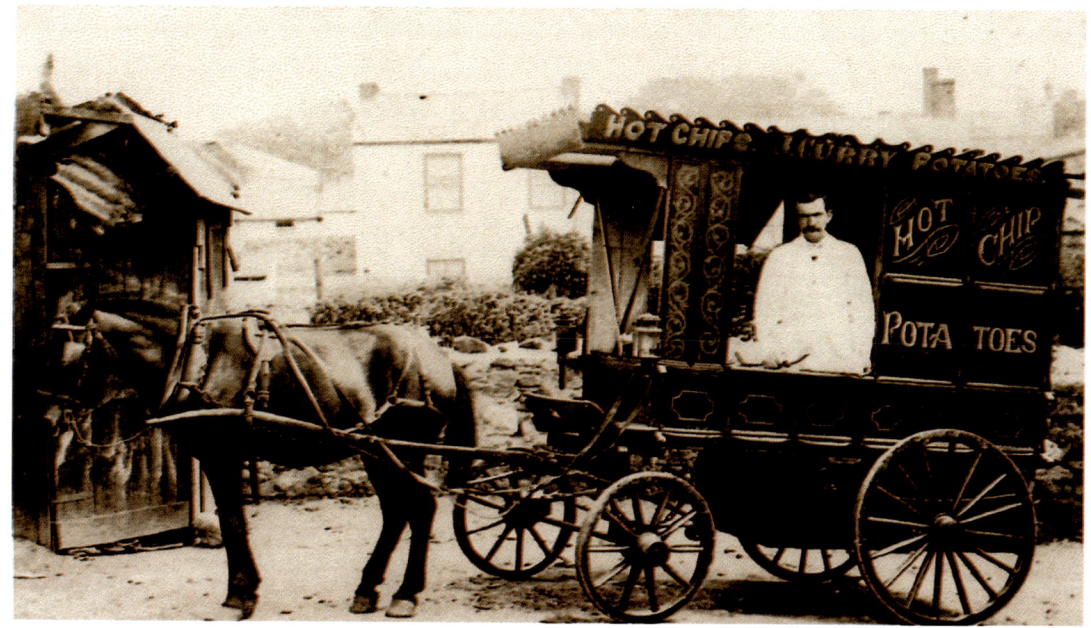

Mr Curry of Redruth is seen here with his little pony and his lovely painted potato wagon in about 1910. Used at night, the cart has candle lamps to get home with. I hope the tumbledown shack is not the pony's stable; if so, he needs to sell more hot potatoes. Anyone for curry and chips?

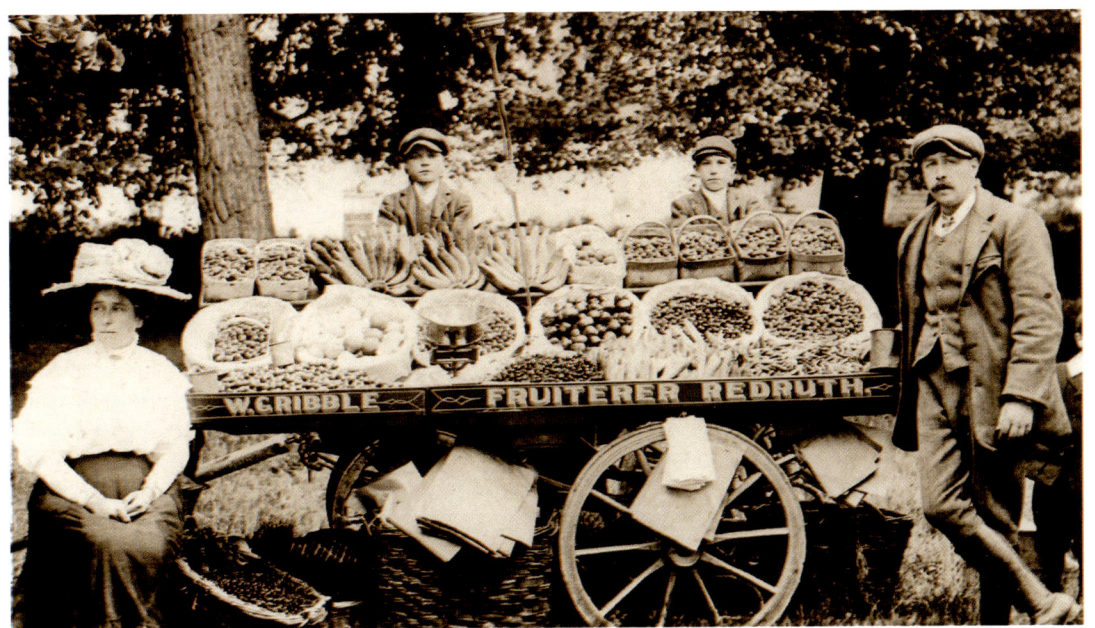

William Gribble, his wife and two young men are seen with their wonderfully turned out fruit and nut stall at an event in Redruth in about 1910 – even the brass scales have had a good clean. With not much in the way of cold storage in those days, the fruit had to be sold, although the nuts on display did not. Let's hope they had a good day, even though the lady isn't smiling and is looking in another direction.

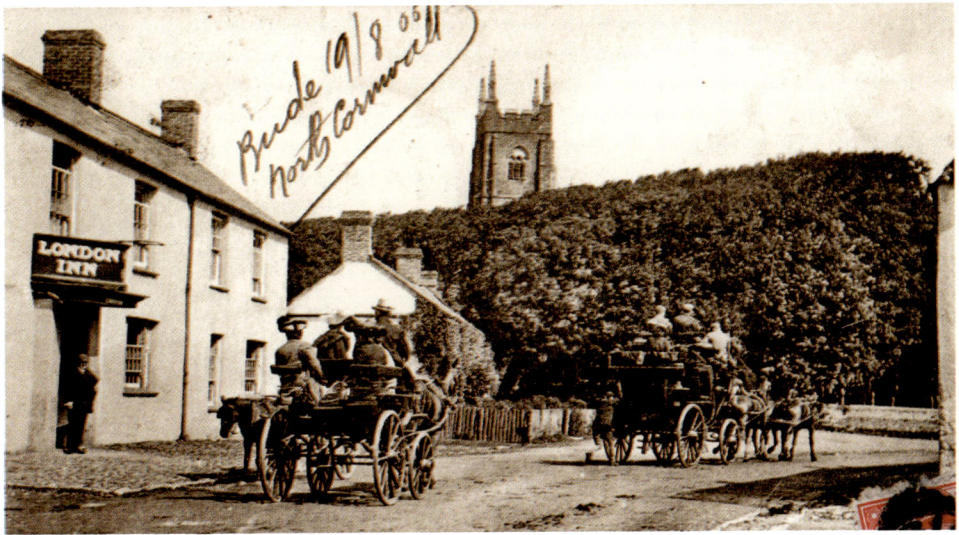

This postcard, posted 20 August 1906 in Bude, shows a coach and pair with passengers and a man either running behind or trying to get a free lift. He is being watched by another horse-drawn wagon with four well-dressed people aboard and a spare horse on the pavement outside the London Inn. The postcard was sent to Paris; written in French, it said the sender was having a good time in Cornwall, the weather was good and wished they were there!

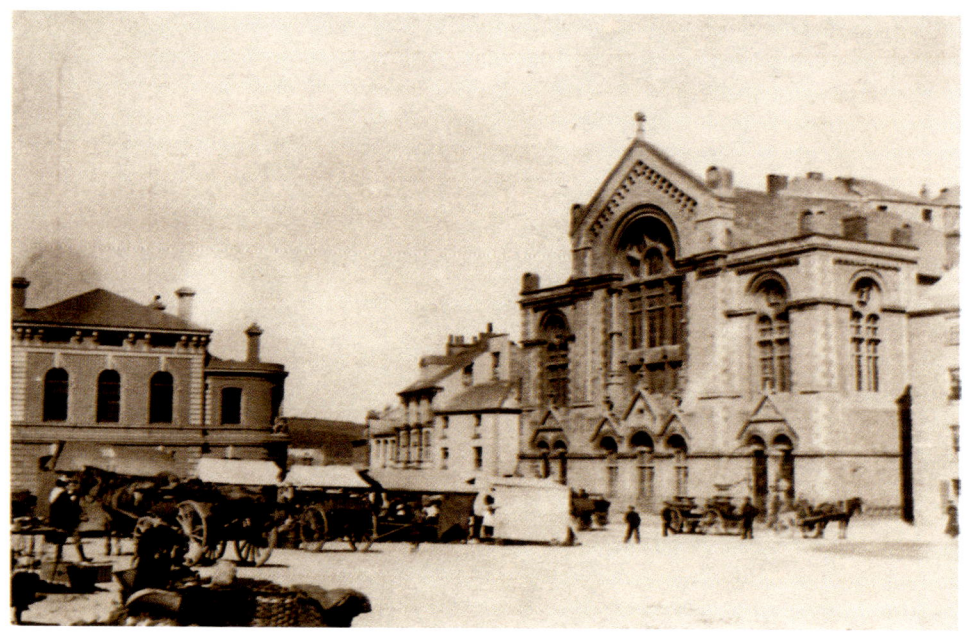

This early photograph of Falmouth Moor, taken on what could well be a lovely sunny day in about 1900, shows horses and carts and what look like several market stalls. To the right, outside the Methodist church, at the bottom of the steps known as Jacob's Ladder, is a carriage perhaps waiting to be hired. In the left hand corner is an early weighing machine with baskets behind it. Is it for weighing fruit and vegetables, or, being a port, might they contain fish?

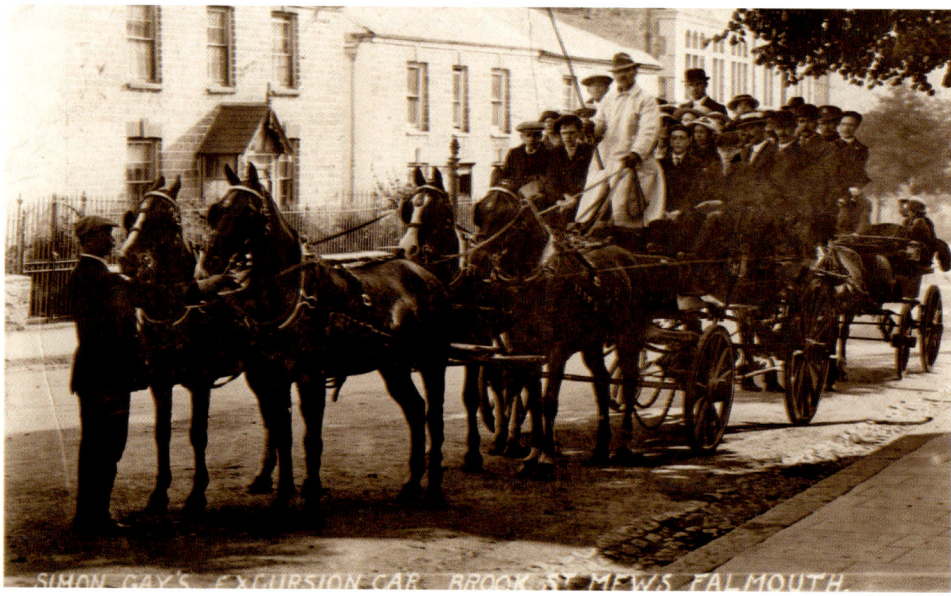

Dated 5 February 1921 and posted from Falmouth to Helston, this lovely Bragg postcard shows a crowded carriage and four horses, known as an excursion car, belonging to Simon Gay (possibly the driver in the white coat). It is leaving Brook Street Mews, Falmouth, for an unknown destination.

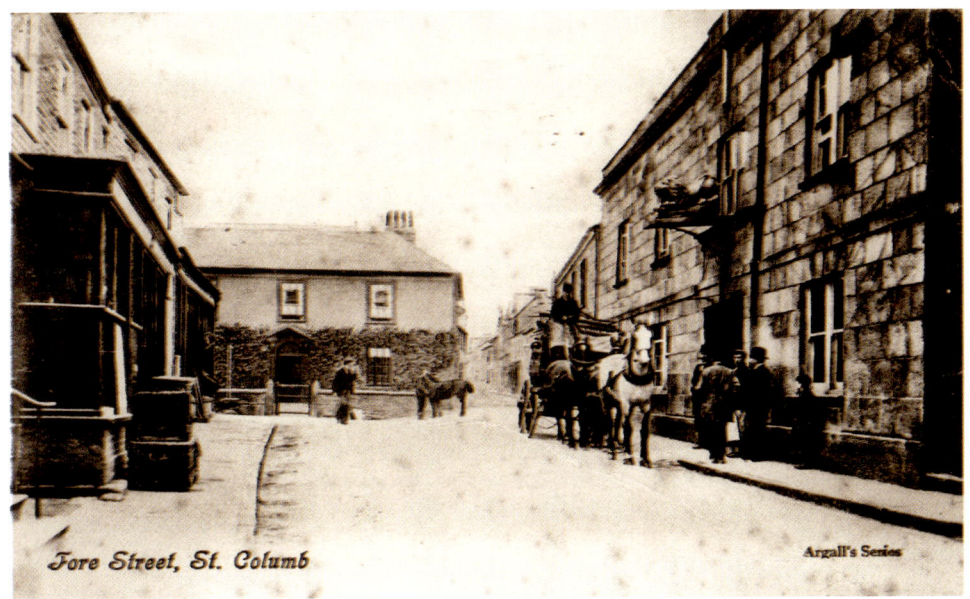

From the Argalls series, this is Fore Street, St Columb Major. Posted to Guildford, Surrey, in 1906, this postcard shows a North Cornwall stagecoach and three horses arriving at the Red Lion Inn. A stone carving of a lion sits over the doorway and a few people are gathered nearby. The shops opposite look to be busy with the wicker or wooden boxes that are on display. I wonder if one of the horses is about to be replaced?

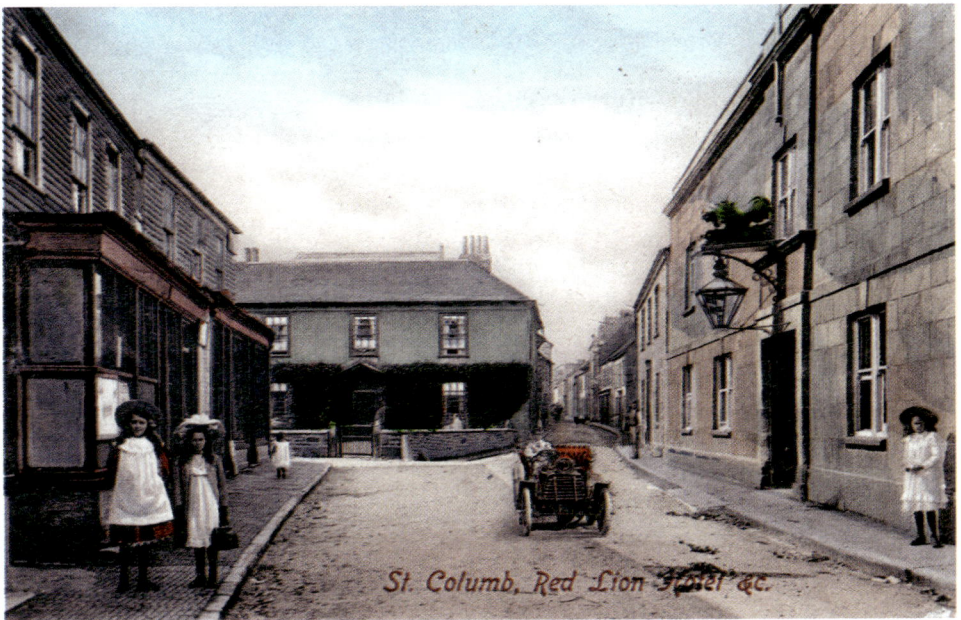

Moving on a few years, this is the same location in about 1910, only the wicker baskets have been replaced with two little girls. The one horse in the background has been replaced with a superimposed car of at least 6 hp; the coach and horses have gone, although the manure has not; and a large lamp is now above the main door.

RED LION Family, Tourist & Commercial HOTEL
ST. COLUMB — W. EYLES, Proprietor

Arrangements made for Tourists to Bedruthan Steps, Vale of Lanherne, Mawgan Convent, Newquay, King Arthur's Castle, Tintagel, Boscastle, and other romantic scenery on the North Coast

TELEPHONE No. 8.   BILLIARDS.   MOTOR GARAGE

Posting in all its Branches. Omnibus meets every train at St. Columb Road Station
The North Cornwall Coach from Newquay to Wadebridge daily, stops here on outward and return journey

Motor Char-a-Banc to and from Truro, Wednesday and Saturday

Moving on again, this advertisement was placed in a Kelly's Directory in 1919 when W. Eyles was the proprietor. The omnibus meets the train at St Columb Road Station and a Motor Char-a-Banc goes to and from Truro but only on a Wednesday and Saturday.

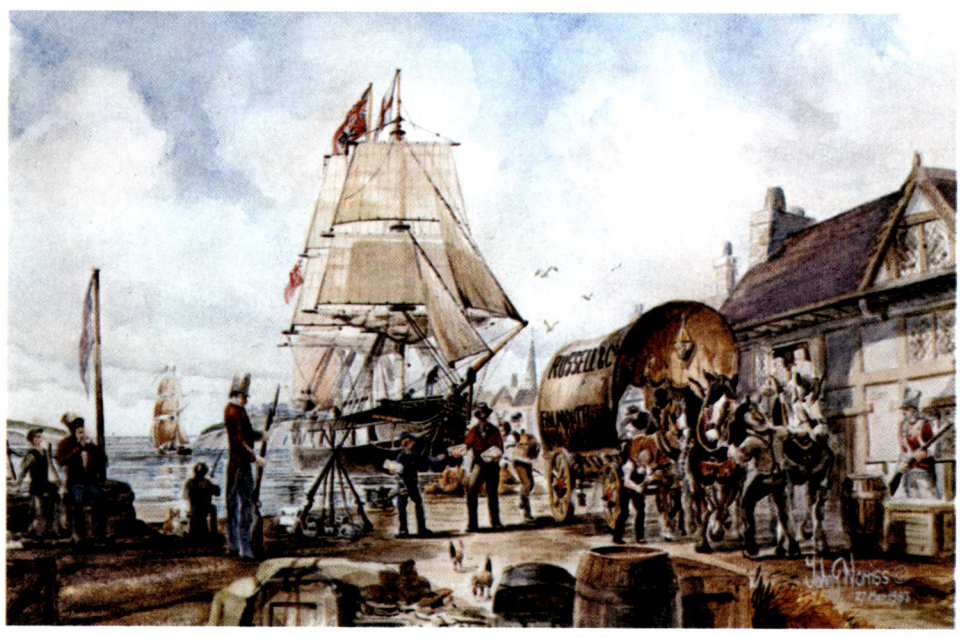

The Falmouth Packet Ship *Francis Freeling*, under the command of Captain James Cunningham, having run the gauntlet of the Spanish vessels, is about to offload mail from the Americas (North and South) as well as gold bullion to Russell's horse-drawn wagon in Falmouth Harbour in 1817. The Falmouth Packet Station was established in 1689 and during the 100 years that followed it grew in importance, providing new services to the West Indies. The *Francis Freeling* successfully fought off American privateers to ensure that the mail and bullion did not fall into the wrong hands. The ship also flies a special flag called 'Post Boy Jack' showing a rider blowing a posthorn to identify herself as a Packet Ship. While the gold is being transferred, several Redcoats are standing by with loaded muskets.

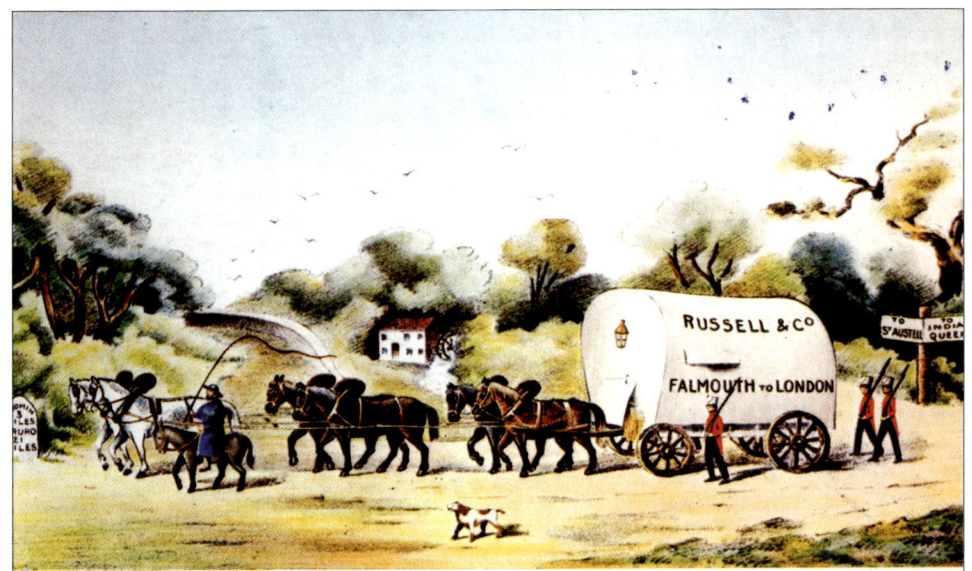

LEAVING THE OFFICES, KILLIGREW STREET EVERY MONDAY AT NOON, AND ARRIVING AT THE CASTLE AND FALCON INN, ALDERSGATE STREET, LONDON, ON THE FOLLOWING SATURDAY JUNE, 1833.

This postcard is not quite what it seems. Although it is captioned as travelling from Falmouth to London every Monday etc., this Russell & Co. Covered horse-drawn wagon with its escort of red-jacketed soldiers is in fact returning to Falmouth, having come over lonely Bodmin Moor and Indian Queens in 1833.

A receipt for 19s 10d, dated 6 August 1832, for goods carried by Russell & Co. every day to all parts of the west of England. The VAN on SPRINGS with GUARDS travels at the rate of SIX MLES an HOUR and has LARGE CHESTS secured for the safety of SMALL PARCELS.

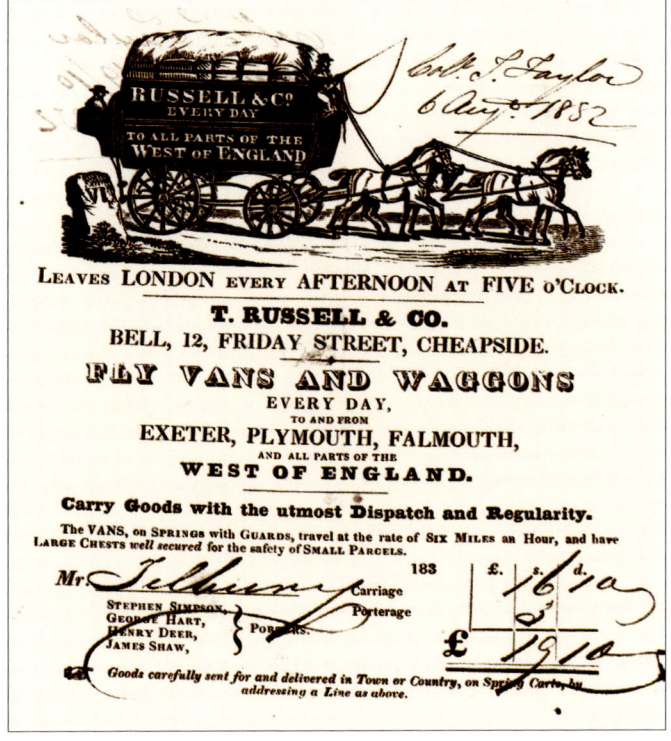

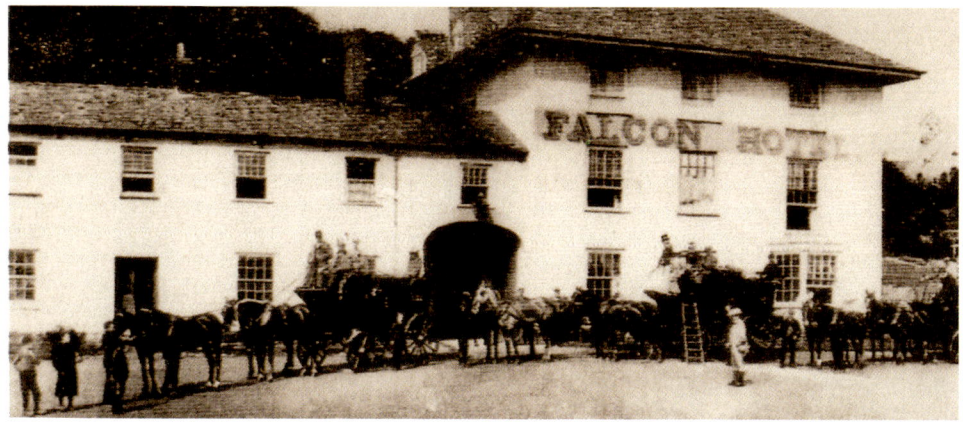

The old Falcon Hotel picture depicts stagecoaches departing for or returning from Holsworthy, Bideford or Tintagel in about 1885.

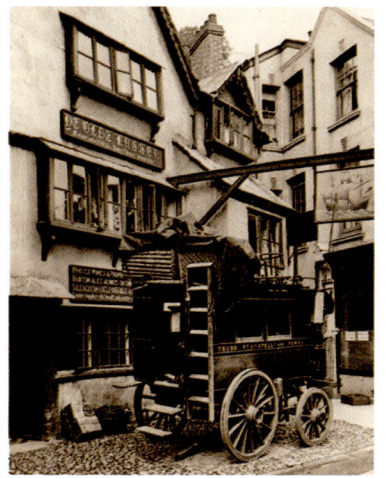

From about 1880 to the start of the First World War, Williams Mitchell of Truro was the proprietor of a horse bus that ran a regular service for two days a week from Truro via St Austell to Fowey, where it remained overnight before returning to Truro the following day. It is seen here at Ye Olde Lugger, Fowey. Entry to the warm and dry inside of the coach is from the back, and the ladder is presumably to place fare-paying passengers in the cold and wet and any luggage on the top.

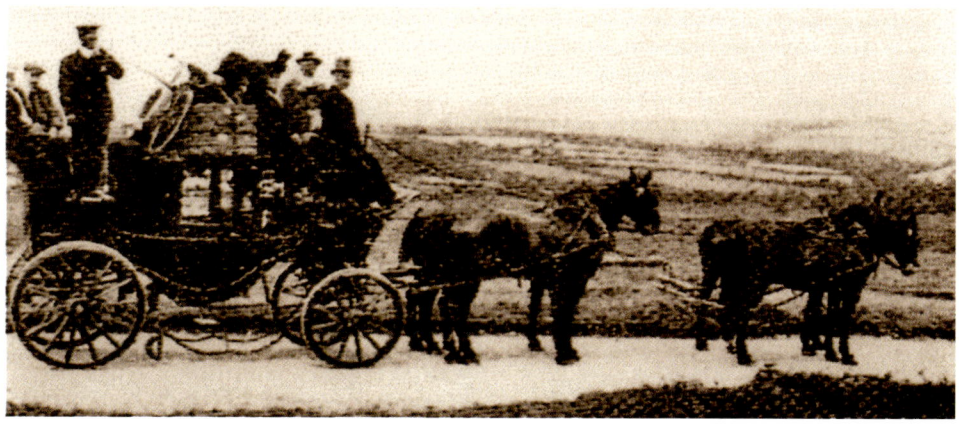

This photograph, taken in about 1900, shows a North Cornwall coach and four crossing Bodmin Moor. Is that a bicycle it seems to be carrying? No-one can be seen inside – perhaps it is too hot!

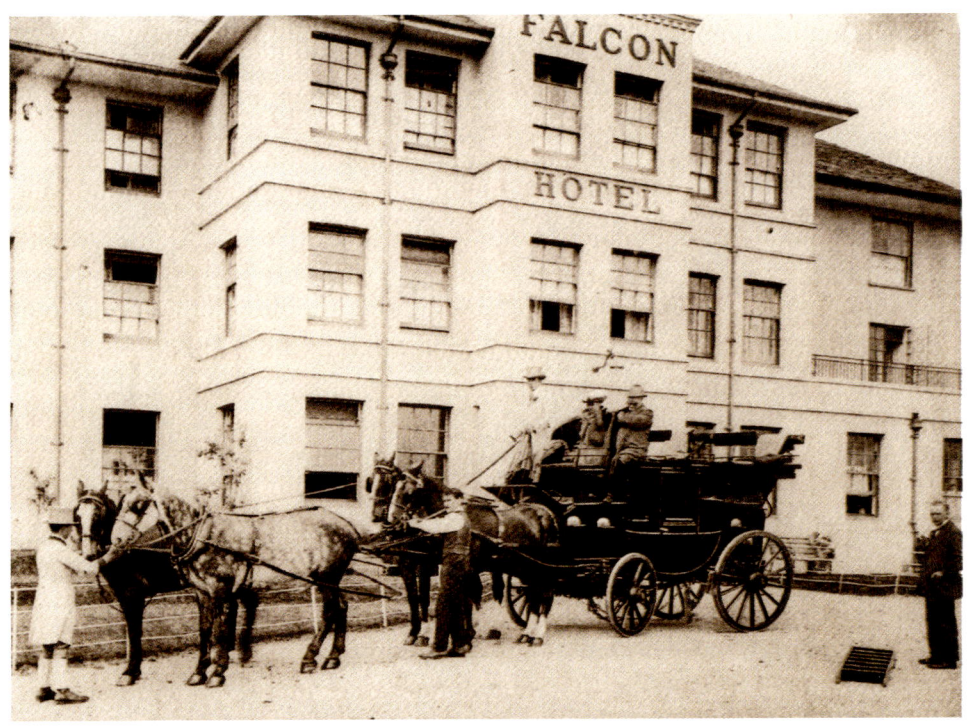

Stagecoaches first made their appearance in Cornwall at the beginning of the nineteenth century; here we see two examples. The first one, above, from about 1900, is seen outside the Falcon Hotel at Bude, near the Bude Canal and a short distance from the lovely sandy beaches. The coach and four are being held steady by a coachman, perhaps waiting for the passengers. As many as possible were squeezed inside the coach, paying twice as much as the ones riding outside. Still in North Cornwall, the lower picture shows another coach and four outside the Wellington Hotel, Boscastle, in about 1913.

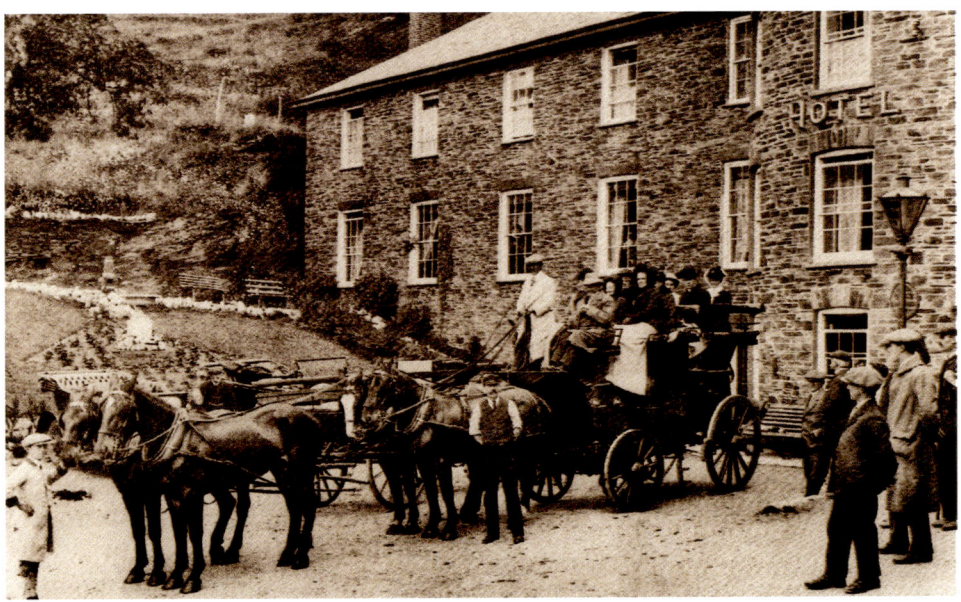

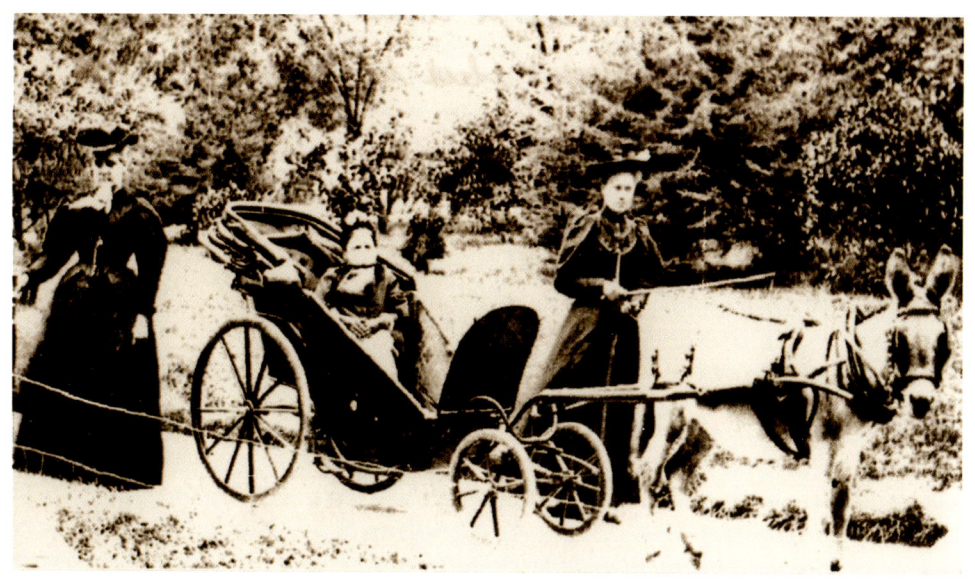

With two hand maidens in attendance, Mrs Cox is being taken for a ride in her donkey cart in about 1890. Either a servant or a relation, one lady in a long flowing dress is either holding a whip or perhaps an encouragement for the animal to move. Whichever it is, no-one seems to be pleased with the situation.

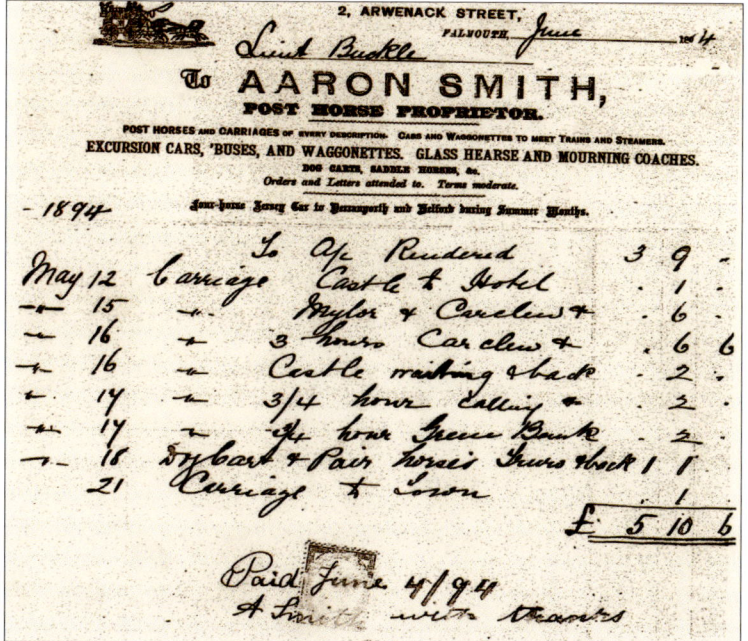

An invoice dated June 1894 from Aaron Smith to Lieutenant Buckle at Pendennis Castle for the cost of hiring a carriage from Pendennis Castle to Greenbank Hotel, to Mylor and Carclew House, waiting three quarters of an hour, etc. It is signed over a stamp by the owner.

REDRUTH AND HAYLE TURNPIKE.

NOTICE IS HEREBY GIVEN, that the TOLLS arising at the several Toll Gates on the said line of road, will be LET by Public AUCTION, at the Savings Bank, Redruth, on *Friday, the 8th day of November* next, at 11 o'clock in the Forenoon, in the manner directed by Act 3rd George Fourth, which Tolls produced the last year the undermentioned sum, over and above the expence of collecting them that is to say, Blowing House Gate, Tuckingmill Gate, Treswithian Gate, Connor Downs Gate, and Copper House Gate, with the bars and chains thereunto attached, the sum of £1204, and will be set up at that sum for one year from 31st December next.

Whoever happens to be the best bidder and taker of said Tolls, will be required to pay one month's rent in advance of the sum agreed on, and be prepared with sufficient sureties to be present (or by letter signifying their consent) to the satisfaction of the Trustees for the payment of the rest of the money monthly in advance, and to abide by such other conditions as shall be stated at the letting

And Notice is hereby further given, that the Trustees will, on the same day, proceed to the discharge of the general business of the Trust.

HENRY ROWE, Clerk.

Dated 3rd October, 1867.

REDRUTH AND HAYLE TURNPIKE ROAD.

WHEREAS no bidding was made on the 8th inst., for the Tolls arising at the several Toll-gates on the above line of road, NOTICE IS HEREBY GIVEN, that the said TOLLS will be SET up again for one year from the 31st day of December next, at a meeting of the Trustees, to be holden at the Savings Bank, Redruth, on Friday, the 13th day of December next at Eleven o'clock in the Forenoon, in the manner directed by an Act passed in the fourth year of the reign of his Majesty George the Fourth, for "Regulating Turnpike Roads,"—which Tolls produced the last year, that is to say,

Blowing House Gate....
Tuckingmill Gate......
Treswithian Gate...... The sum of £1,204 0 0
Connor Downs Gate....
Copper House Gate....

and will be put up at that sum, or such other sum as the Trustees may decide on at such meeting.

Whoever becomes the taker of such Tolls will be required to produce security to the satisfaction of the Trustees, such sureties to be present, or a letter under their hands to be produced for the payment of the money monthly in advance, the first payment to be made at such taking, and also to abide such other conditions as shall then be produced.

And NOTICE IS HEREBY FURTHER GIVEN, that the Trustees, at said meeting, will proceed to discharge the general business of the Trust.

By order of the Trustees,

HENRY ROWE, Clerk.

Dated 11th November, 1867.

Turnpike Road Notices

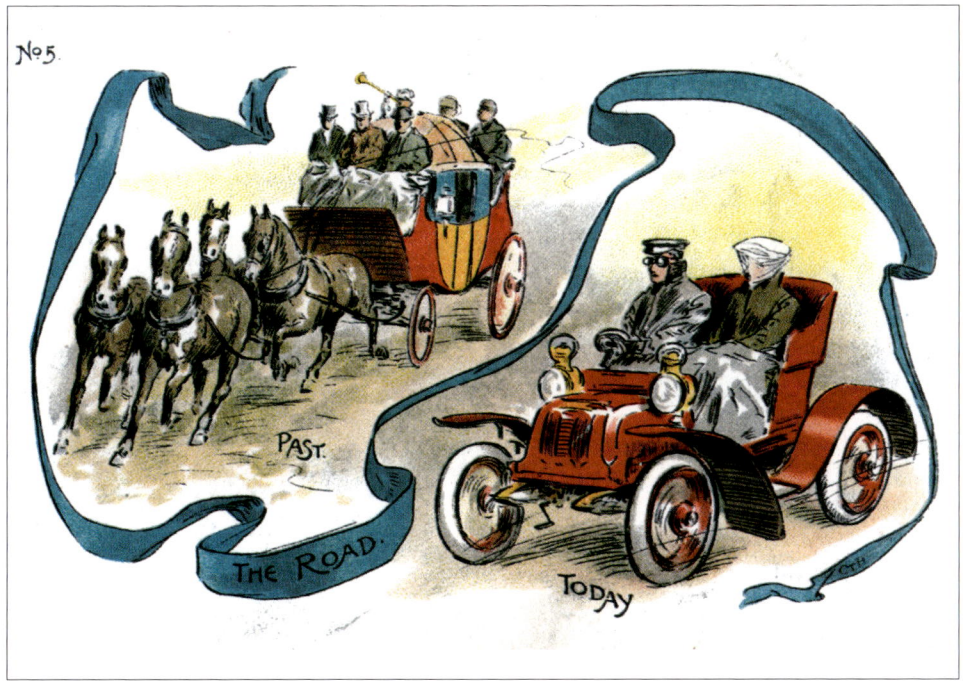

Past and Today – a postcard from the turn of the twentieth century.

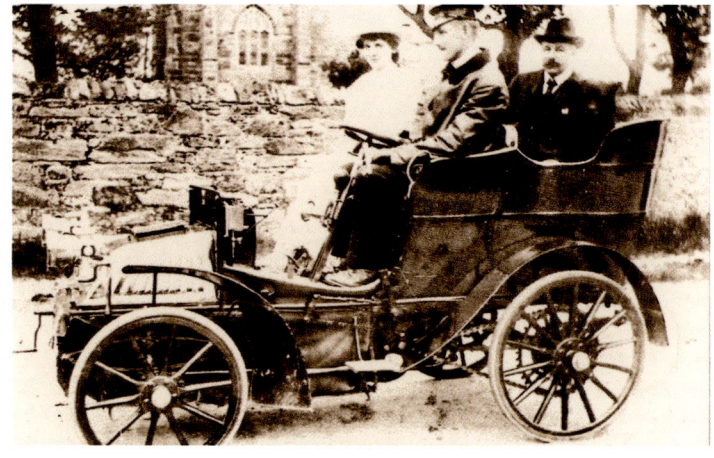

In the early twentieth century the first cars came to Cornwall. This left-hand drive Benz of 7hp, registered AF1, was owned by Dr Downing of Newlyn East, near Newquay. Dr Downing can be seen sitting in the back; his daughter is sitting alongside the chauffeur, Richard Oxnan. The car had a chain drive to the back wheels, which had solid tyres, and a coal scuttle bonnet with a starting handle; the oil drip feed can be seen on the dashboard with a horn on the steering column. There was no windscreen, and no protection against the weather. This picture was taken outside St Newlyn East parish church.

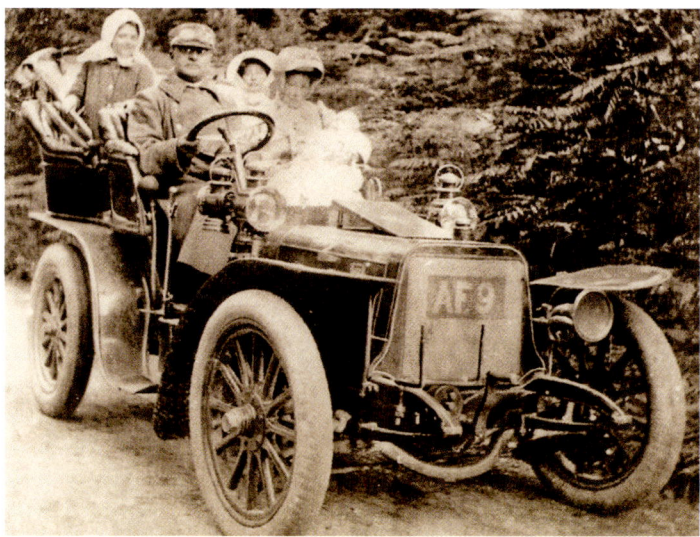

The Rich family is seen out for a ride in their car, an American-designed Duryea built in Britain under licence. Registered AF9, this was a large four-seater of 12 hp with an enormous folding hood, but no windscreen. I think it's of about 1908, but with a 1903 Cornish registration. 1903 is a bit too early for the long horn – the bulb is near his elbow and the other end is under the near-side front mudguard. The tyres are large, almost balloon type; if so, they would be pumped up to at least twice the pressure of today's tyres.

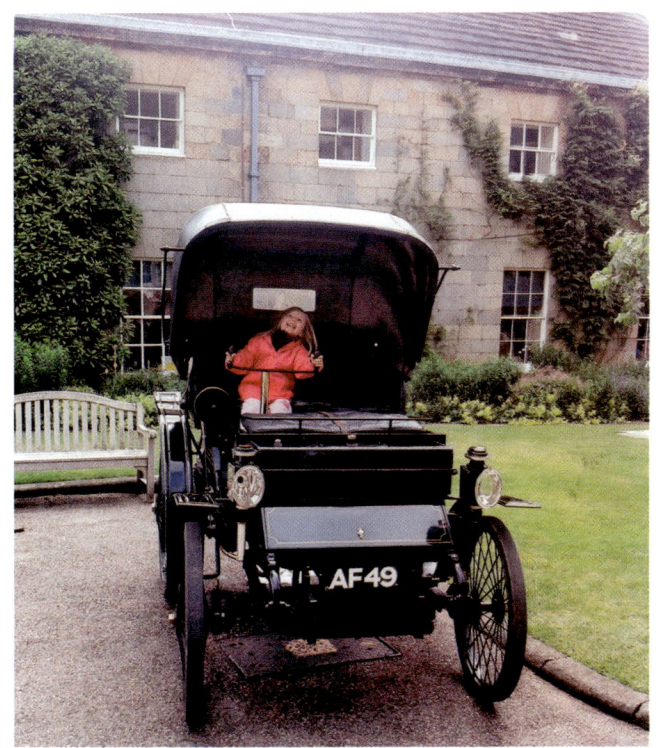

A beautifully restored 2-cylinder, 6 hp Peugeot of 1898 owned by Chris Loder, registered AF49; a lovely young lady is seen here struggling with the tiller steering. This car is running on wire wheels with solid rubber tyres. The model is known as a vis-á-vis four seater because the driver has to look over the shoulder of the person sitting in front of them. The candle lamps have been restored to perfection, with the reflectors silvered. I think perhaps the mirror is a necessary extra. The hood gives protection from behind but the Brighton road rain can beat straight at you.

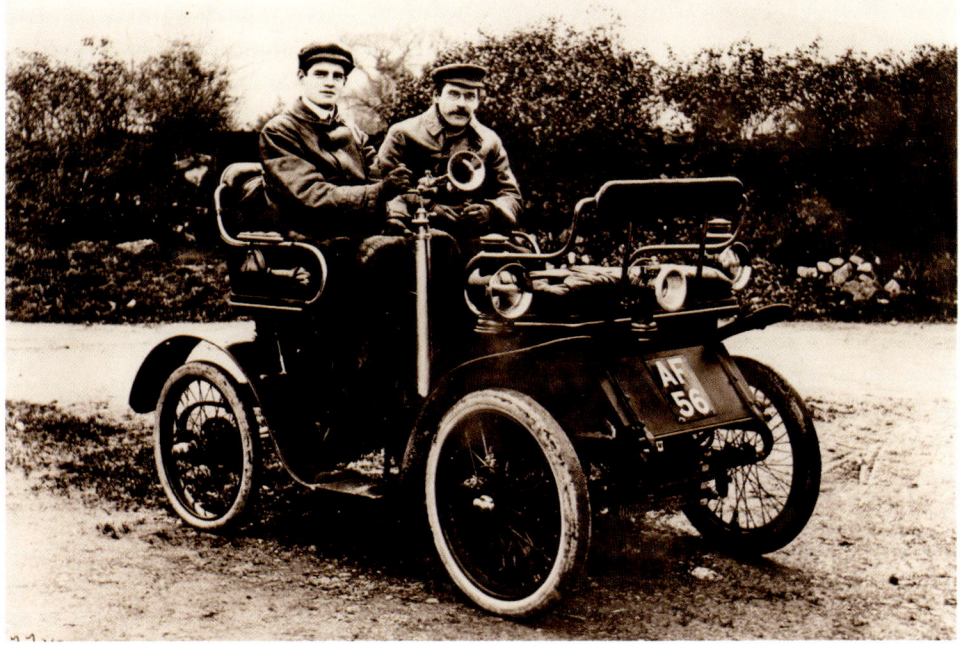

Dr A. Gregor of Overdale, Penryn, owns and drives this 1904 De Dion-Bouton vis-á-vis with tiller steering on wire wheels. For night driving, the car has three forward-facing oil lamps. This De Dion carries its own make of engine of 4½ hp. AF 56 has its sound of approaching attached to the steering column.

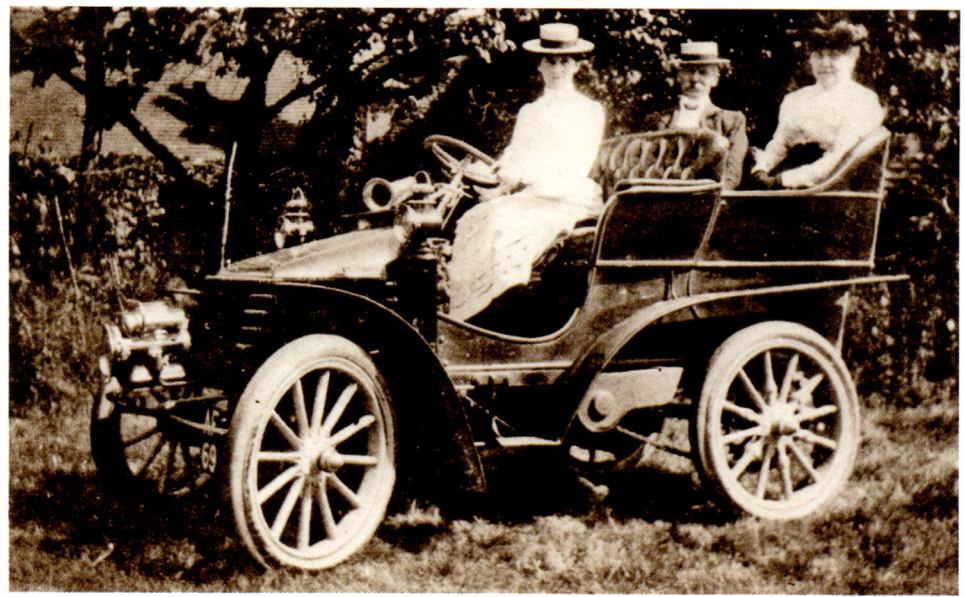

The first Wolseley motor car, a three-wheeler, was made by Herbert Austin in 1897. From 1901 to 1914, the company was known as Wolseley Tool & Motor Co. Ltd. In the top picture, the owner of this vehicle, Thomas Blamey of Veryan, is seen sitting in the back seat. AF 69 produced 8 hp and was a four-seater, painted green with a yellow lining. The lady in the driver's seat could well be his daughter. The car had a chain drive to the rear wheels, two oil side lights and a huge acetylene lamp to the front. AF 85 was a similar car, owned by Dr Bertie James Mayne. Dated 1906, the car's registration was transferred from a 1904 7 hp Star. Sitting in the driving seat is the doctor's mechanic and chauffeur. Another beautiful old motor car.

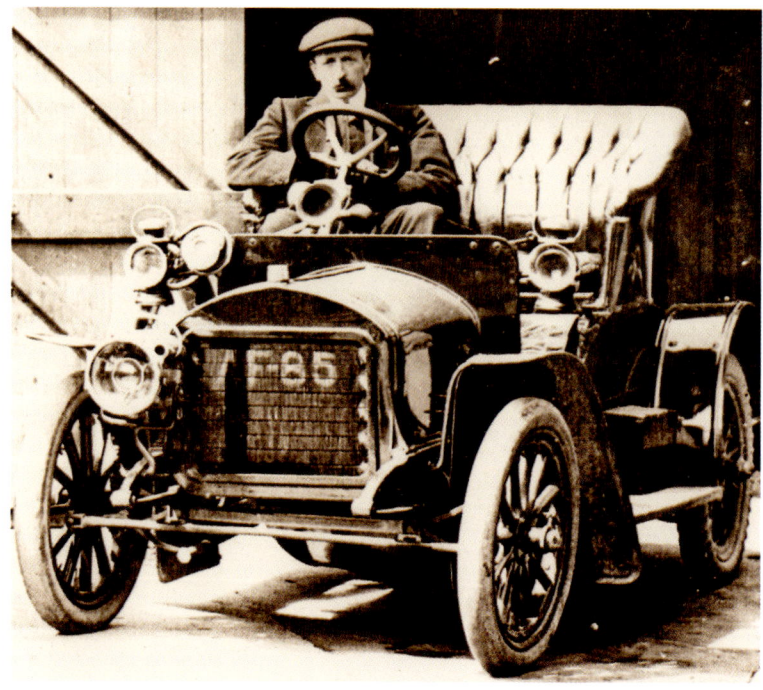

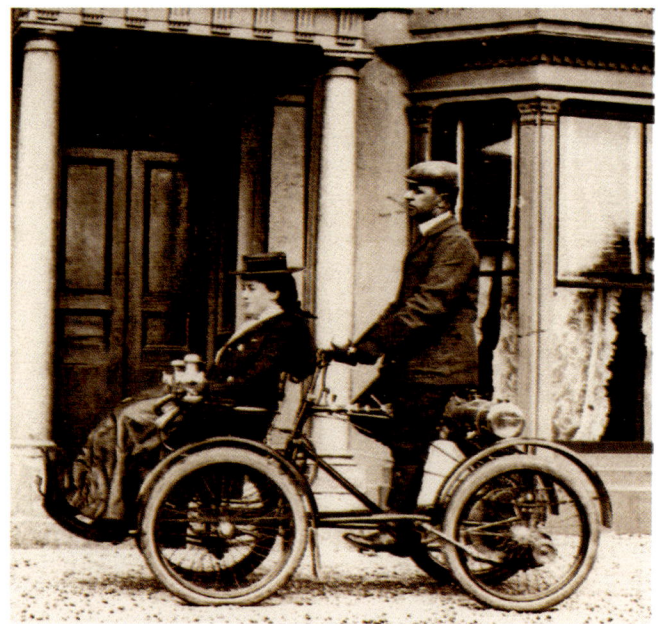

A 2¾ hp De Dion engine Progress Quadcycle, AF 77 was registered in April 1904 by Fred Rich, Tolgus, Redruth. Progress started making cycles, as did a lot of other firms of that era. The pretty young lady is sitting in the front seat known as the 'mother-in-law's seat' because it was the one nearest the accident if you were unlucky to have one. With no protection whatsoever, it must have been unpleasant driving in the rain. The company went into liquidation in 1903.

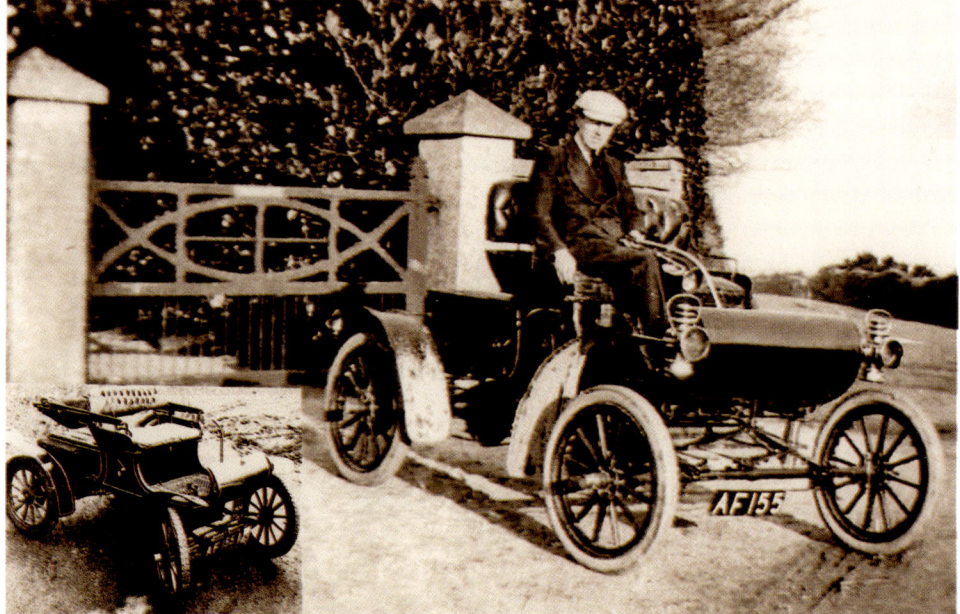

Physician and surgeon Charles Edward Abbot of Roche, St Austell, was the first registered keeper of this Oldsmobile with its curved dash. AF 155 was a replacement for the pony and trap, simple to drive and very reliable. This image was taken in 1905, when it was almost new; current owner Andrew Smith of Cheshire would one day like to take it back to Cornwall, where the house and gates still stand. Inset is the same car, with the added luxury of a hood without any lamps or hooter. While on display at Brooklands during the Second World War, it was severely damaged; gathered in a number of tea chests, the owner restored the car in the early 1950s. Made in Michigan, USA, this car produced 5 hp and had tiller steering; the starting handle was beneath the driver's seat.

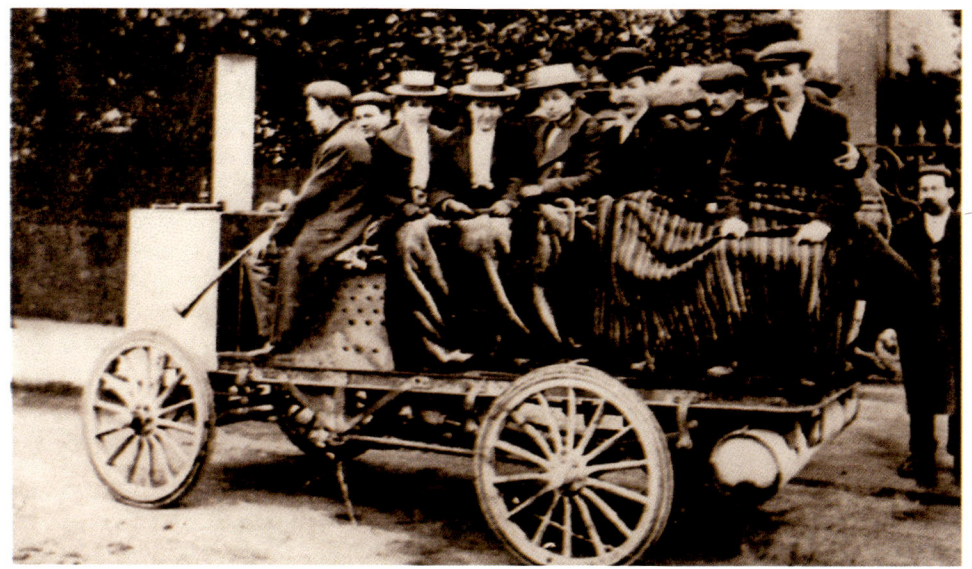

Vivian Bickford, born April 1870 in Camborne, graduated from Cambridge University in 1892. After getting married he set up a business as a liquid fuel apparatus manufacturer. The new craze for motorised transport interested him, so in 1901 he constructed his own vehicle, known as the Okodyne. Later the same year he built his first steam lorry, naming it Pyrodyne. A local newspaper reported that he made trial runs in the town in his 'home made motor car' because motor vehicles were not licensed until 1 January 1904. The first registration for a Pyrodyne was AF 145, on 12 July 1905; spelt as 'Pyrodene' with an 'e' not a 'y', it was described as a 12 hp steam wagon with a flat platform, 19.5 cwt, painted dark red and licenced to the Bickford Smith Fuse Works, Tuckingmill, Camborne. The second was AF 182, registered on 13 February 1906 as before: a flat platform with rail, 12 hp, 35 cwt unladen weight, dark green. Another two steam wagons were produced as well as the Okodyne, registered AF 24. By 1906 Bickford had ceased to produce vehicles but had opened the Bickford Motor Company in both Basset Road and Pendarves Road, Camborne. By 1912 the company ceased trading and on 23 April the entire stock was auctioned. Vivian Bickford died in 1918, aged only 48.

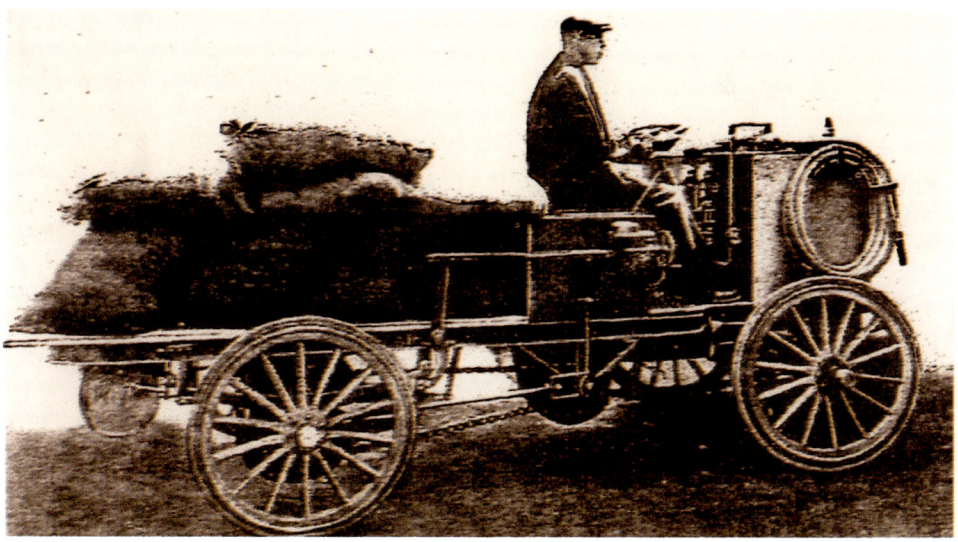

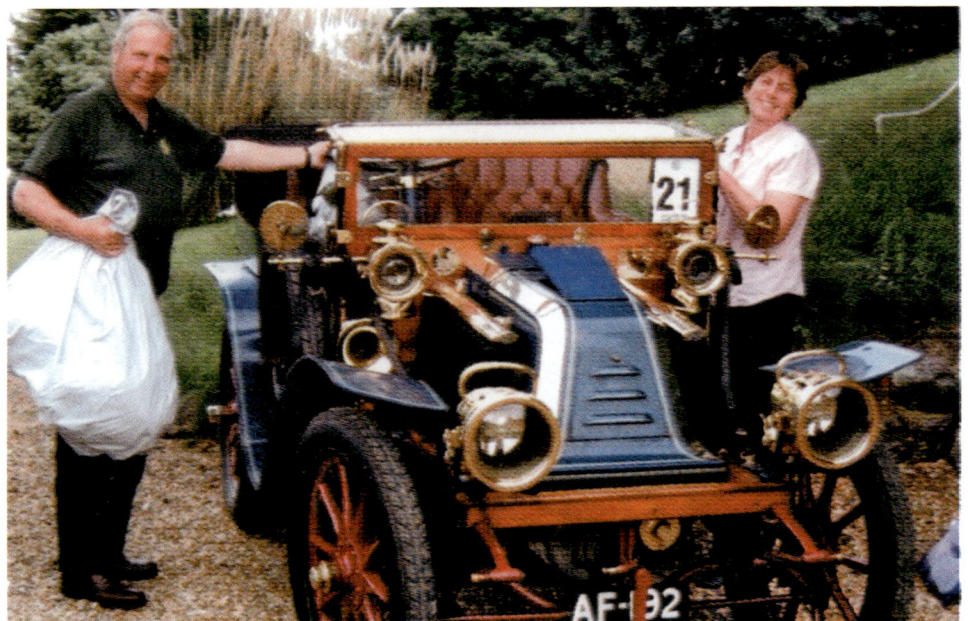

This French-made Renault twin-cylinder 10 hp tonneau, AF 192, belongs to Mr and Mrs Watson. This wonderful veteran car has taken part in many London to Brighton runs as well as club rallies. The brassware must have required a lot of elbow grease – it's well turned out and a credit to them.

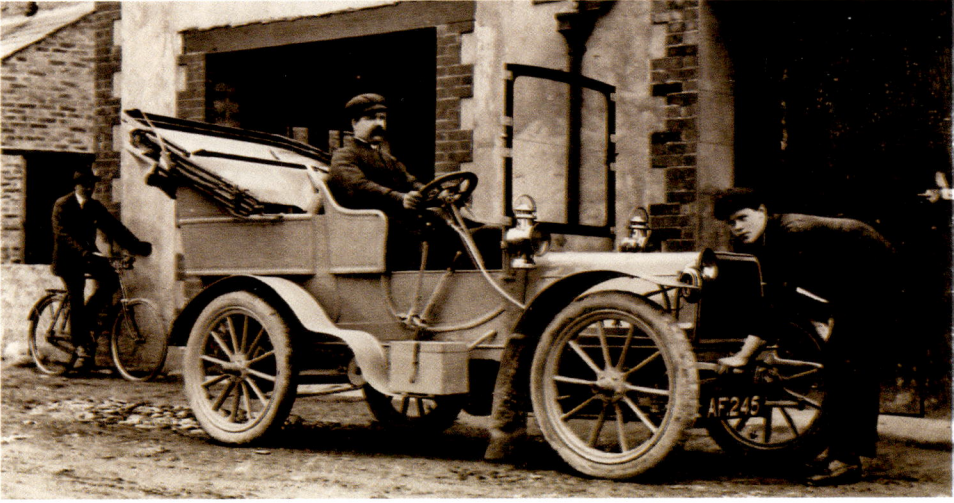

Made in Antwerp, this Minerva dates to 1904 or 1905 and produced 6 hp with a chain drive to the rear wheels. The Minerva Company started off making bicycles in the late nineteenth century, and then progressed to making their first car in 1900. The scene here shows a young mechanic starting the engine by hand. This car was advanced; so much that it has a windscreen and also a folding hood. Access to the driver's position is via the front passenger's door, with outside gear change and hand brake. The gleaming brass lamps and boa constrictor horn bulb under the steering wheel make AF 245 rather a nice motor car. William Easom, a Penryn motor dealer, is seen in the driving seat.

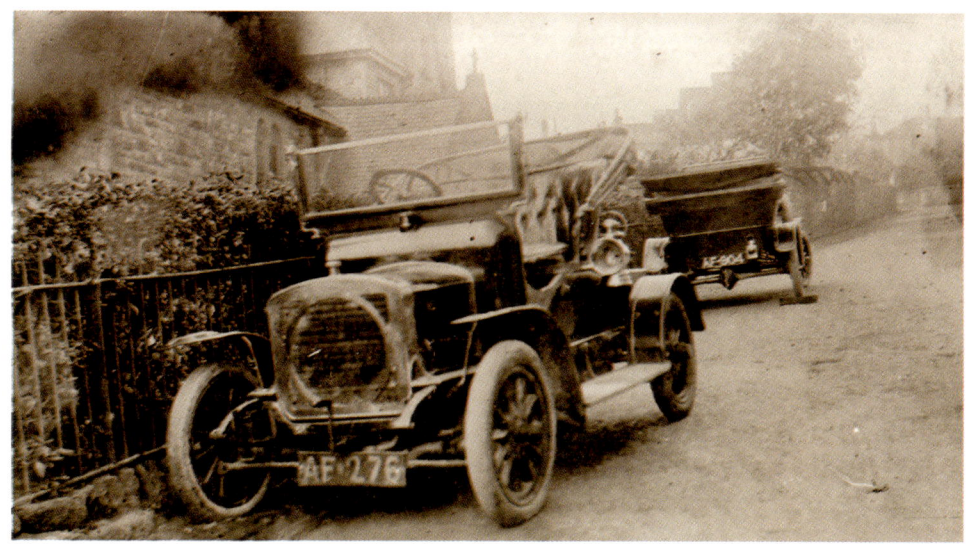

AF 276 was made by Singer & Co. Ltd, Coventry. They began as a bicycle and motorcycle manufacturer, making their first car in 1905. This was a 15 hp, 3-cylinder machine designed by Alex Craig and made under licence from Lea-Francis. Only cars with front vertical engines were listed in 1907, the smaller ones having T-head White & Poppe power units; with the windscreen and large brass oil lamps, this one dates from about 1907. There is another car behind, AF 904, with a nice square rear lamp, dated 1912; it must have dodgy brakes because why is a brick placed behind the rear wheels?

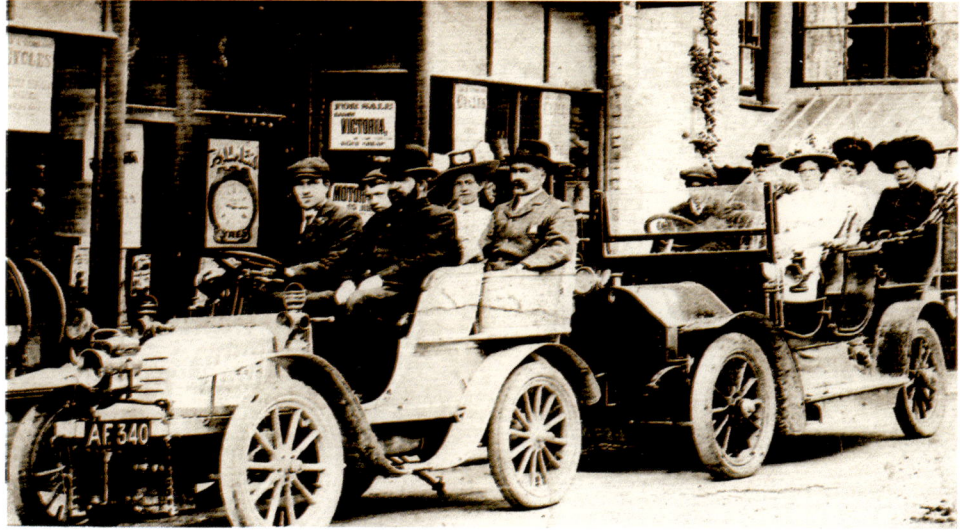

Setting off for a ride, AF 340 from 1905 is an Adler of German origin. The vehicle behind it is possibly a Humber; its number plate, although unreadable, is sure to be Cornish. Fully loaded, the cars are waiting outside Powell's shop at St Columb. Some of the adverts are interesting: there is a light Victoria (a small car) for sale, very cheap; motor cars for hire; bicycles for sale or hire; and the Palmer tyre sign and clock tells us it is 10:15 a.m. What is hanging down between the wheels and mudguard on the front car? Let's hope for the people in that front car that it didn't rain when this was snapped in 1908.

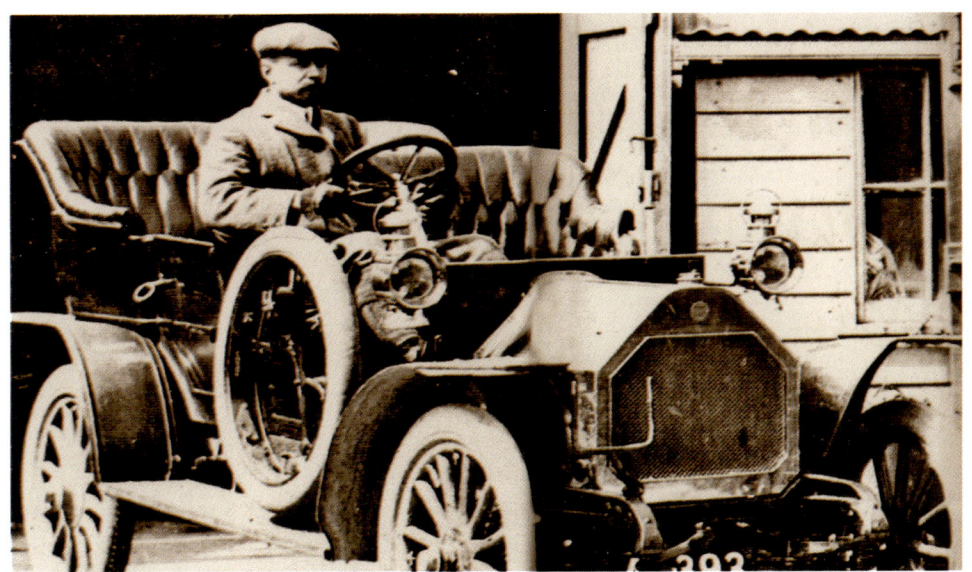

Here Dr Bertie James Mayne can be seen in the driving seat of his 14 hp Belsize in January 1909; AF 393 was painted green with black lining. The spare wheel stops him from climbing into the driver's seat, so access is via the passenger side. Rear riders have the luxury of being able to enter their seats by small doors on each side. The leather button back upholstery, probably red in colour, looks in perfect condition. His other car, a Wolseley, AF 85, has been shown earlier.

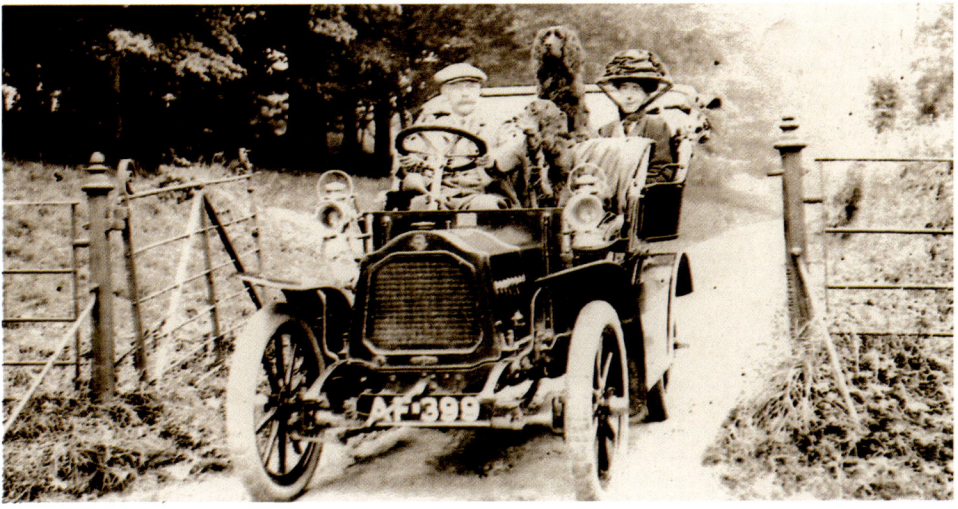

Made in France, this 1904 De Dion-Bouton of 8 hp, a single or perhaps even a twin cylinder open motor car, looks well turned out and gleaming. The De Dion company started in 1885, building steam vehicles; they built petrol engines which were used by any number of other car companies to power their motor vehicles. There is so much more that could be written about this company that it would take several books to explain everything they produced for motor cars. A small 3.5 hp engine was developed that could drive a four-seater car, then the different types of gear boxes, back axles, etc. AF 399 would almost fly. The two guard dogs look well used to riding with the owners.

No. 226   *Duplicate*

MOTOR CAR ACT. 1903.

LICENCE TO DRIVE A MOTOR CAR.

County (Borough) of *Cornwall*

George Henry Rapson, of *New Street, Penryn.* is hereby Licensed to drive a Motor Car for the period of twelve months from the *Thirteenth* day of *August* 190*4*, until the *Twelfth* day of *August* 190*5* inclusive.

Signed (a) *Christopher L. Coward*

N.B.—Particulars of any endorsements of any Licence previously held by the person licensed must be entered on the back of this Licence

CLERK OF THE COUNCIL.

IMPORTANT

N.B.—This Licence should always be carried, as failure by the Driver of a Motor Car to produce a Licence when demanded by a Police Constable renders him liable to a fine not exceeding £5. (Sec. 3 (4).)

In the event of the loss or defacement of this Licence a duplicate can be obtained from the Council on the payment of a fee of One Shilling.

Renewals of Licence.

This Licence (Licence No. *226*) granted by the Council of the County (Borough) of *Cornwall* under the Motor Car Act, 1903, is hereby renewed, so as to be in force for twelve months from the *13th* day of *August 1905* until the *12th* day of *August 1906* inclusive.

Signed *Christopher L. Coward*

Note.—If the holder of the licence furnishes the County Council with his licence for the purpose, the renewal must be entered upon the licence. It will otherwise be a seperate document.

CLERK OF THE COUNCIL.

Possibly only the 226th person in Cornwall to drive – a real pioneer of motoring.

Even in sunshine this proud couple, Mr and Mrs Williamson, looks splendid and ready for the off in their 12 hp, 4 cylinder 1909 Star, AF 440, built in Wolverhampton. Star produced their first car in 1898, with a single cylinder, water-cooled 3.5 hp engine. All Stars up until 1914 were extremely well made, as is the one in the picture. The lovely pair of big brass lamps are very impressive, as is the champagne or umbrella holder behind the driver; the rear view mirror is a necessity.

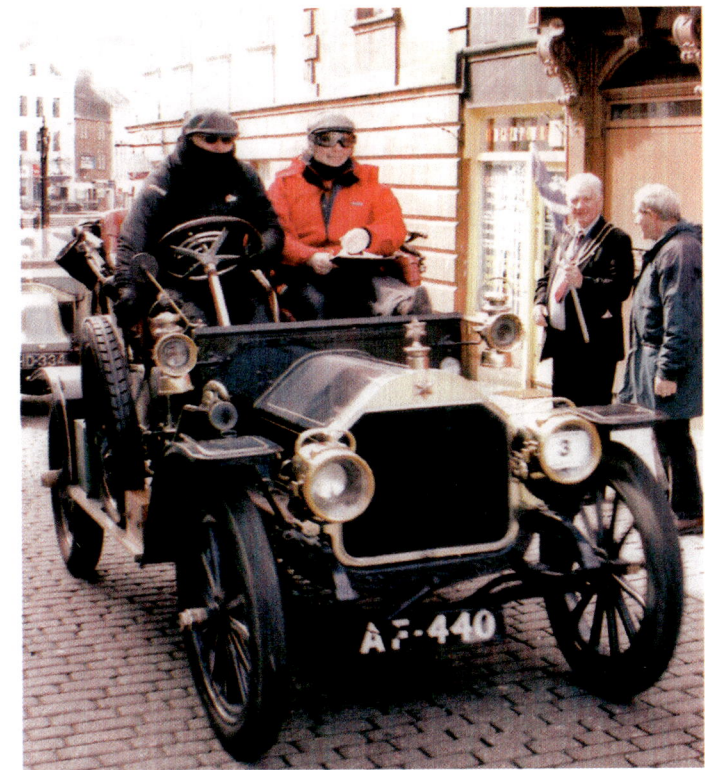

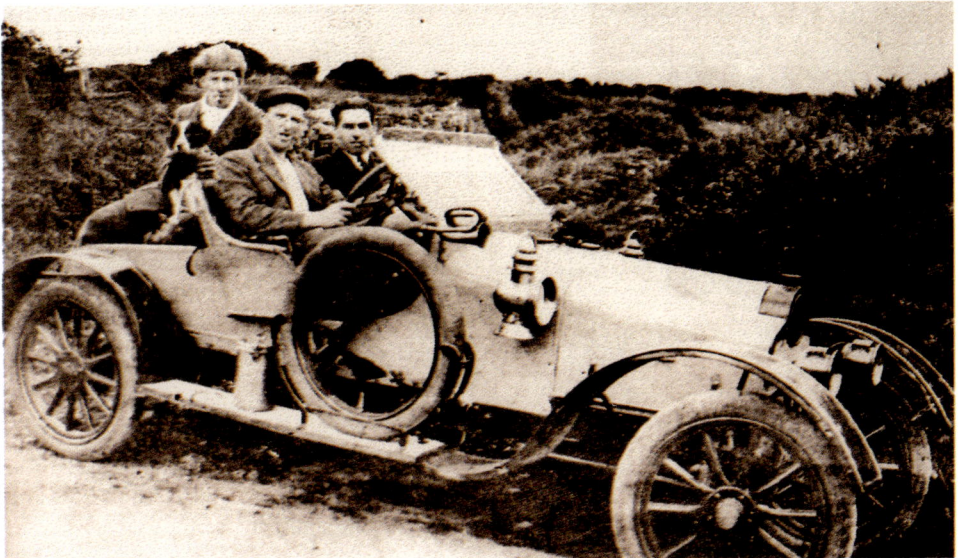

Until 1920, the power output of the single cylinder engine in the Sizaire Naudin was poor. Then the power was increased by enlarging the bore and by lengthening the stroke. Having reached the limit, it was replaced with a small long-stroke four with overhead inlet valves. The single cylinder engine lasted until 1923. AF 632 (1911), a small, sporting French voiturette, had a transverse leaf spring with sliding pillars. The first owner was a Mr Wright of the Castle Hotel, Launceston, with Rover the dog hitching a ride.

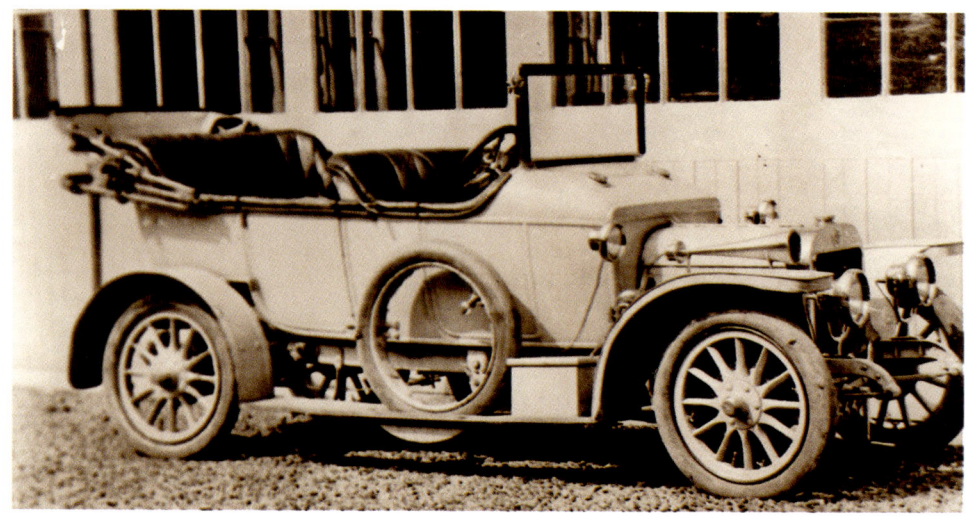

Built in Glasgow in 1912, Argyll's 15 hp tourer helped to make them the fifth biggest motor manufacturer in Britain. The 'Flying Fifteen' with its James engine had single sleeve valves and front wheel brakes. AF 653, seen here in this photograph, has a full set of electric lamps, including the scuttle; they were fork mounted and 'bell' shaped. It also has an electric horn of considerable length and a spare, bolt-on wheel and tyre.

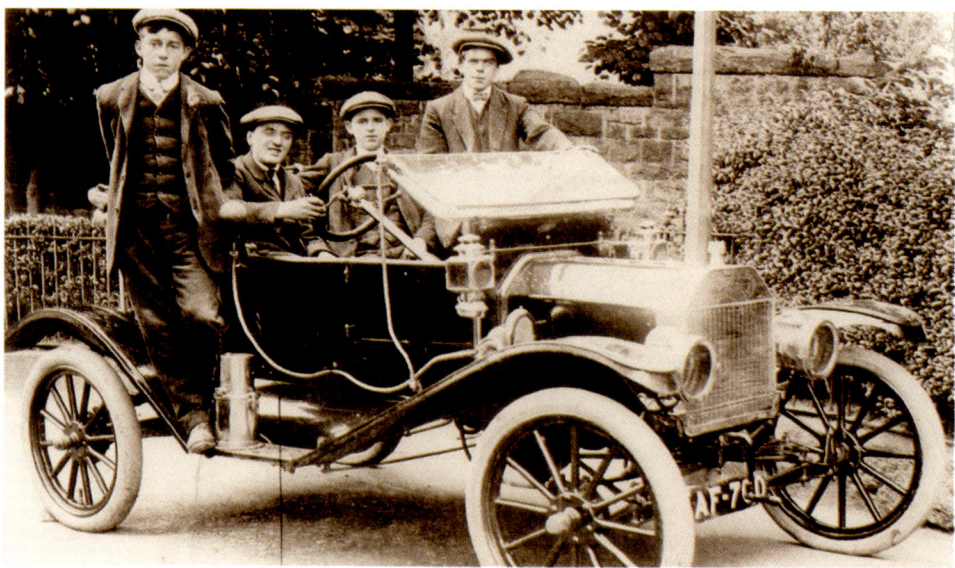

The starting handle gets in the way of reading the number plate on this Ford Model T – is it AF 700 or another number? With an 18-year production run, the 'Tin Lizzie' put the world on wheels – 15 million were made between October 1908 and May 1927. It had a 2.9 litre, 4 cylinder side valve engine with a top speed of between 40 and 45 mph capable of doing between 25 and 30 mpg. In 1911 a British factory was opened in Manchester. Between 1914 and 1925 black was the only colour available; in 1917 the original brass radiator was replaced by a black one. I wonder if this was a family outing on the day the car was bought new, with a gleaming, polished radiator and bulb horn, square paraffin oil carriage and front acetylene lamps. Each of the men and boys sports a hat and neck tie.

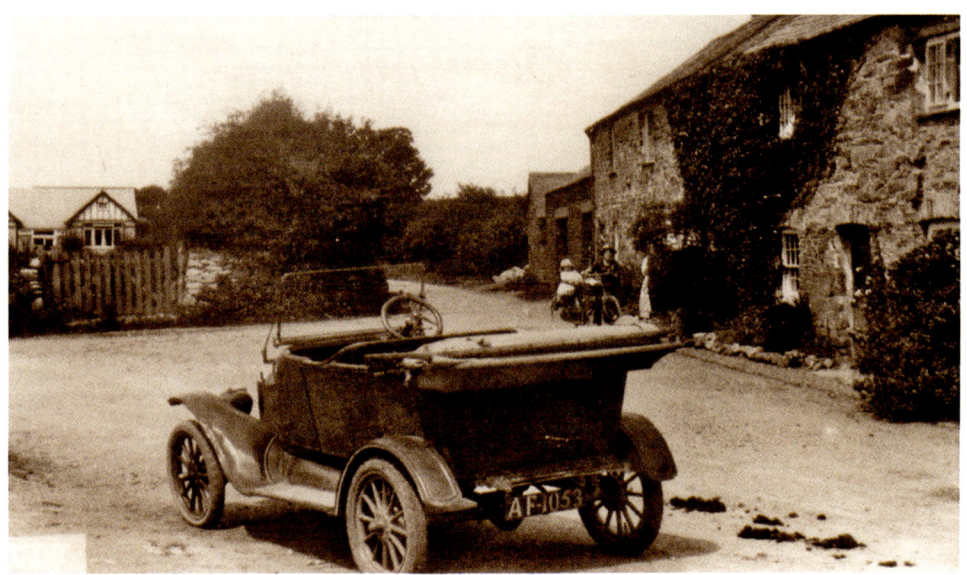

In the background a little child rides on their parent's bicycle, perhaps a little envious of someone's car parked in the foreground. AF 1053 was a British-built Ford Model T, seen here in St Tudy, North Cornwall, in 1912. It looks as if a horse had recently passed by.

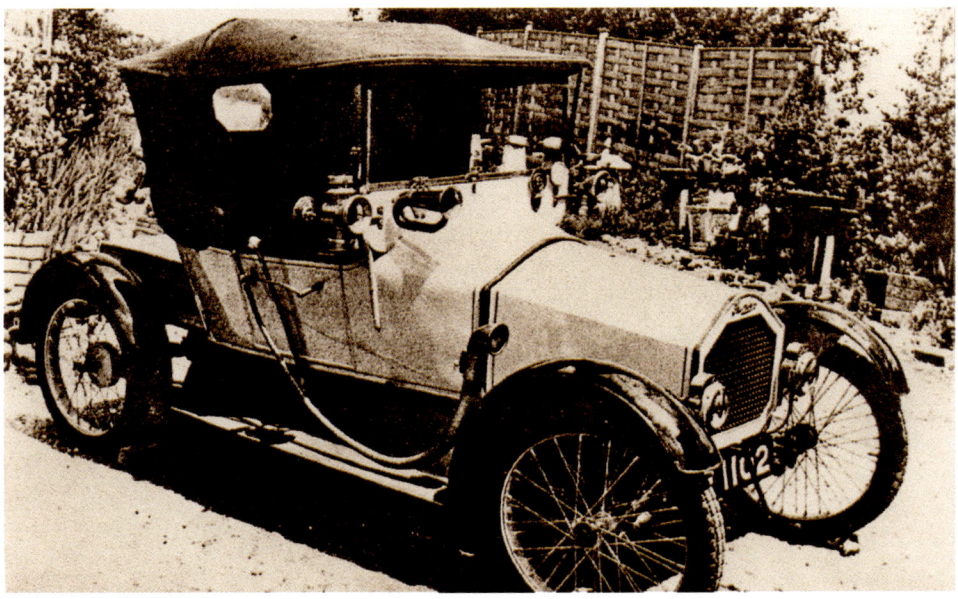

Painted light green, this 8 hp 2-seat baby Humberette dates from 1913. Registered AF 1102, it cost £120, and for an extra £15 it could be bought with a water-cooled engine. With its hood up for winter protection, the little rear window looks almost just a spy hole. Running on wire wheels with very narrow tyres, there were brakes on the rear wheels only. A stone has been placed under the front near side wheel to help stop the car rolling forward. There is outside gear change and a long boa constrictor horn as well as a bulb horn and brass lamps with a rear view mirror. Stand by to be saluted by the patrol man when he sees this beautiful little car coming with its AA badge on display.

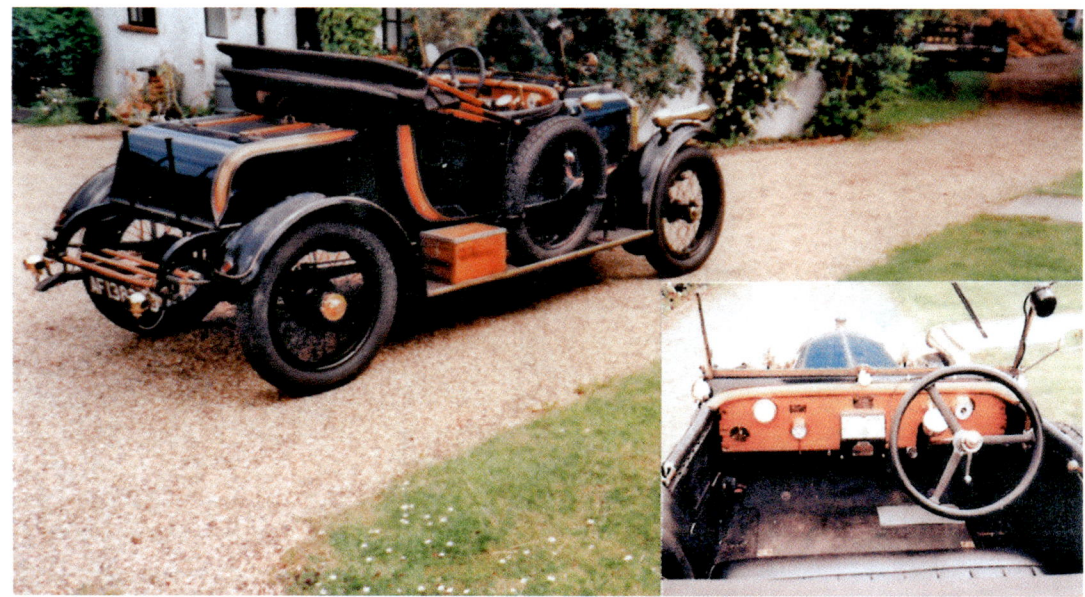

AF 1328 is a 1914 two-seat Turner 12/20 hp now owned by John Lawson of Purley. It was first owned by a gentleman who served in the army but unfortunately did not return from duty during the First World War. Many years later, after the death of the widow, the car was found in a builders' yard by Mr R. Thwaites of Truro, who towed it away on a bar because the brakes were useless. The original spark plugs were in place, though, and the side curtains still in wrappers. Under the thick layer of dirt, the little car was once painted a mustard yellow; after plenty of elbow grease it was repainted in Oxford blue with cream wheels. After a long overhaul of the mechanics, the engine started quite easily, almost invariably starting on the second swing of the handle. The long and often steep hills around the Camborne and Redruth area were nothing to this little car, which is unique as it's the only known 12/20 hp Turner existing in the world. Not a lot is known about its owners, only a doctor in Somerset who used it locally. The present owner, Mr Lawson, then bought the car, which is completely original, with lamps and horn, etc. as the day it was manufactured in Wolverhampton. The photograph shows that the car is in pristine condition, well looked after and used. The inset shows the view through the windscreen going up Camborne Hill, coming down.

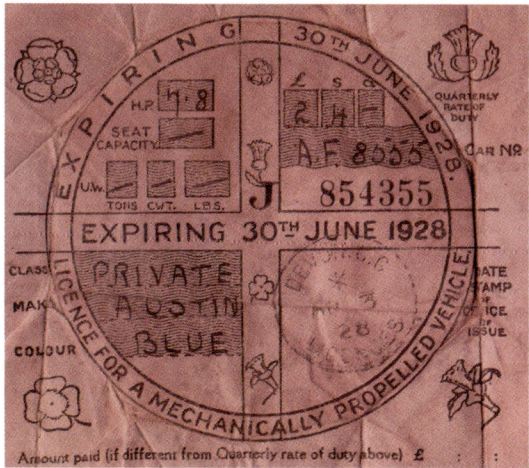
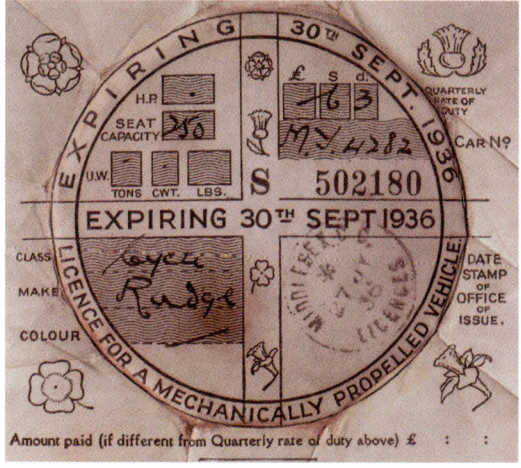

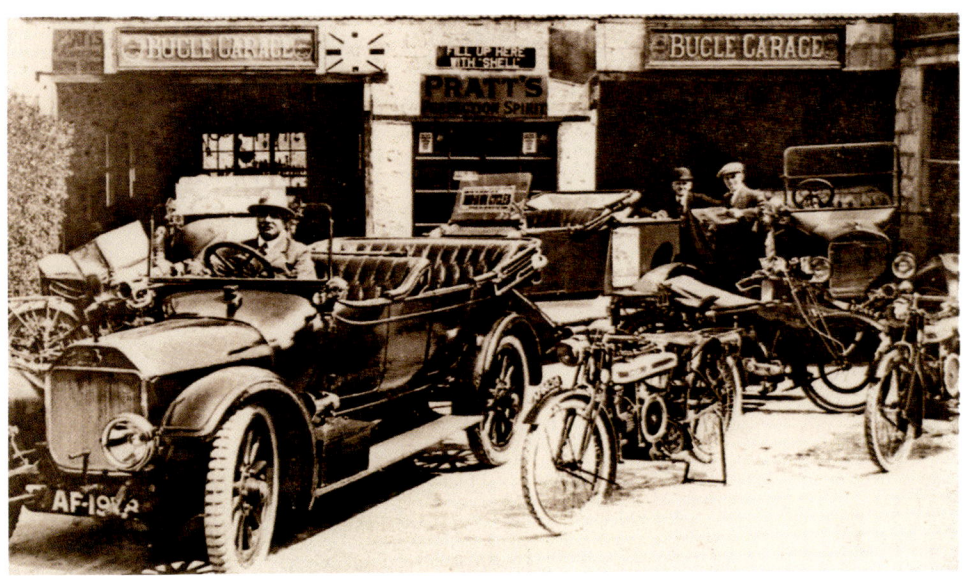

A Swift 15 hp four-seater tourer (AF 1978), two Douglases (AF 6626; the other is unreadable), a Rudge (AF 5664) and a Ford Model T help to make up this remarkable picture, assuming they are all for sale in this 1920s view of a Bugle Garage. Pratt's Perfection Spirit or Shell petrol are available to fill up with here before leaving. The gentlemen in view could be salesmen, or perhaps the gentleman in the bowler hat is one of the owners, the Tonkin brothers. All the machinery looks to be in extremely good condition.

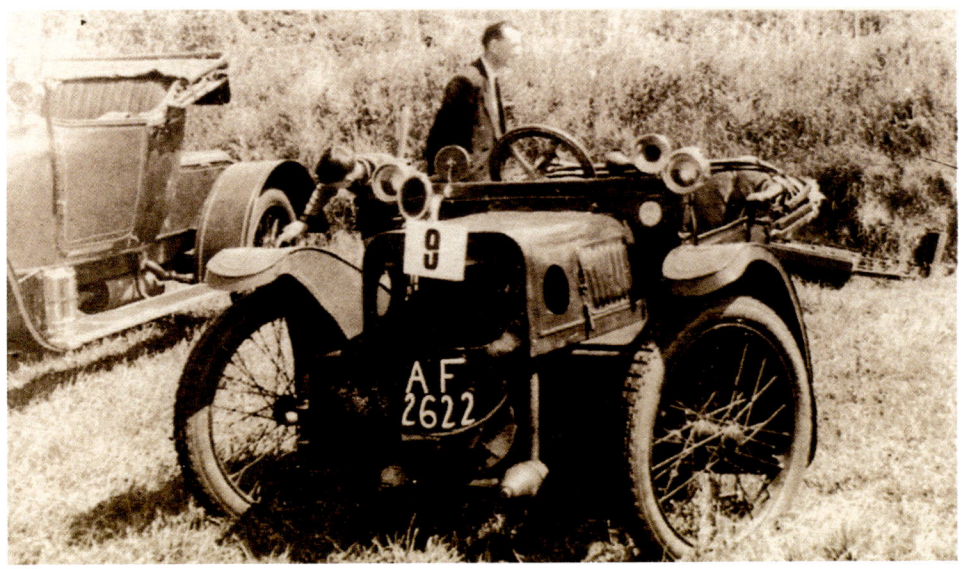

A 1913 three-wheel Morgan (seen here at a later date), AF 2622 was made in Malvern. A two-seater runabout, it had a two cylinder, 8 hp engine. From 1910, this was an air-cooled V twin motorcycle engine of 1,100 cc made by JAP. The Morgan's road-holding was above average, and because it was safer than most it became popular with sportsmen. In 1914 a Grand Prix model, the first competition model, was produced, and in 1920 a four-seater was listed. With small brass lamps, a hood and a mirror, this one looks very good.

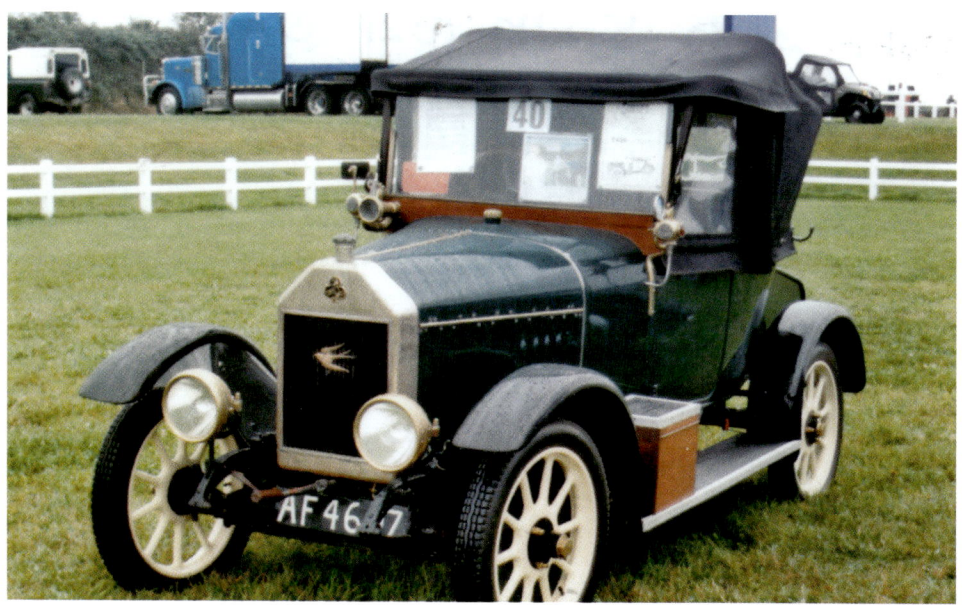

The Swift Motor Company built their first car in Coventry in 1900, progressing from sewing machines through to bicycles, motor tricycles and quadcycles to cars. This photograph shows a Model ED 10 hp Radford engine two-seater with a dickey seat sporting a three-speed, gate-change gearbox. It belonged to Thomas Hoskin of Bodmin and was registered AF 4607 in the summer of 1921. After many years, passing through several owners (some unknown), it came to Victor Crebe, who attempted to restore it. The new owner bought it mostly in boxes, with several pieces missing. Taking at least eight painstaking years, he lovingly restored the car, replacing the rare missing parts. In 2001 it passed its first MOT in time to attend the Swift Car Centenary in Coventry.

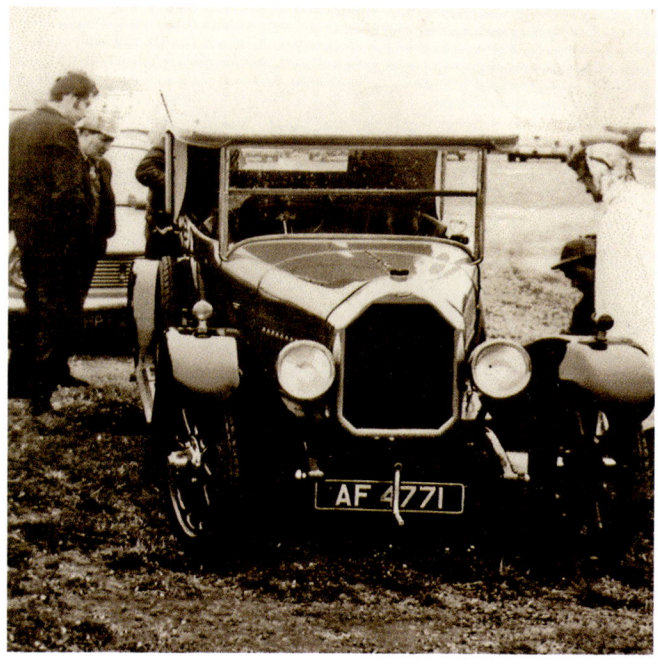

Lands End was where this Humber was snapped during the summer of 1975. After the First World War, Humber of Coventry concentrated on solid family cars noted for their excellent workmanship. All-weather equipment was supplied and side valved engines were used up until 1922. Painted in 'Camel', this four-seater is being admired by Peter Moyle and the author. AF 4771 is believed to be a 18 hp Chummy first registered in 1921/22; it has been fully restored by M. Lane, a garage owner.

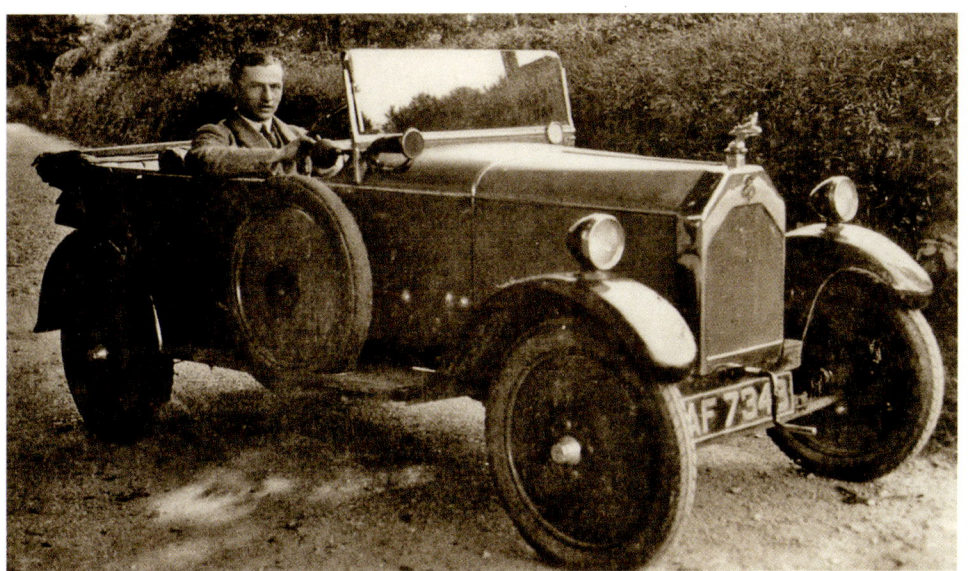

Initially, Swift's cars used the De Dion engine. A four cylinder engine of Swift's own make was introduced in 1904. This Swift of the early 1920s (AF 7343?) was a four-seater made in Coventry. The Swift 10 was redesigned in 1923 with a detachable head and coil ignition; a three-speed gearbox was added in 1925 and it reverted to a magneto engine. Access to the driver's side is via the front passenger door, with a spare wheel fixed to the running board. It also sports a hood, bulb horn, electric lights and a mascot on the radiator (a swift, of course).

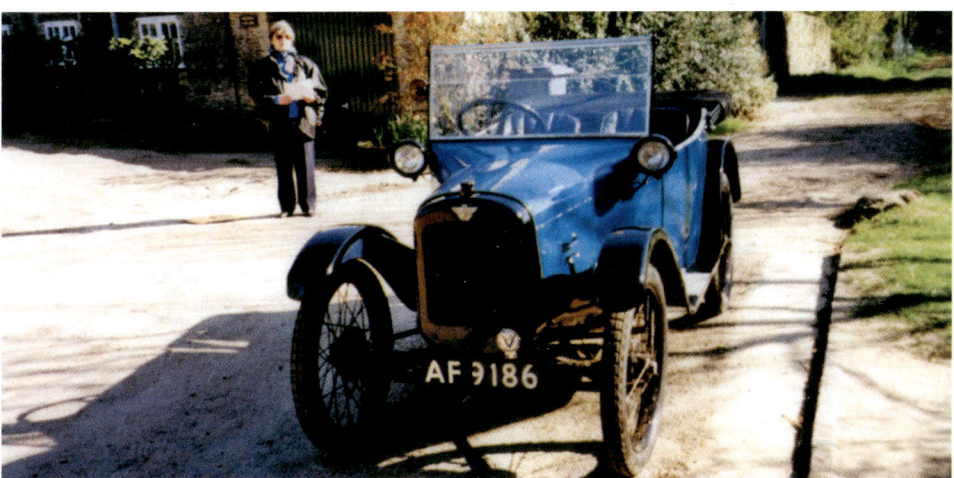

This charming little Austin 7 of 1923 was registered AF 9186 in 1924. The Chummy first came on the scene in 1922, developed by Herbert Austin for the masses. More often than not, it was the first little car that a lot of working people owned instead of a motorcycle. It was a four seater (normally two adults and two children) and came complete with an all-weather hood and side screens, electric lamps on the scuttle (in later models the lamps moved to the front), brakes on all four wheels and a foot brake connected to the rear wheels. The detachable wire wheels had non-skid tyres, and the petrol tank would hold four gallons. A member of the Vintage Sports Car Club, the owner of this pretty little car, which cost a little over £100 when new, is G. St John.

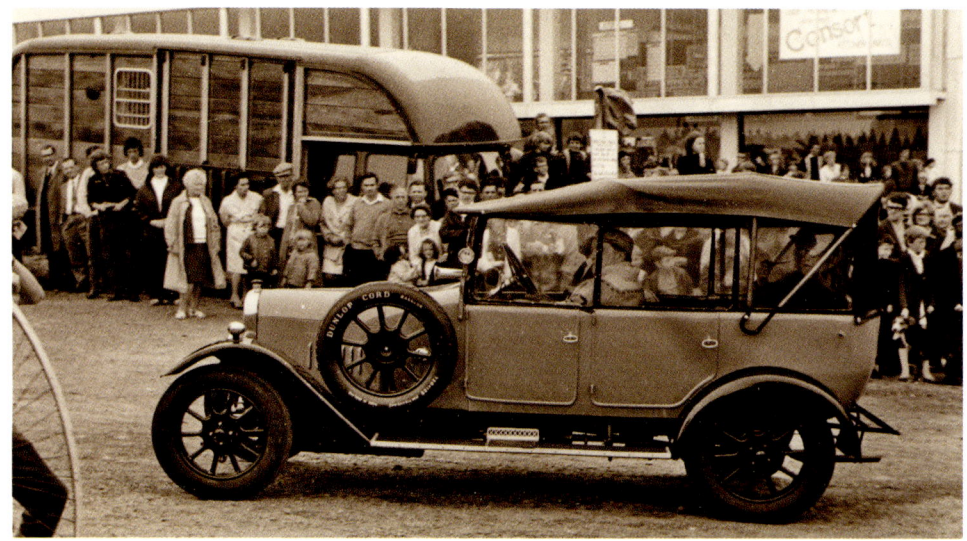

Photographed at a vintage car rally at Penzance in the late 1960s, this really beautiful 1924/5 Clyno, RL 1726, is owned and driven by Willie Pendray of Camborne. The early cars were built by Clyno Engineering Co., Wolverhampton. They used a 1,400 cc four-cylinder Coventry-Climax engine and a three-speed gearbox, utterly reliable. Sales outstripped other assembled marques. Four wheel breaks were offered as an optional extra and the deluxe models, of which this is one, were known as Royals. Dunlop cord tyres came as standard. With Arthur Bunn as co-pilot, don't forget to wipe your feet before entering the passenger's side with the mat provided.

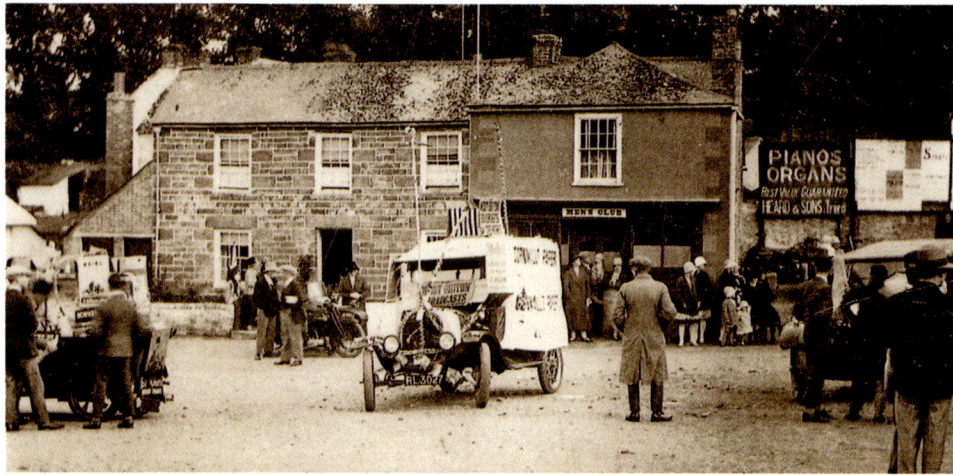

Snapped in Lanner, this picture looks like an assembly of vehicles about to go into a carnival parade. The gaily decorated vehicles are undistinguishable, although some registered plates are readable. In the centre could be either a large four-seater car or a van, RL 3027, marked 'West Briton Broadcasts'. Could it be the loudspeaker van? To the left of the AF-registered motorcycle, on the extreme left, is another little car; on the right hand side is a large car with another AF registration. Looking at the young ladies outside the Men's Club, we can see the type of hats worn at the time, dating the picture to around 1925. Meanwhile, Head & Sons of Truro guarantee the best value for pianos and organs.

This Austin Clifton Tourer was registered as RL 6325 on 30 July 1927. This beautiful car was once exported to Belgium before being brought back by its present owner, Roger Lewis, who managed to retain its original number. The car is well looked after and maintained by the owner. It was originally bought from Ernest J. Powell of Broad Street, St Columb, whose nameplate is still on the dashboard. This 1,800 cc four-seater was one of the hardest-wearing machines of all time.

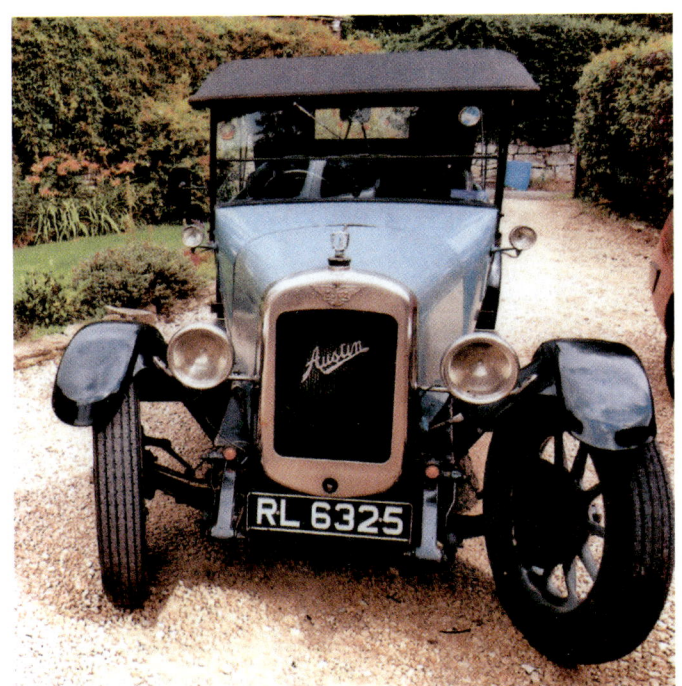

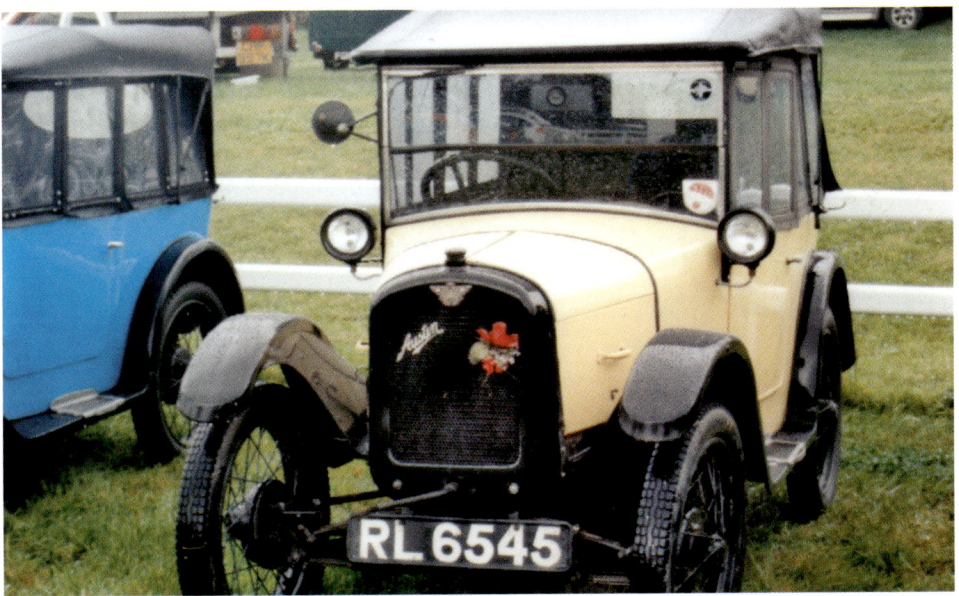

This lovely little Austin 7 Chummy was first registered in September 1927 with the plate number RL 6545. It was first owned by a Mr James of Bugle, staying with him for ten years. It had quite a number of unknown owners in the 1960s and 1970s and was in a very poor condition when it was bought by its present owner, Regina Jarmin, in 1993. A considerable amount of money was spent restoring this delightful little car, which passed its first MOT in December 1996. Nicknamed 'Annie', it is now in regular use. 'Annie' was driven from Lands End to John O'Groats and back in the early 2000s, taking four days up and 28 hours back home to Cornwall at an average speed of 31 mph and 38 mpg, doing 1,760 miles in five days.

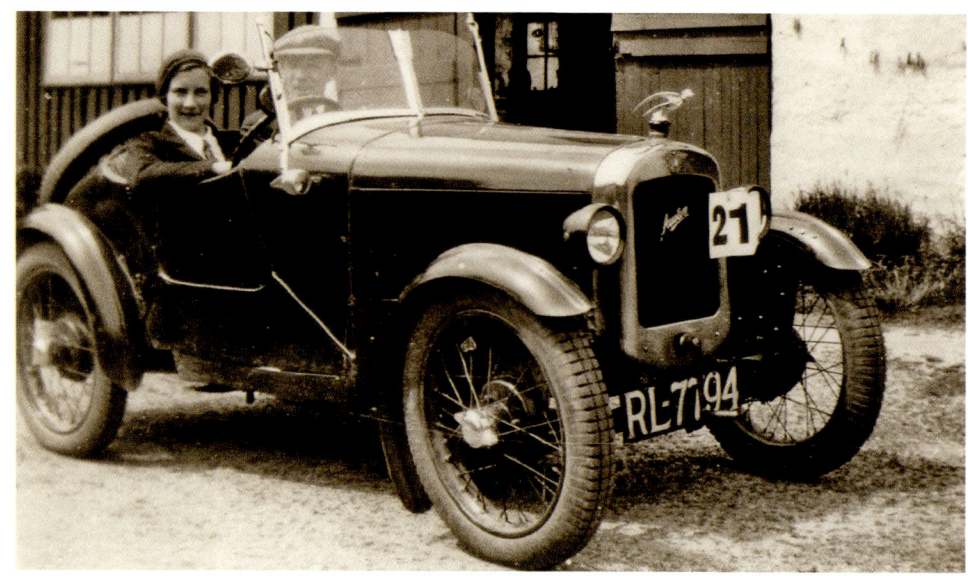

Mrs Doris George is seen here preparing to take part in the Lelant Trial in 1932. Registered in late 1927 with the number RL 7794, this delightful little two-seater Austin Nippy with a Gordon England beetle-back body has the number 21 attached to a headlight. It was very popular with sportsmen, costing £175 complete with raked steering column and gear lever, shock absorbers, speedometer, fan and electric starter. The car in the picture has spoke wheels, knock-ons and, fitted to the radiator cap, a mascot; perhaps it came from Halfords, which sold several types of mascots. The passenger could be her father.

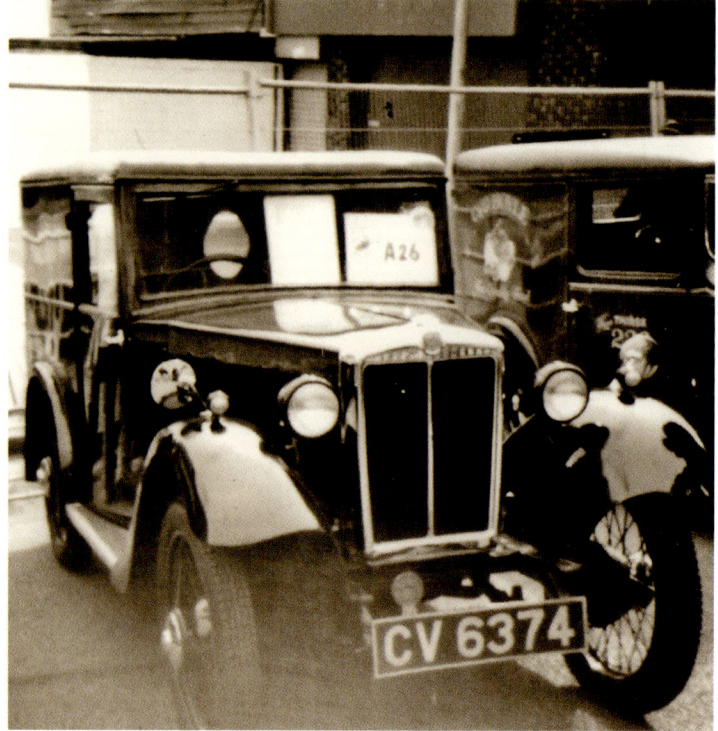

This lovely little van, CV 6374, dating from about 1930, is seen at a rally with the number A26 in the windscreen. The little oval windows must have been difficult to see through when driving although it has a nice pair of wing mirrors.

Mrs Doris George must have been well pleased with her little Nippy because after selling it she bought another Austin 10 or 12, this time a saloon four-seater, registered CV 1110 in 1928/29. On 13 July 1932, with Edith Barrond, she left the Lands End Hotel in rain and fog and set off for John O'Groats. What an undertaking by two ladies when it was a big day out if anyone went to the seaside for the day. With a full tank of petrol and all the food they could take, they set off for a big adventure: Penzance, Launceston (fog gone), out of Cornwall, on to Bristol (no rain) then the Midlands, crossing the border into Scotland. Taking eight days, without any breakdowns, but with several punctures which they had to repair themselves, having to buy a new tyre in Scotland, they arrived at their destination. The picture is dated 21 July at John O'Groats. It is known that they stayed the night there, setting out the next day for Cornwall and home. Unfortunately, they did not keep a record of how much petrol etc. they used but still, what an undertaking – no motorways or bypasses then and garages were few and far between in Scotland. With the rain and fog starting off, it is believed that they came home quicker – well, it is downhill!

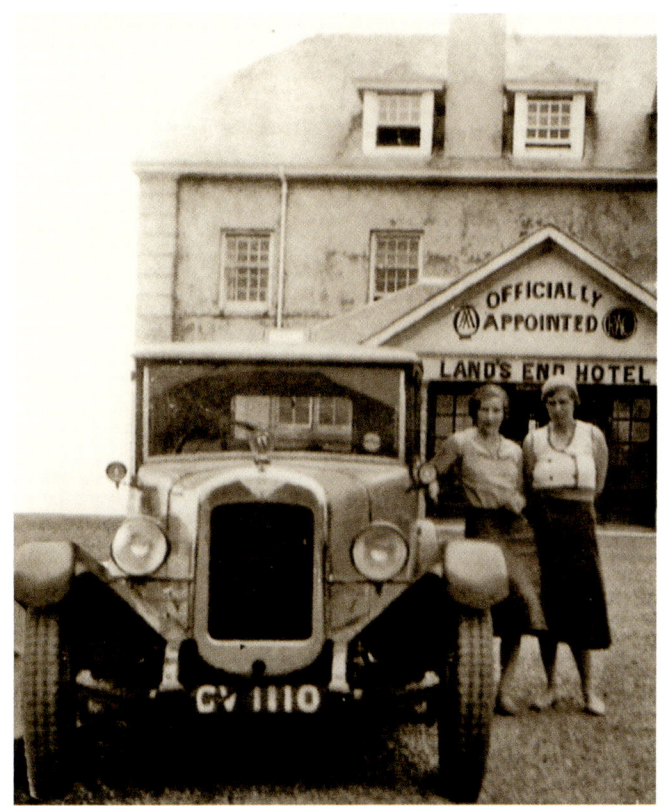

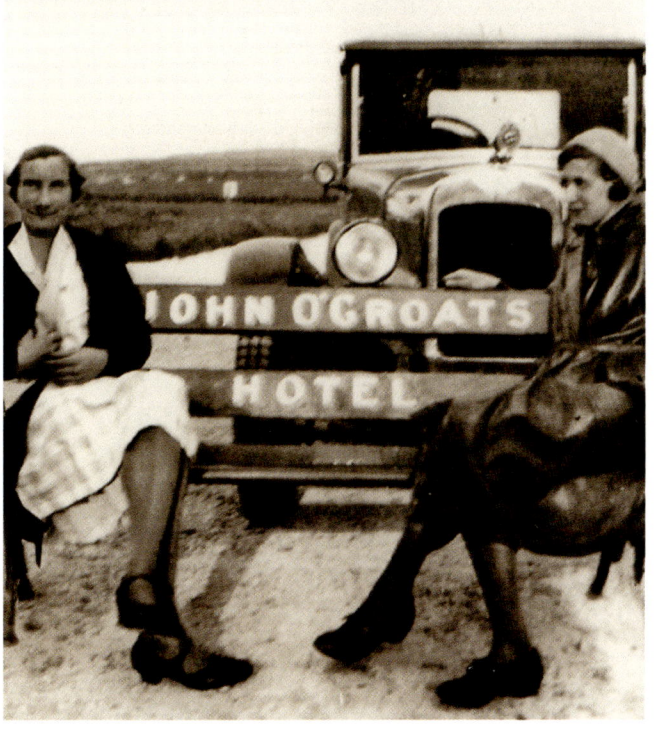

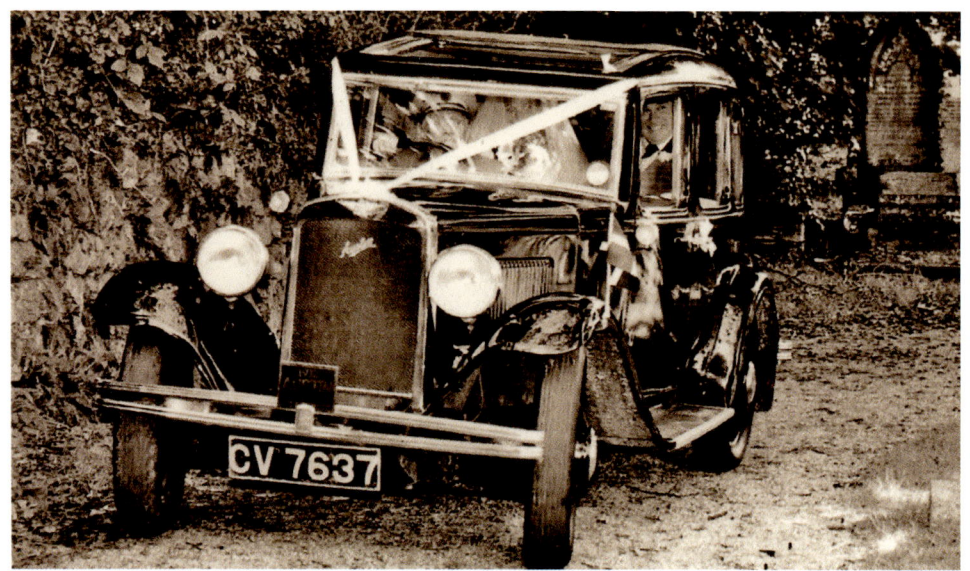

This well-known car, an Austin 12/4 registered CV 7637 in 1932, belongs to Roy Bunt. A motor mechanic like his father before him, he is the same age as this adorable car. The Austin came into his ownership from a local farmer via a member of the Steam Engine Society for £16, a lot of money in the 1960s. Towing it home on a rope to Camborne, he set about restoring it. The leather interior is still original, as is the rubber on the running board. Mr Bunt's skill as a motor mechanic enabled him to do most of the work himself. He and his car have taken part in several episodes of *Jeeves and Wooster* and also in Joanna Lumley's *Coming Home*, filmed in Newquay. Once, on a trip to London, the car was looked after by a policeman, parked on double yellow lines, while he looked around Madam Tussauds. This beautiful looking car is an ideal choice for weddings and special occasions, as can be seen in the snapshot. What do you give your father for a birthday present, a man who loves old cars and machinery in general? They decided on a stained glass window. Over the years the colour in the glass has faded a little, but it is still very impressive.

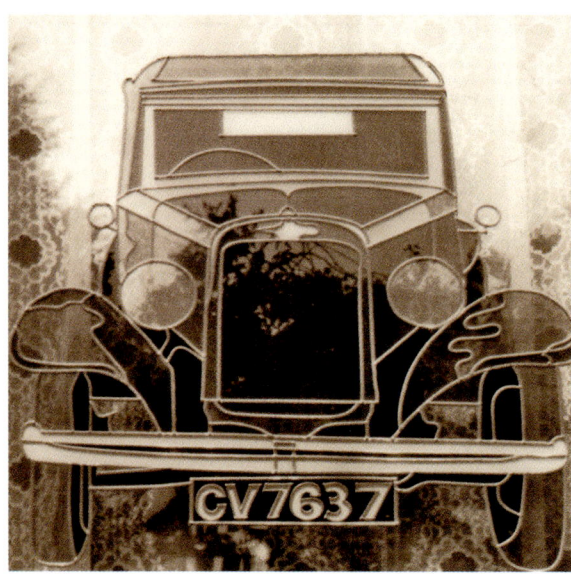

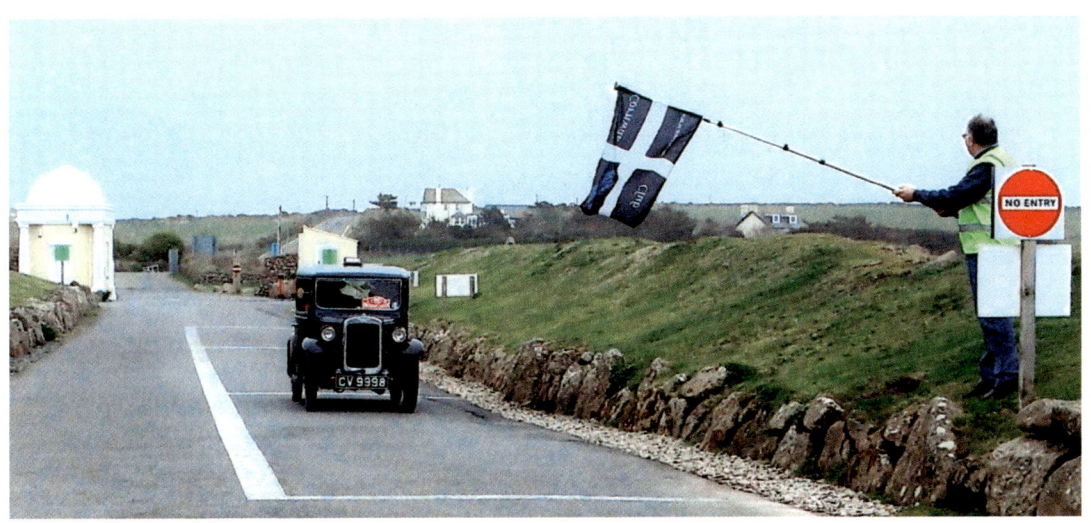

To celebrate the ninetieth anniversary of the launch of the Baby Austin 7 in 1922, Sandy Croall drove his seventy-nine-year-old motor car back to Lands End from John O'Groats. CV 9998 was registered in March 1934 to Les Hingston, who sold it to a lady from Probus in 1952; buying it in 2001, the present owner is only the third person to own it. The weekend before Easter, with the car loaded with all types of spares, the plan was to travel from home at Mousehole to Shrewsbury, then to Hamilton, and on to Inverness, and finally John O'Groats. Driving through snow at Shrewsbury and high winds most of the way made it very uncomfortable – with no heater in the car, it became very cold indeed. Departure from John O'Groats was 9.30 a.m. on Easter Saturday; without many garages, particular attention was paid to fuel consumption, and fog was encountered along the way. When he stopped for fuel, he would also have something to eat. The car ran smoothly but the solo effort was beginning to tell. Between Bristol and Exeter there was light rain. Driving solo for so long, he nodded off for a few seconds, then pulled into a lay-by and slept for a short while. With 110 miles to Lands End, the A30 seemed almost clear and he made it to Lands End with five minutes to spare, doing the run in under 24 hours. The top picture shows the Austin arriving at Lands End at 9.25 on Easter Sunday, and the bottom picture shows the same car about to leave John O'Groats at 9.30 on Easter Saturday.

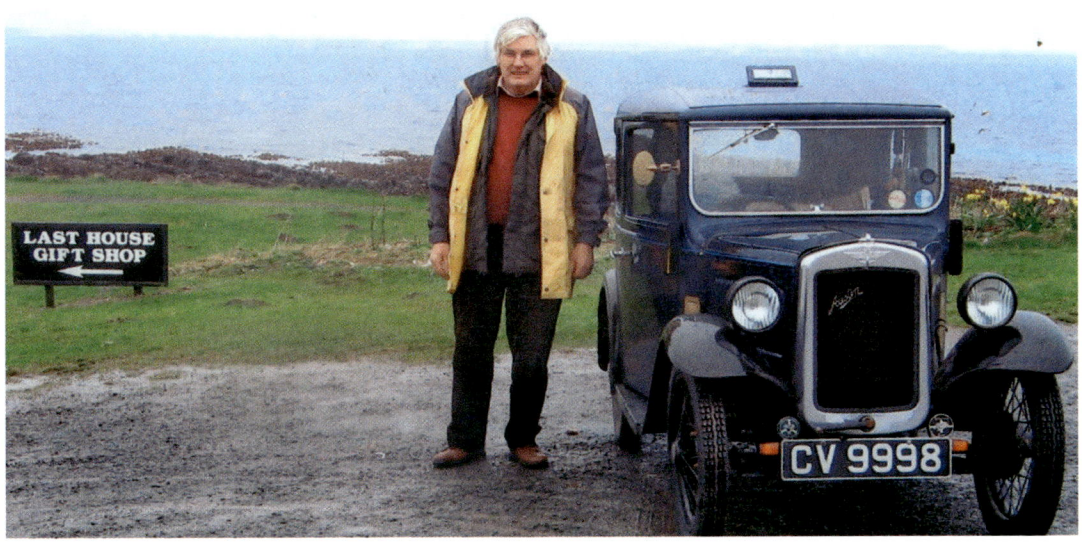

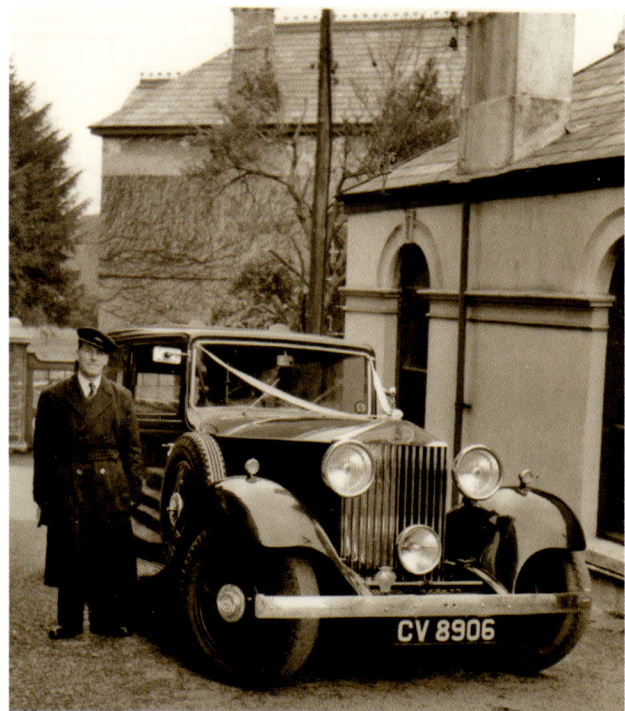

Is the chauffeur waiting for the bride and groom? This beautiful Rolls-Royce 20/25 model was registered CV 8906 in 1934. The Rolls-Royce was the result of a meeting between Henry Royce, a manufacturer of electric cranes, and the Honourable C. S. Rolls, a pioneer motorist. In 1931 the company bought Bentley Motors. Sir Henry Royce died in 1933 and the entwined 'R's of the radiator emblem were changed from red to black, supposedly in mourning. With huge Lucas P100 headlights also supporting an Automobile Association badge, I wonder if the car is reliable?

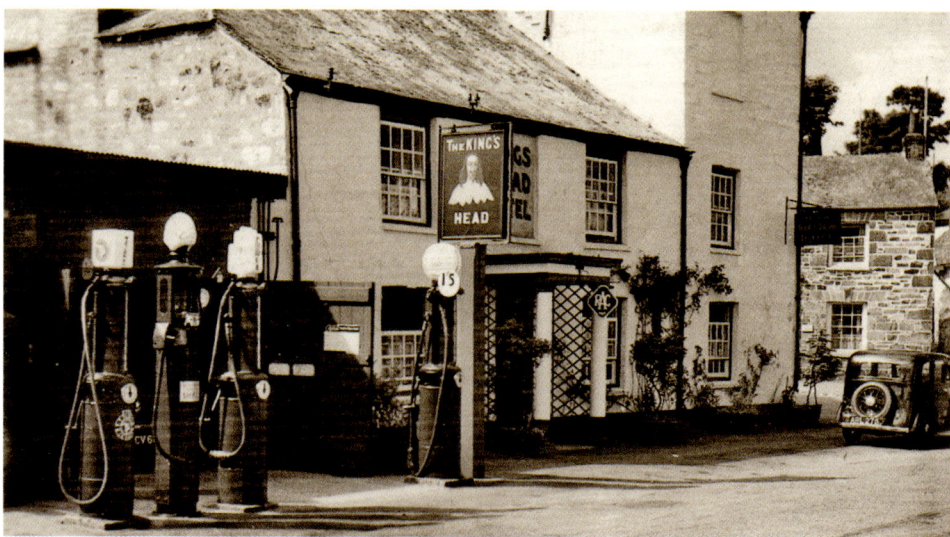

Those were the days – 1s 5d per gallon, with a choice of either Power, Shell, National, or Essolene, all from hand-operated pumps with glass globes that were lit at night. This was Potter's Garage, next door to the King's Head Hotel in Chacewater, between Redruth and Truro. This snap was taken in the early 1940s. To the right is the rear end of an Austin car, registered ARL 275 from 1934, outside the King's Head, where an RAC sign is on the right hand pillar of the entrance. Between the National and Shell petrol pumps can be seen part of a number plate, CV6 – it could be George Potter's own car or another brought in for repairs. The garage closed in the early 1970s and was completely dismantled. With long shadows and open windows in the hotel, it must have been a long, hot summer's day.

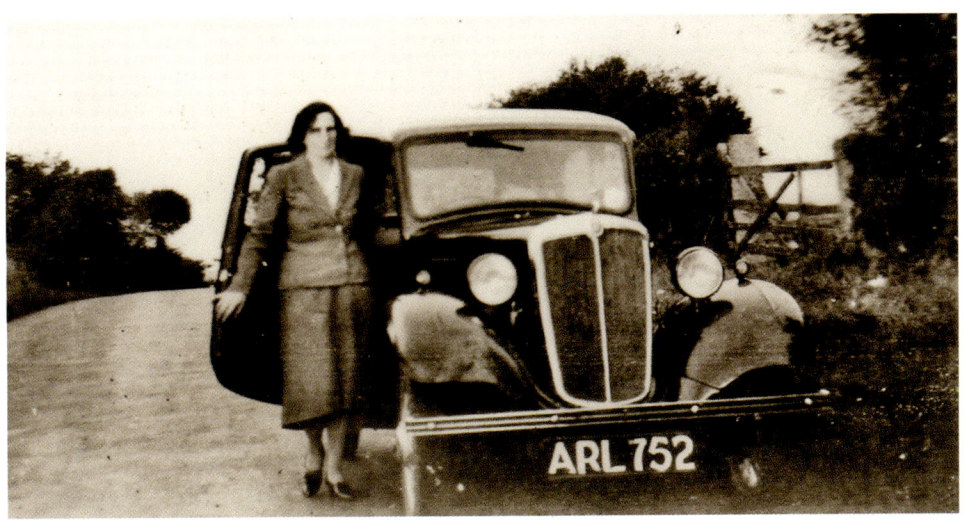

ARL 752 is seen here in a country lane somewhere in Cornwall; this 1934 Morris 8 has stopped for the lady driver to have her photograph taken by her passenger before moving off again for their destination. This Morris, made in Cowley, pioneered the semaphore-type traffic indicators. It became a best-seller, with a 918 cc, side valve, series one Morris 8 retailing at £132 10s for a fully equipped saloon. This helped Morris to reach their first million cars by 1939.

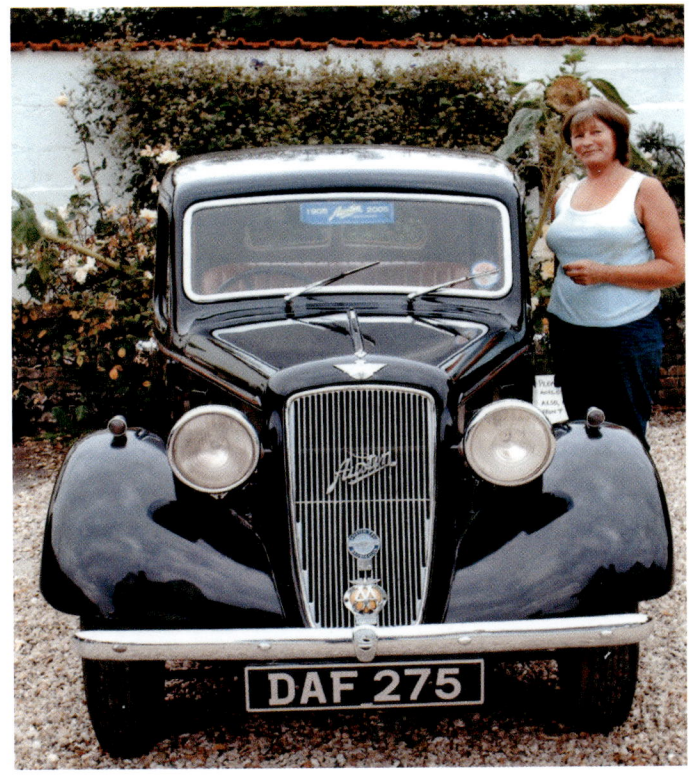

The blue badge between the AA and Austin badges is the Austin 10 Owner's Club badge; the owners of this delightful 10 hp Cambridge, Mr and Mrs Steve Veal, are members. Registered DAF 275 in 1937, it was supplied new from Martin's of Looe and even though it has had several owners it has never been outside East Cornwall and has certainly never crossed the Tamar. At one time the then owner was about to take the car to Beaulieu to sell; when he pulled into a local garage to fill up, the owner bought the car from him there and then, restoring the car. It came into the hands of the present owners in 2002 and I am told by both that it is a real pleasure to drive and goes as well as it looks.

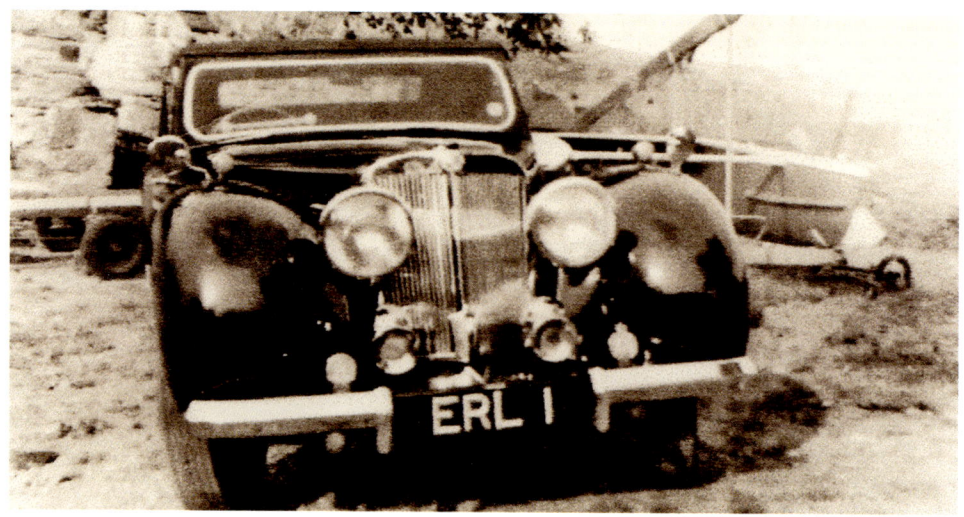

This Triumph Roadster, ERL 1, was made in May 1948. Its first owner was Charles Giffard of St Austell. His elder son Miles, born in 1925, played Minor Counties Cricket for Cornwall and was educated at Rugby School. He hated his father, who told him to give up a nineteen-year-old girl he had developed a serious relationship with. Having been refused permission to use the car, he got drunk and, using a piece of lead pipe, murdered both his parents, tipping their bodies over the cliff at the bottom of the garden (his mother was still alive). He then fled to London in ERL 1, where he was arrested. It took the jury 35 minutes to find him guilty and he was hanged in Bristol in February 1953. After several previous owners, the present owner, John Rhodes, bought the car in 2011, bringing it back to its present standard.

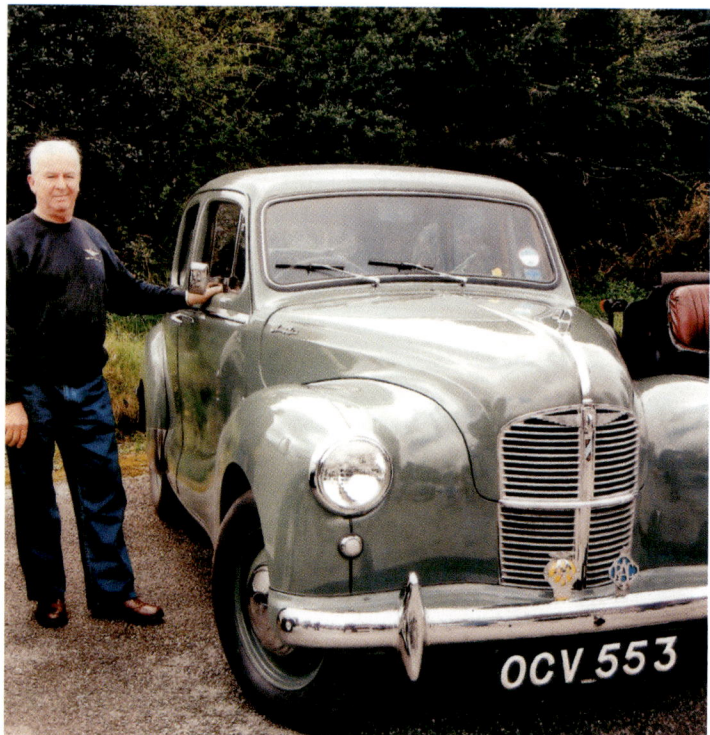

Once owned by a Camelford lady, this Austin A40 Devon, made in 1949 but registered in 1951, looks splendid in its highly polished finish. It has been restored and repainted and is now owned by A. Bowyer, who is only the third owner. OCV 553 has a 1.2 litre engine with overhead valve and is independtly sprung at the front. It sold well in the US, helping Austin to sell over 85,000 cars.

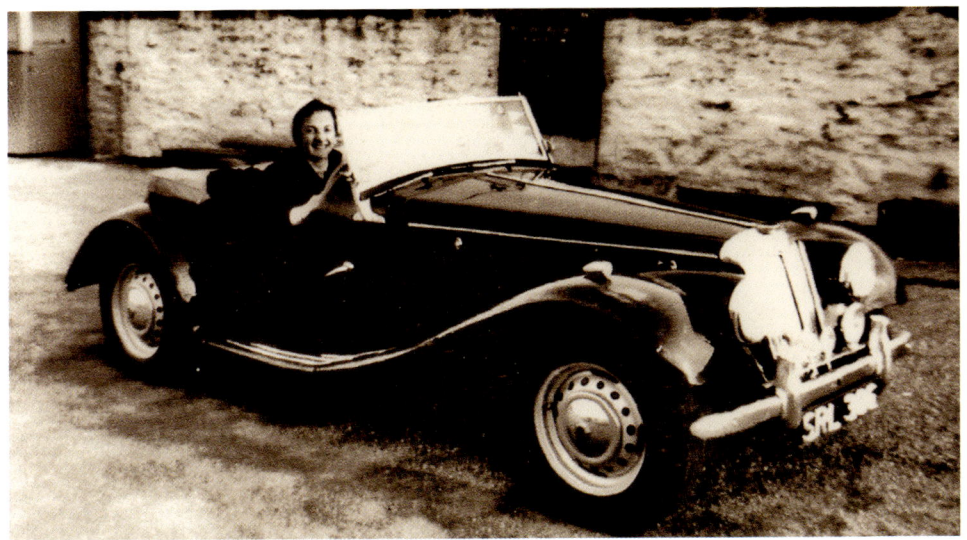

This 1954 MG TF bearing the registration number SRL 366 is seen here being driven by Mrs Mill Seward at St Mawes. The TF of 1953 was the first MG production car to incorporate aerodynamic principles. It was fitted with a 1.3 litre engine but a 1.5 litre version was optional. With a badge bar and over-riders on the front bumper, this sports car looks very desirable with the hood down on a nice summer's day.

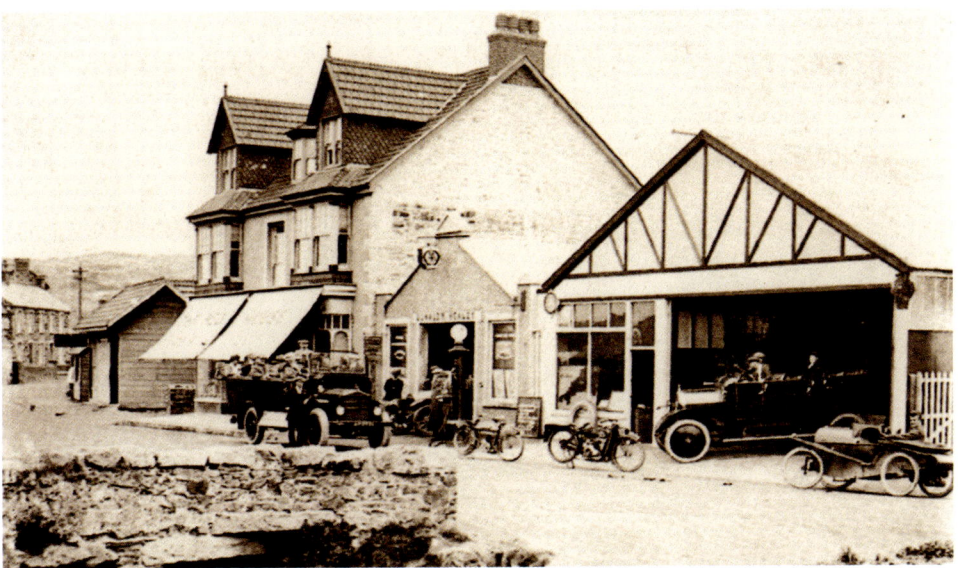

Born in Perranporth in July 1898, Donald Healey became interested in all things mechanical at an early age. Upon leaving school, he joined the Sopwith Aviation Co. at the nearby Brooklands racing circuit. He volunteered for the Royal Flying Corps, earning his wings in 1916; he was invalided out at the age of 18 after being shot down by British anti-aircraft fire. In 1919 he opened the first garage in Perranporth; this photo from the 1920s shows that same garage. On the left is a Garford eighteen to twenty-seater Blue Livery bus registered AF 3771; then there is a Shell petrol pump; then a four-seater large car with solid wheels (possibly a Trojan) coming out of the garage; on the extreme right is a Carden cyclecar.

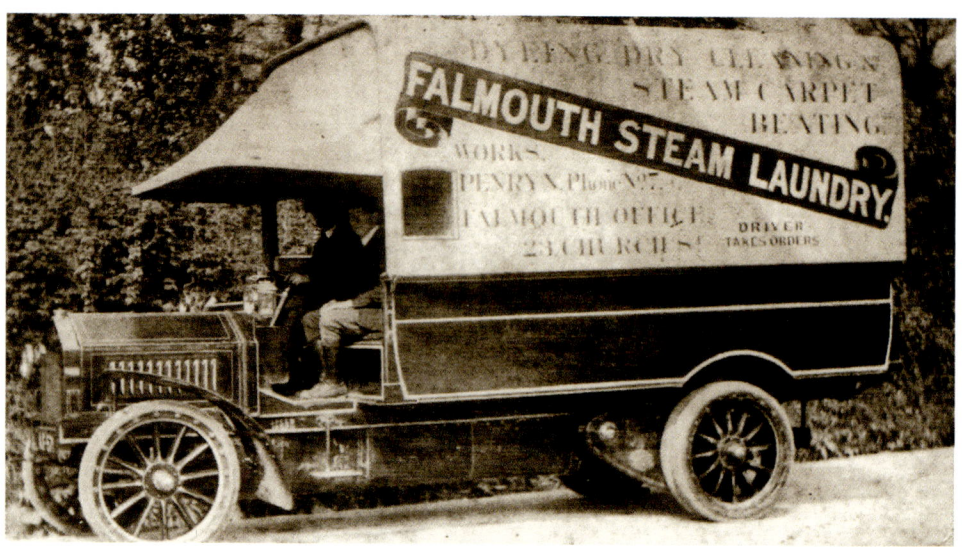

Although the offices of the Falmouth Steam Laundry were at 23 Church Street, Falmouth, the works were at The Praze, Penryn. It had all the water it needed from the stream flowing from Treluswell to wash the clothes. The sign written on this large vehicle is: 'DYEING, DRY CLEANING, STEAM CARPET BEATING, FALMOUTH STEAM LAUNDRY WORKS PENRYN PHONE NO.7 FAMOUTH OFFICE, 23, CHURCH STREET DRIVER TAKES ORDERS.' The registration number is hard to distinguish but looks like AF571, which would make it pre-1910. The Laundry representative would call with a grey fibre box to place the dirty linen in. After a short while the linen would be returned, gleaming and ironed – a door to door service. The manager at one time was Pearse Rodgers.

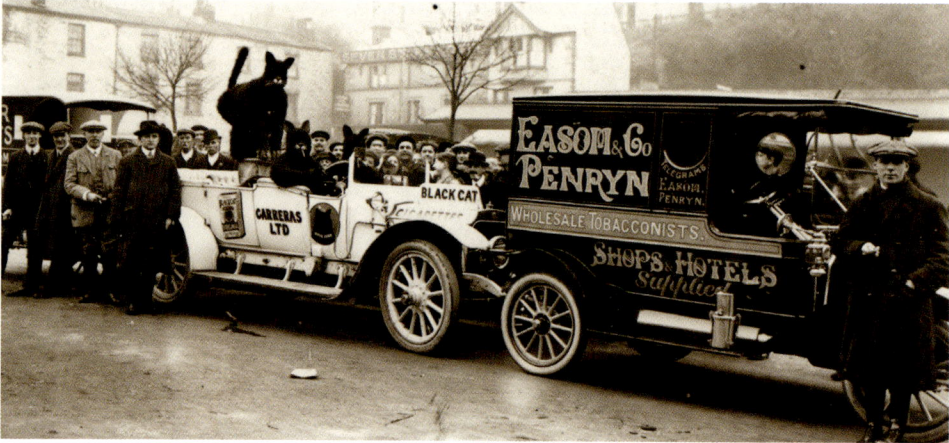

Advertising Black Cat Cigarettes, Carreras Ltd are posing here on The Moor, Falmouth, with three men dressed as Felix the Cat in the white-painted motor car. Behind and ahead of them are two Ford Model T vans belonging to Easom & Co., Penryn; not only were they motor experts, they were wholesale tobacconists, supplying shops and hotels. There being no driver's door, the driver climbed in from the passenger's side of the van. The container on the running board is an acetylene generator to supply gas to the lamps. See how difficult it must have been to control the van, with all the levers on the steering column. Although no registration numbers are visible, I feel sure they would have been Cornish from around 1910.

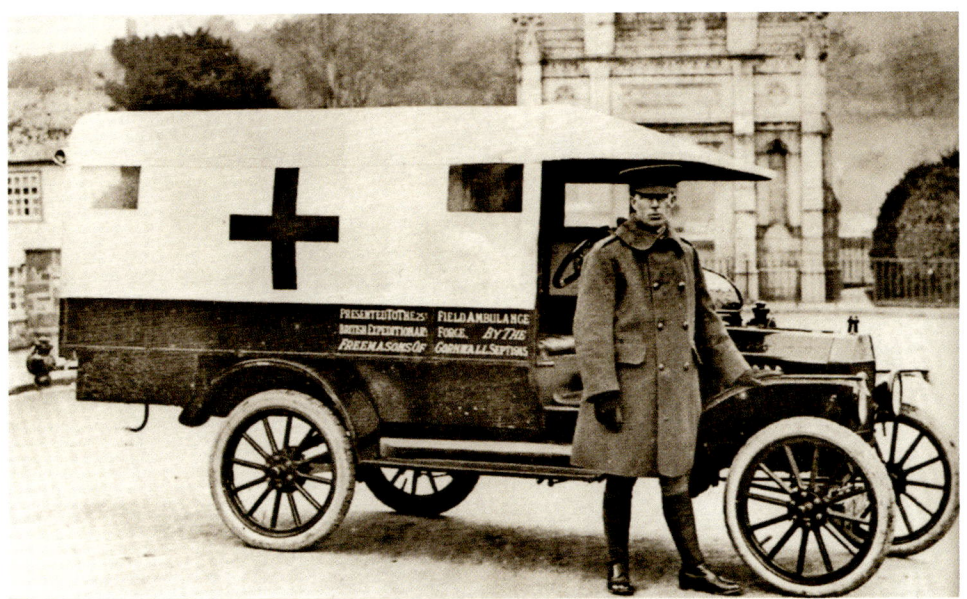

This Ford Model T with an electric head lamp and oil side and rear lamps is seen at Helston. Although the number plate cannot be read, it would have been Cornish because it was presented to the British Expeditionary Force as a ambulance by the Freemasons of Cornwall in September 1915. The driver is standing proudly alongside his vehicle. It was this type of little van which, when used by small businesses, consigned the horse and cart to history.

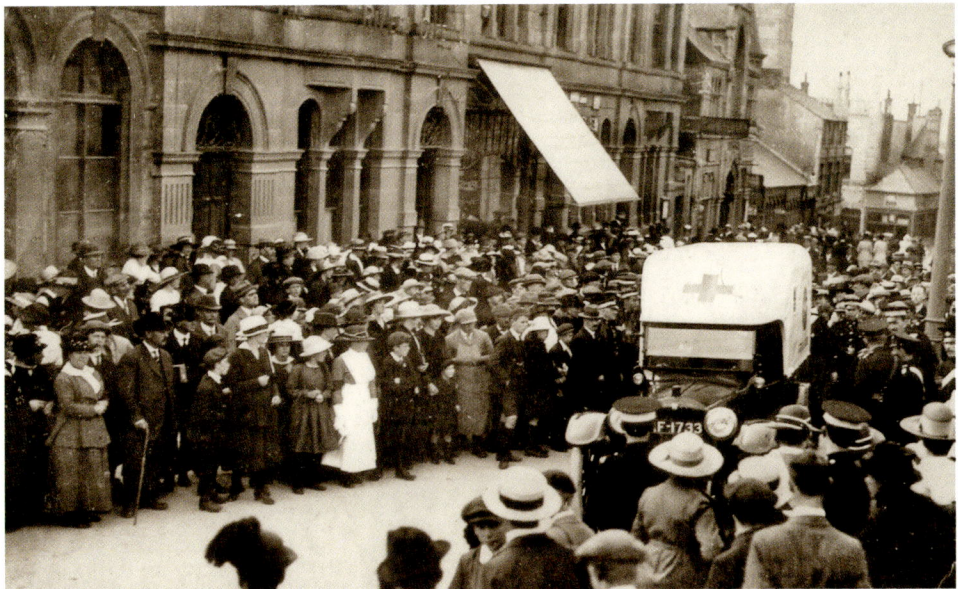

An enormous number of people, all in their best finery with hats and bonnets, have turned out in Alma Place to meet and greet a new vehicle for the Redruth branch of the St John's Ambulance Brigade after the First World War. AF 1733, the registration number on the front of the radiator, is plain to see.

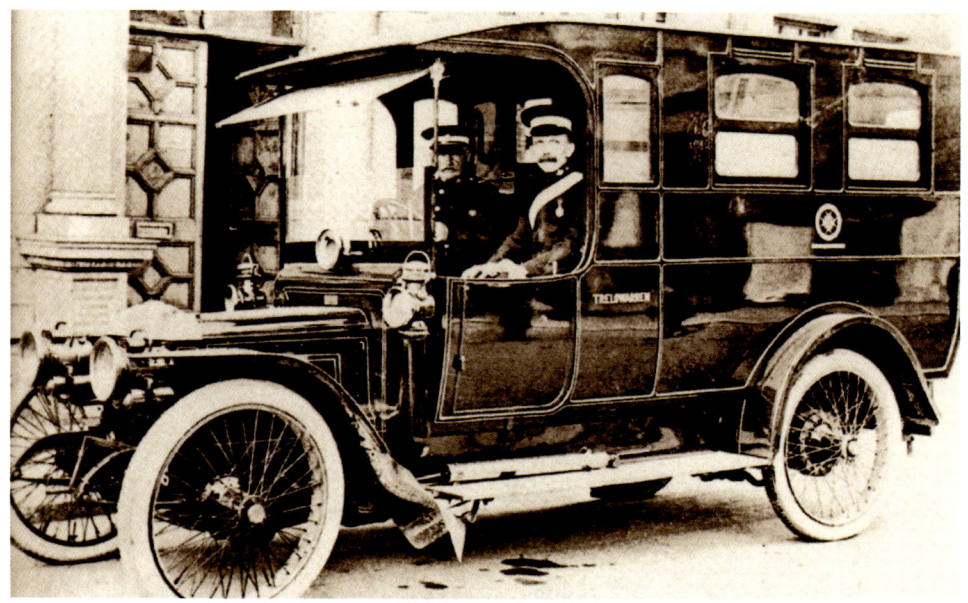

Trelowarren is the name given to this new vehicle for the Camborne Ambulance Brigade on Saturday 18 May 1918. The Cornish registration number was AF 1988. It was photographed outside the council offices, driven by William Wood with Mr Quintrell alongside him. This type of conveyance was often built on a large car chassis; looking at the large wire wheels, it might have been a Bentley or Daimler chassis in this case. The sign writing and lining, hand painting, etc. are superb, as are the lovely sets of large acetylene gas and oil lamps.

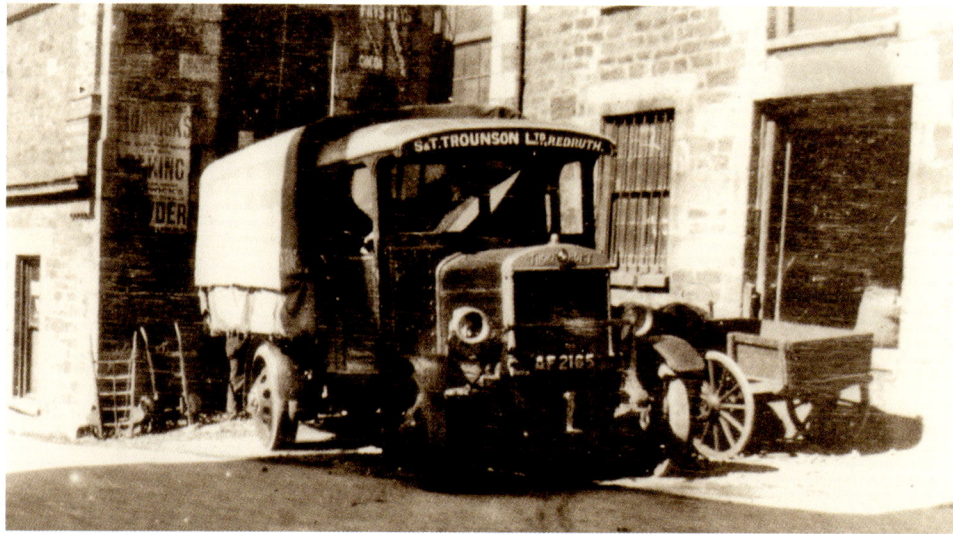

At the back of this wholesale and retail grocer's business in Fore Street, Redruth, S&T Trounson's Thornycroft lorry, AF 2165, is waiting to load or unload its contents on a nice sunny day in the 1920s. The legs of a gentleman can be seen behind the canvas back, with two sack trucks and a hand cart nearby to help him if needed. The lorry has acetylene gas lamps and there are solid tyres on the wheels. The building is still there, but the enamel signs for Fry's Chocolate, etc. are not.

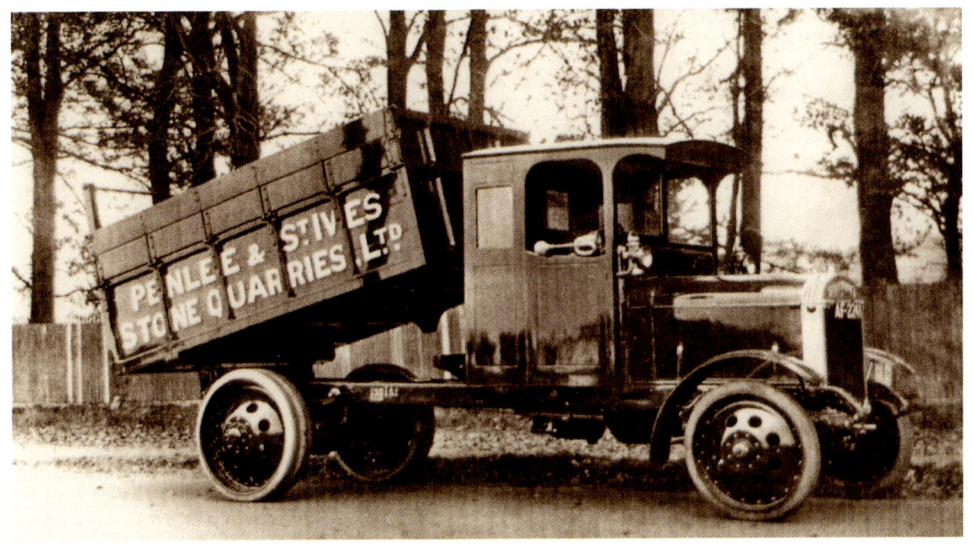

Penlee & St Ives Stone Quarries proudly display their brand new Thornycroft tipper lorry, registered AF 2241 in about 1920. It is still on solid tyres, double to the rear, with brass paraffin lamps and a bulb horn at the driver's elbow.

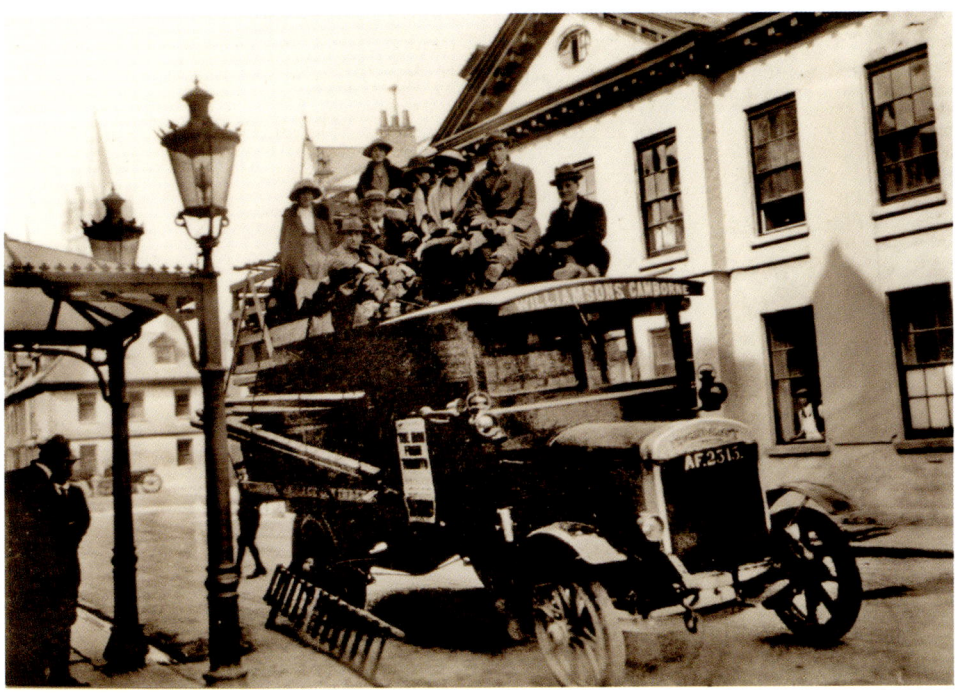

This Thornycroft lorry, AF 2313, is seen outside the theatre in Truro when it was almost new, in about 1915. It has a pair of oil lamps, a bulb horn and a single acetylene lamp. Heaven only knows what all the people are doing on top of the rubbish, with a ladder on the ground. The cast iron street lights are long gone, as is the canopy. A horse and carriage appear to be behind the left hand column and one of the spires of Truro cathedral can be seen behind the lantern of the same post.

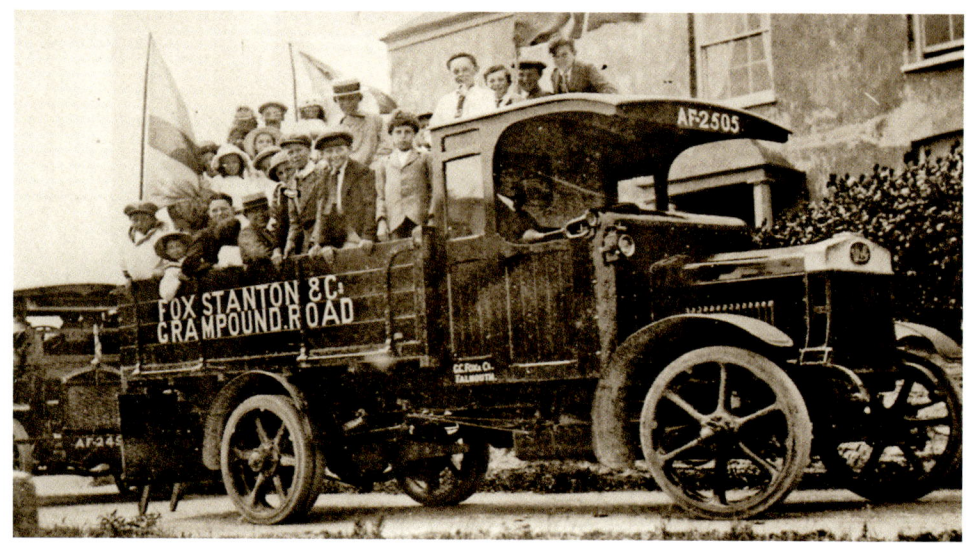

This W&G lorry was on loan for a short while, for what is believed to have been a church outing at Gerrans. The lorry belonged to G. C. Fox & Co. of Falmouth, which became Fox Stanton & Co. They also had a branch at Penryn, down by the side of the river, the Budock side of the bridge, where vessels could tie up and unload cargoes of timber for the company. The registration, AF 2505, dates it to around 1920. The heavy cast wheels and solid rubber tyres, oil lamps, and bulb trumpet horn make it complete. Behind it can be seen AF 2494, a smaller lorry from Portscatho.

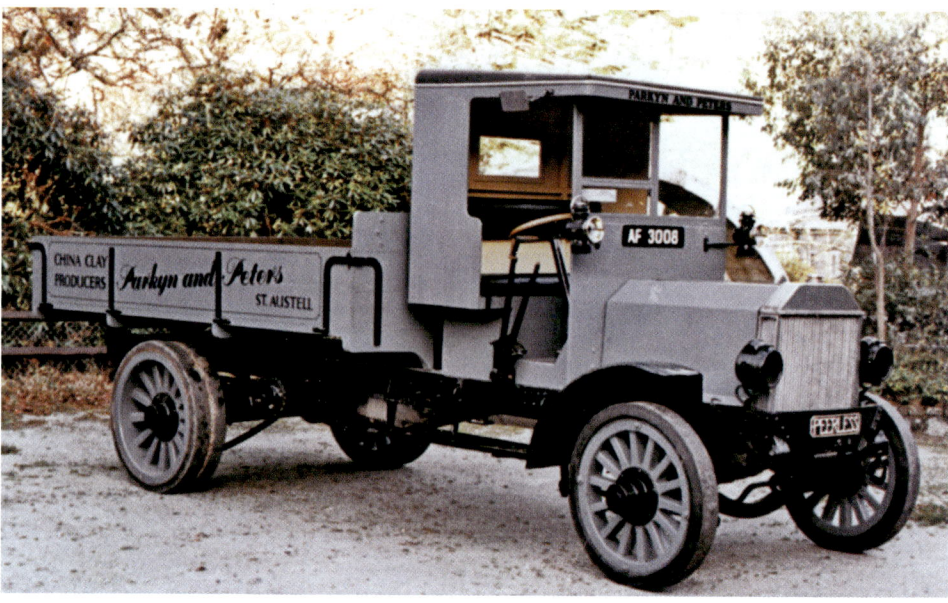

An American Peerless 4½ ton lorry from 1916, AF 3008 was owned by Parkyn & Peters, who were China clay producers at St Austell; restored by Mr Roberts, it can be seen at the Wheal Martyn Museum. It had chain driven double rear wheels, heavy wooden spokes and solid rubber tyres, acetylene gas head lamps and oil side lights and with the hand brake and gear change outside, it must have been difficult to drive.

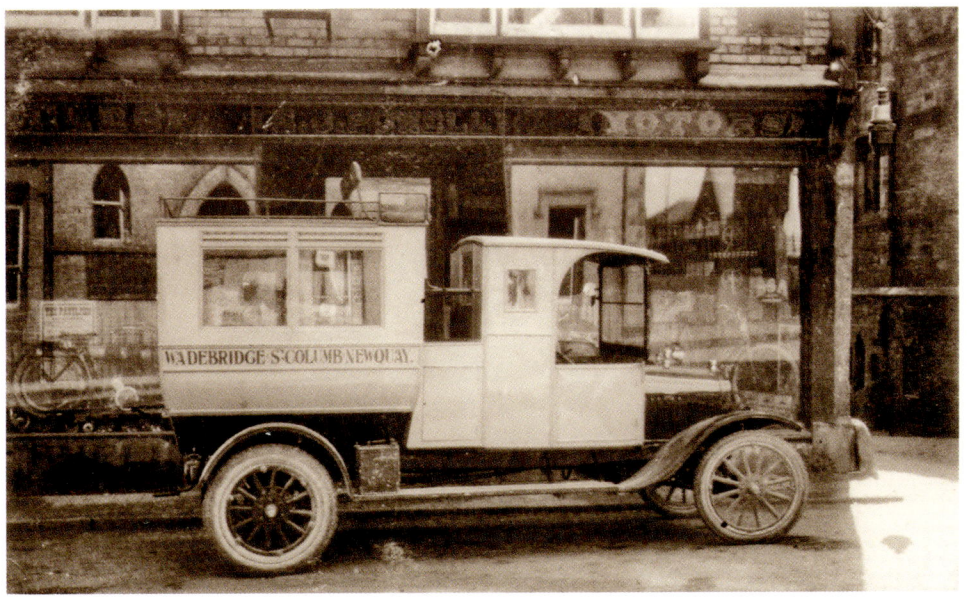

Snapped outside E. J. Powell's cycle shop in St Columb, this Ford Model T of about 1910 or 1912 can be seen in another photograph, where its registration reads AF 3?11. It could be the local ambulance, serving Wadebridge, St Columb and Newquay. It looks like there is a small acetylene cycle lamp attached to the vehicle and a 2-gallon petrol can on the running board. A spark plug can be seen hanging off a bracket on the corner of the shop window and according to the poster there is something on at The Pavilion.

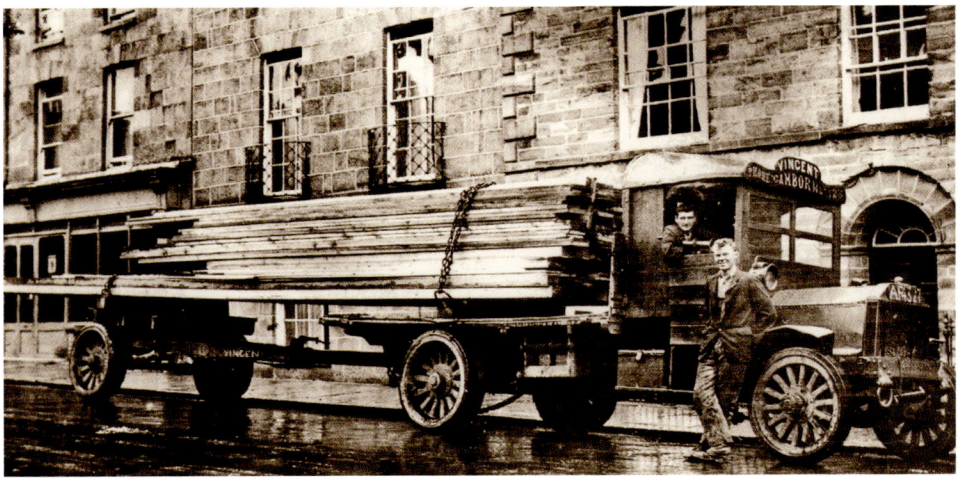

Snapped in Lemon Street, this Peerless lorry was made in the United States, possibly for the War Department, but now carries the registration AF 4327, from about 1920. Like most lorries made for really heavy work, the wheels were made of large wooden spokes and had solid rubber tyres. The lorry, owned by Vincents of Camborne, is seen towing a two-wheeled trailer to take the weight of the extra-long planks of wood.

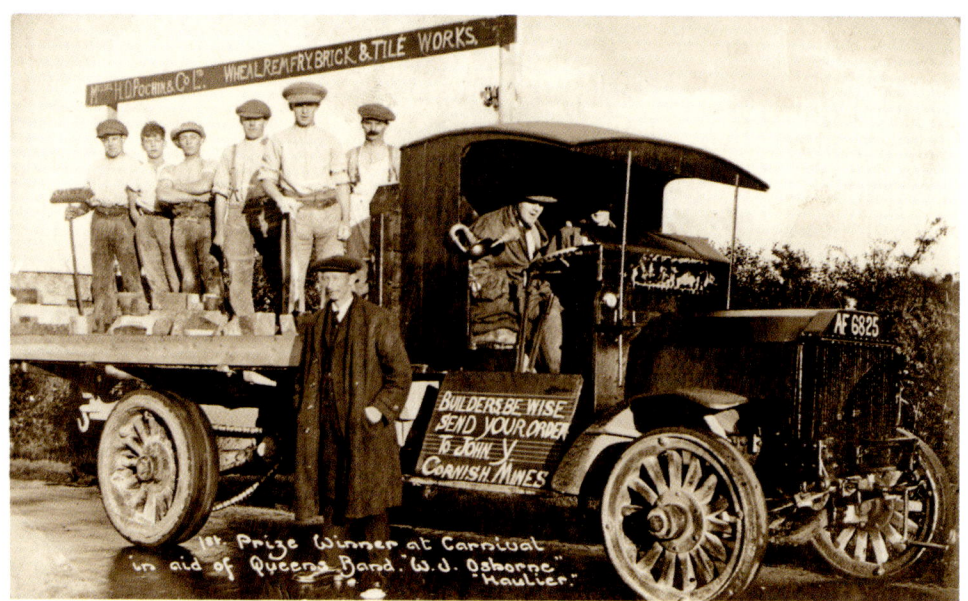

Messers H. D. Pochin & Co. Ltd, Wheal Remfry Brick & Tile Works, as it says, were first prize winners at the carnival in aid of Queens Band (Indian Queens). W. J. Osborne was the owner of the 1920s Ford Model T lorry AF 6825, which had a chain drive to the back double wheels. But builders be wise, send your orders to John Y. Cornish Mines.

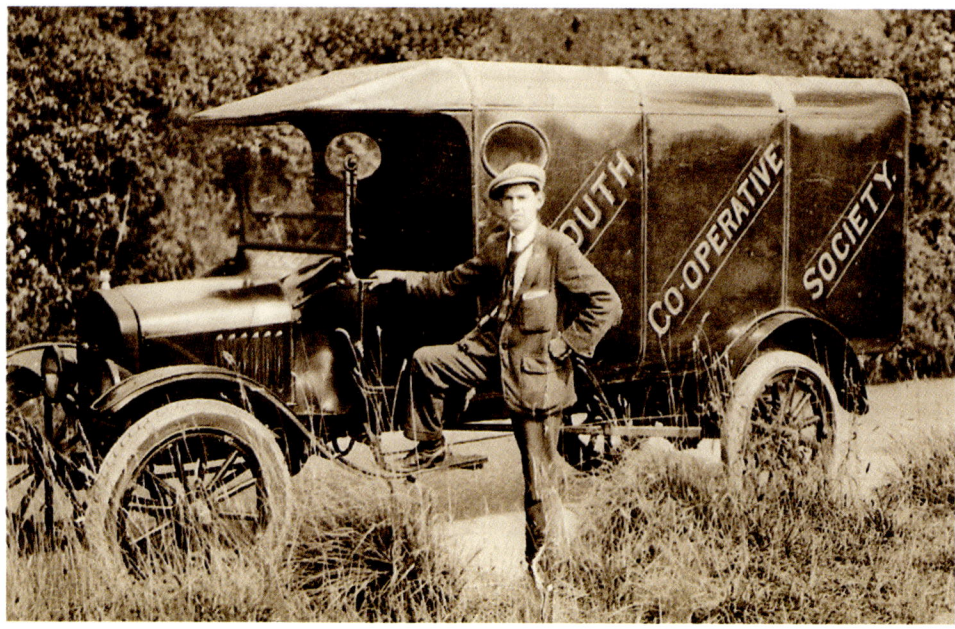

The registration number below the windscreen on this Falmouth Co-Operative Society Ford Model T van is only just readable – is it AF 8943? With the typical Ford headlamps and the shape of the radiator cap, this van could almost be new. The driver, posing with his loose tie and cigarette, is believed to be Ted Richards, making the van 93 years old.

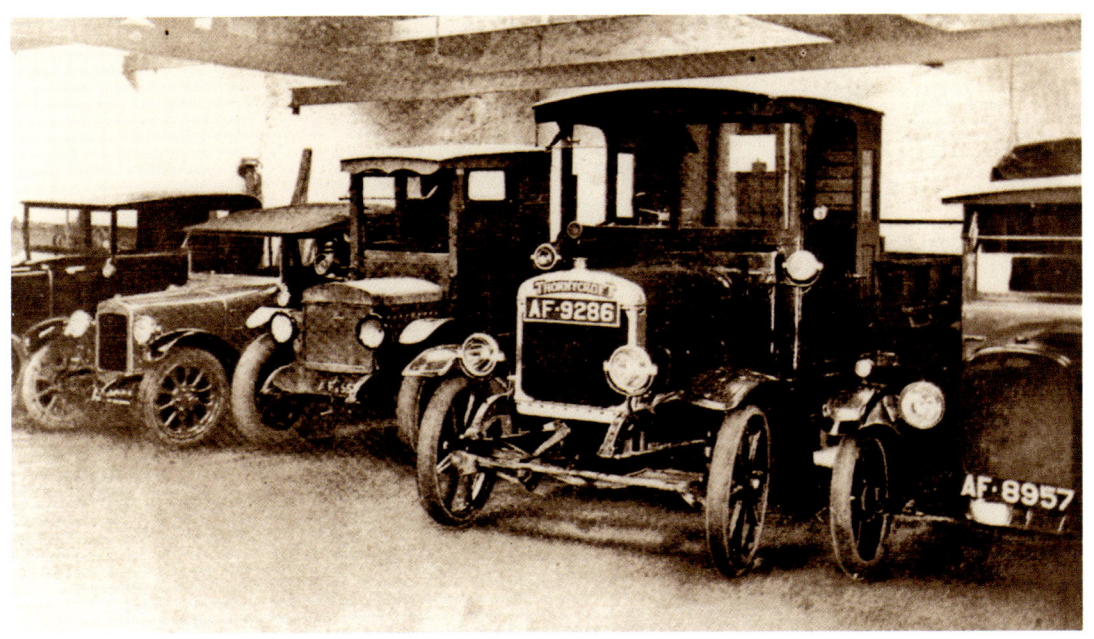

This image from the mid-1920s shows a Thornycroft lorry, AF 9286; a Chevrolet, AF 8957; a Maxwell flat truck; and an Austin car, all gathered for storage or repair at a commercial garage somewhere in Cornwall, or are they for sale?

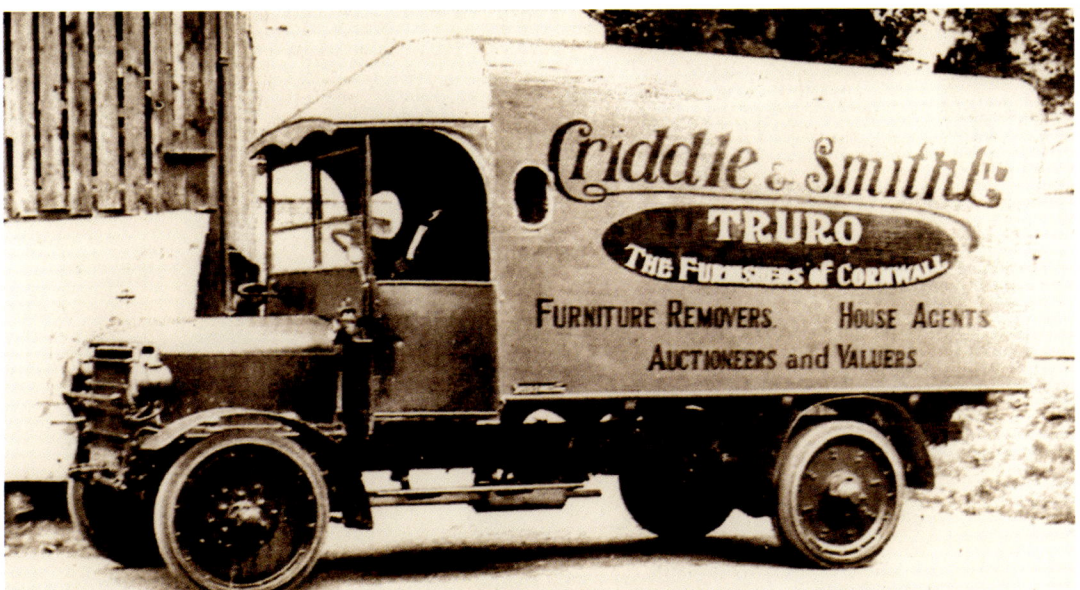

Built on what is believed to be a Daimler chassis, this Criddle & Smith lorry was one of the first motorised vehicles to be used by the firm after it finished with horse-drawn wagons. It had solid wheels and tyres and used both acetylene and oil lamps. The number of the lorry is thought to have been AF 9885.

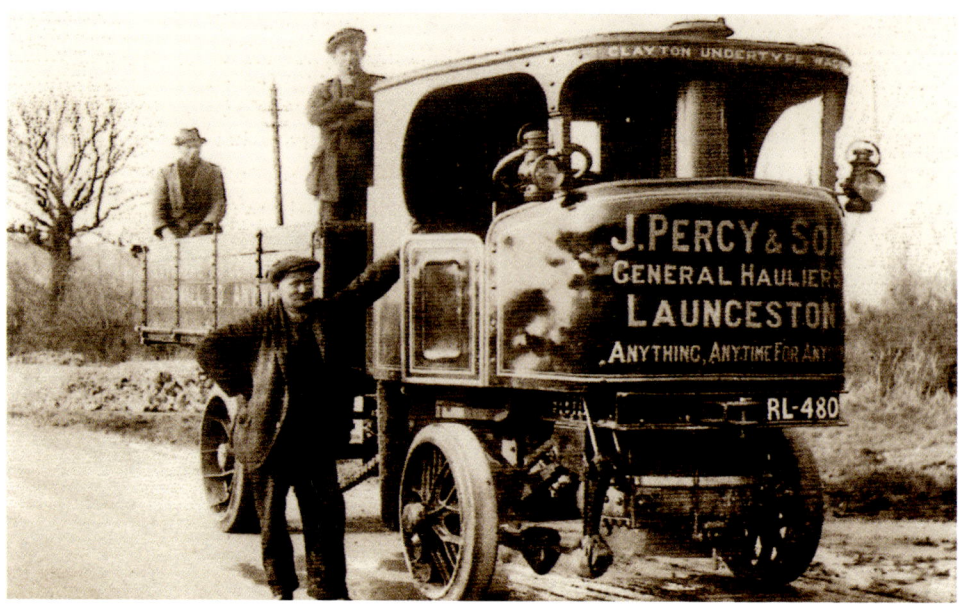

New in 1925 and registered RL 480, this Clayton Three-way Tipper seen here working in North Cornwall was believed to be made in Cornwall but nothing more is known except that it was bought by J. Percy & Son, who were general hauliers; they advertised their work as 'Anything, Anytime, Anywhere'. Chain-driven to the rear wheels and running on solid tyres, it is not known if it was steam or petrol powered, but it had lovely brass 'Lucas King of the Road' oil lamps.

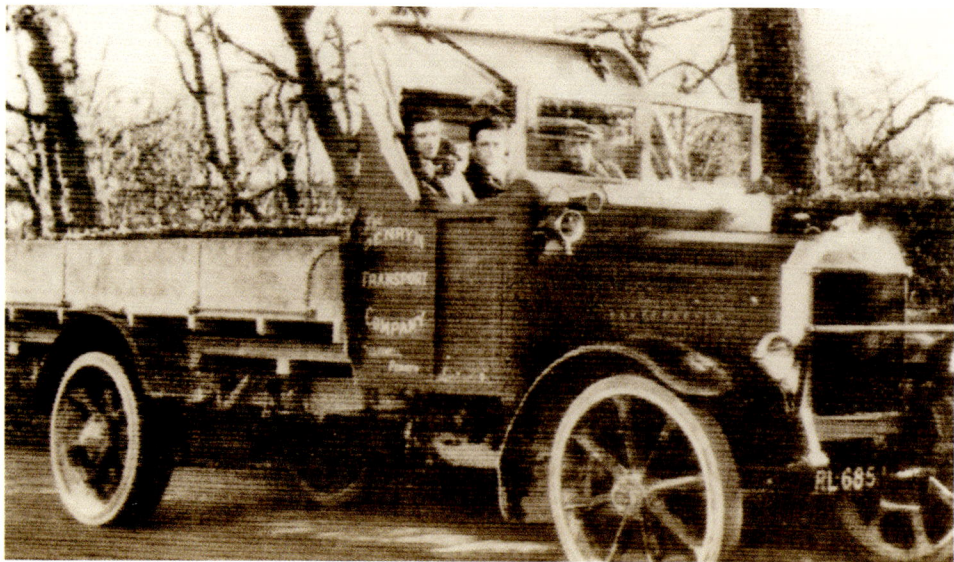

With drop sides for easy loading and unloading, this 1926 Dennis lorry belonging to the Penryn Transport Co. of Treluswell could carry almost any dry freight. Registered as RL 685, it ran on solid tyres although pneumatics had been used on Edwardian motor cars and motorcycles for some time; it also had electric and oil lamps and also a bulb horn. It must have been fine weather when this photo was taken with the driver's hood open.

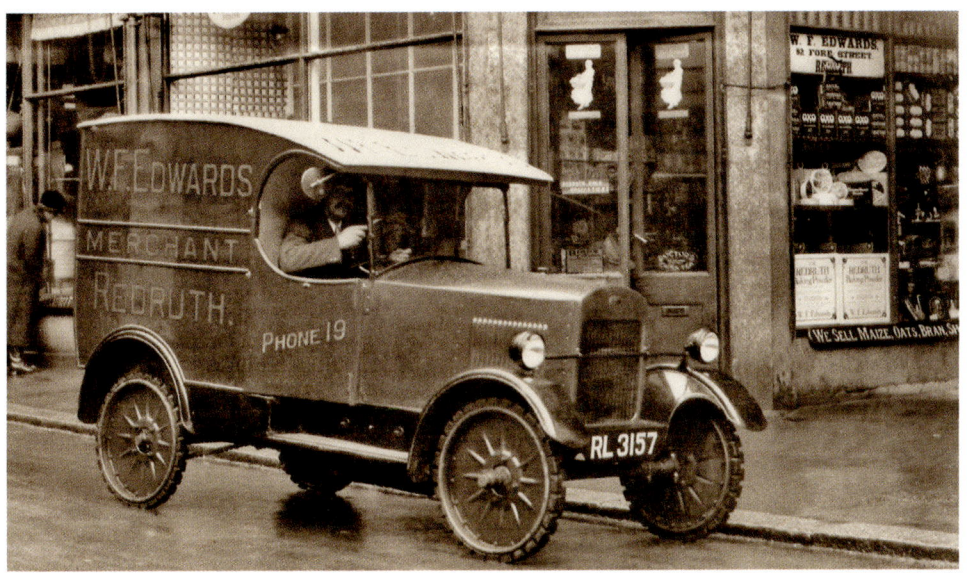

The sign written on this lovely little Trogan van says 'W. F. Edwards, Merchant, Redruth Phone 19'. Running on narrow, solid tyres, it had a 2-stroke, 4-cylinder slow-revving engine with good pulling power, and good hill climbing ability in particular. Registered RL 3157, it dates from about 1925 and would have cost less than £120 when new. As a merchant, they certainly sold almost everything from maize, oats and bran to furniture polish and Oxo as well as Redruth rock and Redruth baking powder, all at 92 Fore Street. They have long gone and the shop is empty.

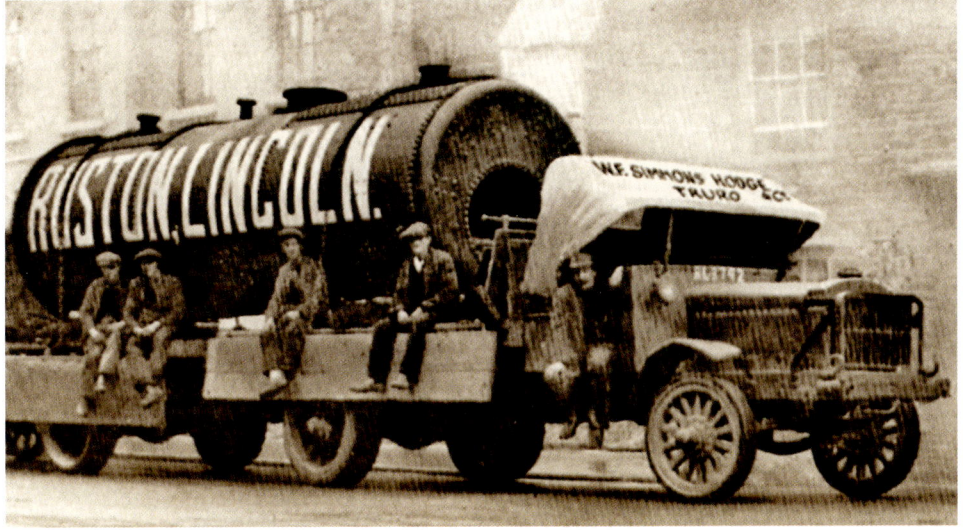

This huge lorry from Truro registered RL 3792 belonged to W. F. Simmons Hodge & Co. It could be a 1926/27 Scamell and is being used to move a large round tank marked 'RUSTON LINCOLN', the name of a firm which made ships' boilers and other engineering parts for large projects. To take the weight, a four-wheeled trailer is being used; it must have been terrible to drive and steer with solid tyres on the front and pneumatics behind.

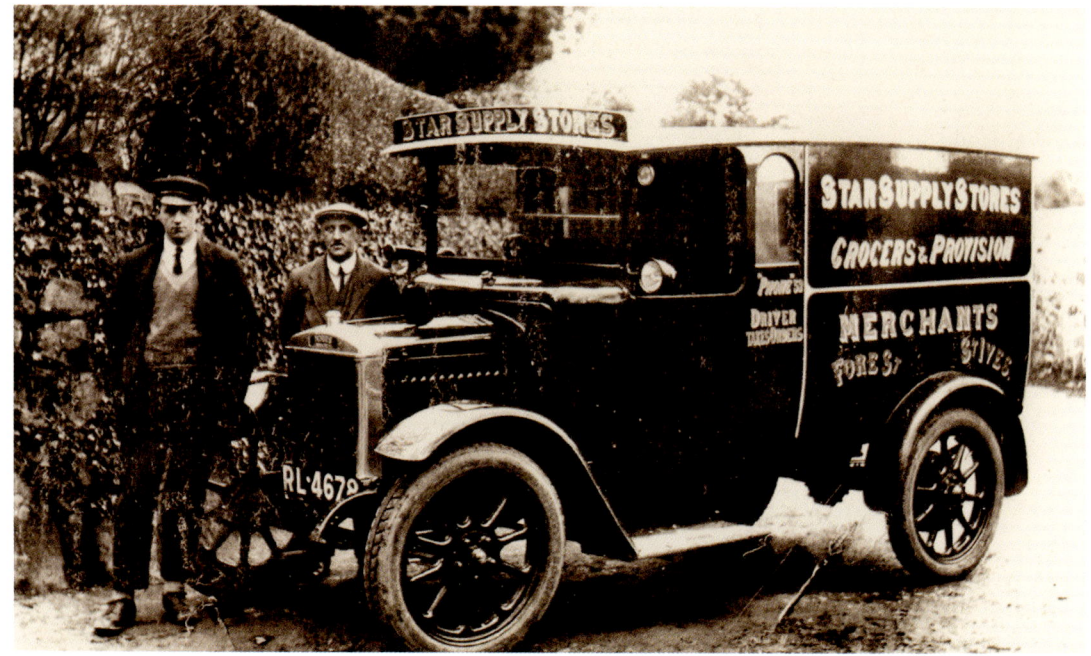

This lovely Morris Commercial van had only a pair of side lights to illuminate the way in the dark. Dating from about 1925, this vehicle registered RL 4678 has been chosen by the Star Supply Stores, Grocers and Provision Merchants of Fore Street, St Ives Phone No. 52. The driver is taking orders.

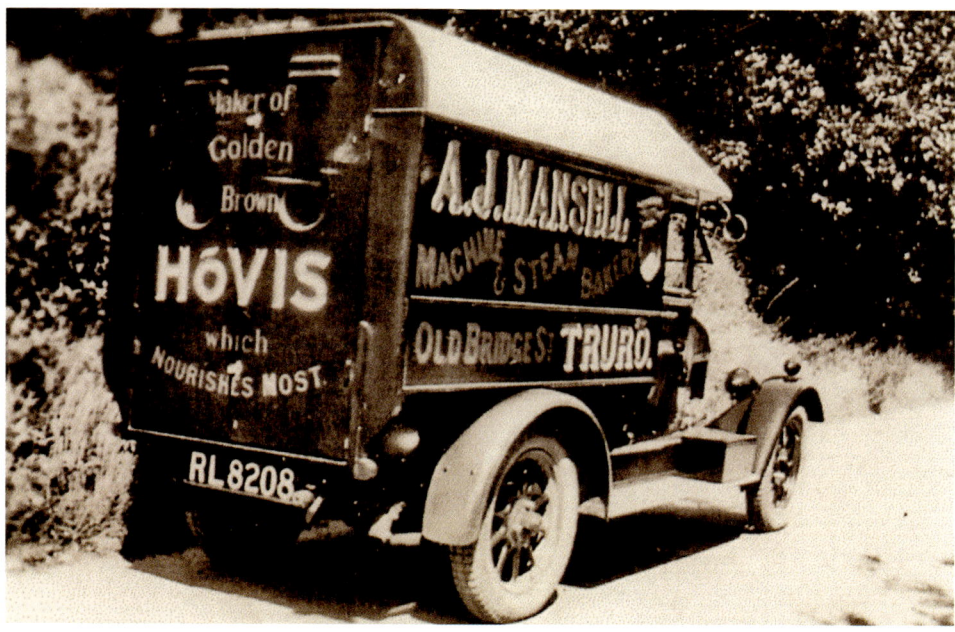

A. J. Mansell, Machine & Steam Bakery of Old Bridge Street, Truro, preferred this Morris van, RL 8208, for his deliveries, advertising Golden Brown Hovis. This scene from the late 1920s is a long way from when he started with his horse and cart.

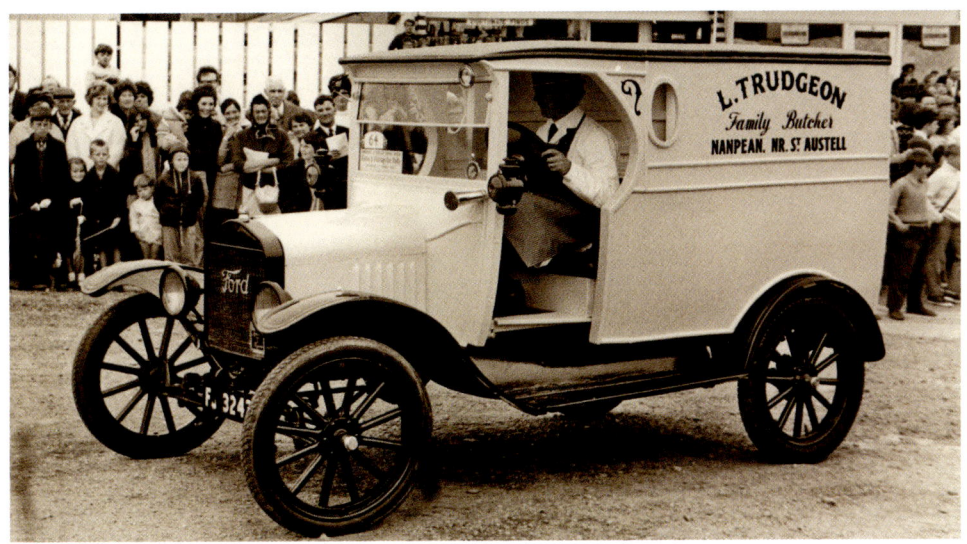

Les Trudgeon, Family Butcher from Nanpean, St Austell, is seen here with his left hand driver Ford Model T. The head lamps are the same as the one seen in Falmouth but the shape of the van body back from and including the windscreen is different: oval windows rather than the round ones seen in Falmouth, and no running boards. He also has 'Bun' type oil side lamps and a bulb horn. Les is seen dressed in his butcher's apron and the whole turnout is to his usual standard – perfect. The notice in the windscreen says 'Mount Charles Band Week Fete and Vintage Car Rally' with his number, 64, from when this snap was taken at a 1970s rally at Penzance. It's a pity that it isn't a Cornish number but the van dates from the mid-1920s.

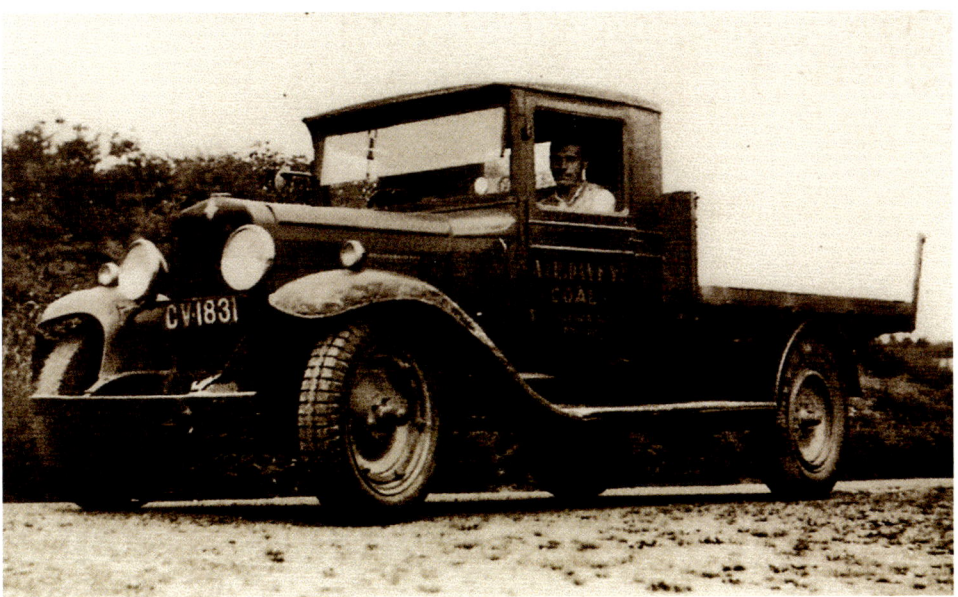

Arthur F. Davey, Coal Merchant of Truro, is seen here in the passenger seat of his drop-sided American Chevrolet lorry. CV 1831 would date from 1929 and was well used, as the dents in the front wings show.

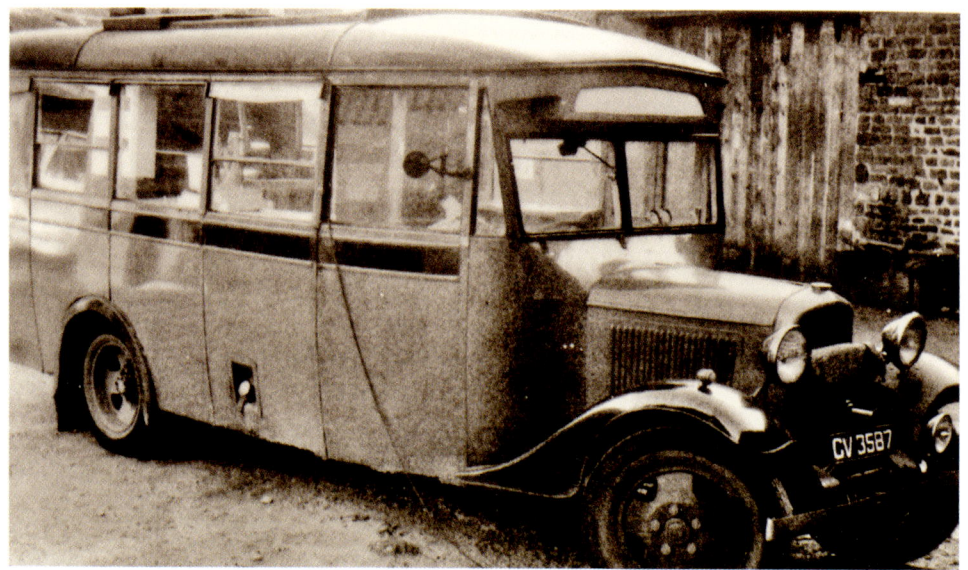

This small vehicle could at one time have been a bus with a split windscreen. Now it has been converted into a mobile fish and chip shop with the number CV 3587. Looking through one of the windows, you can see the machine which, when its handle was pulled down, changed potatoes into chips!

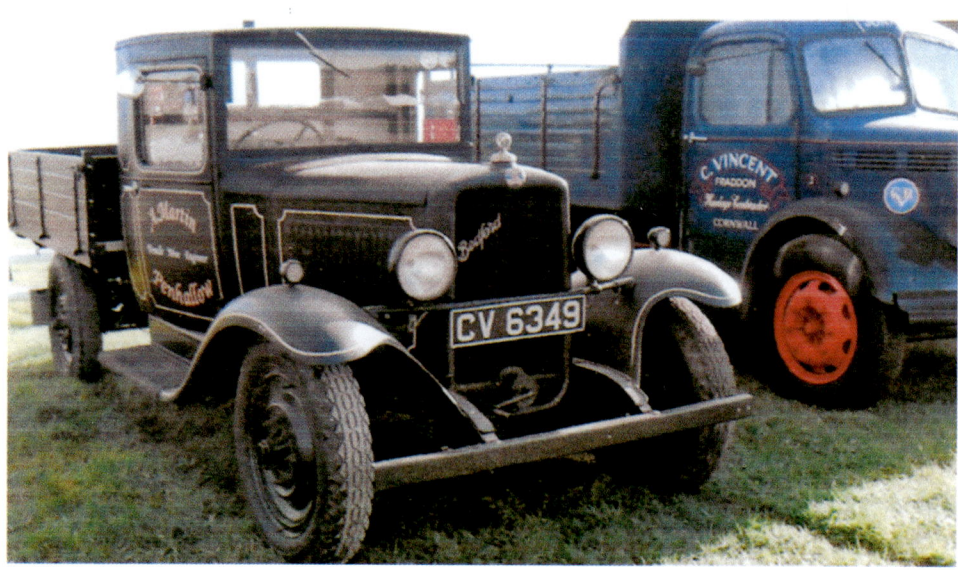

CV 6349 is a lovely restored 2-ton drop-sided, open Bedford lorry owned by A. Martin, an engineer from Penhallow. It is seen next to a red-wheeled lorry owned by C. Vincent, a haulage contractor from Fraddon, with a split windscreen. Both have almost perfect painting and lining.

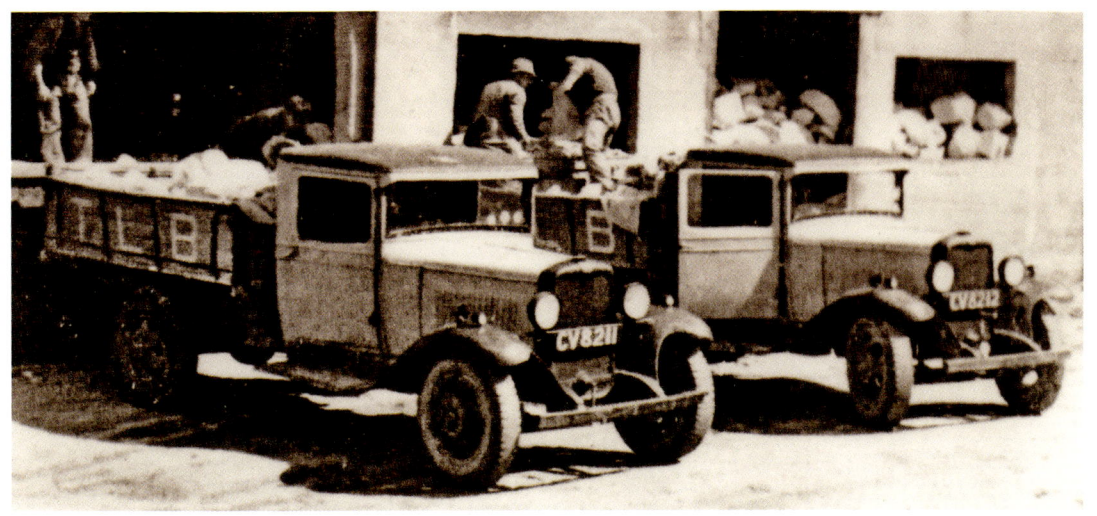

CV 8212 is seen here with its younger brother, CV 8211. This pair of Bedford 2-tonners owned by TL&B are pictured with full loads of China clay. The licence numbers date them to 1932/33.

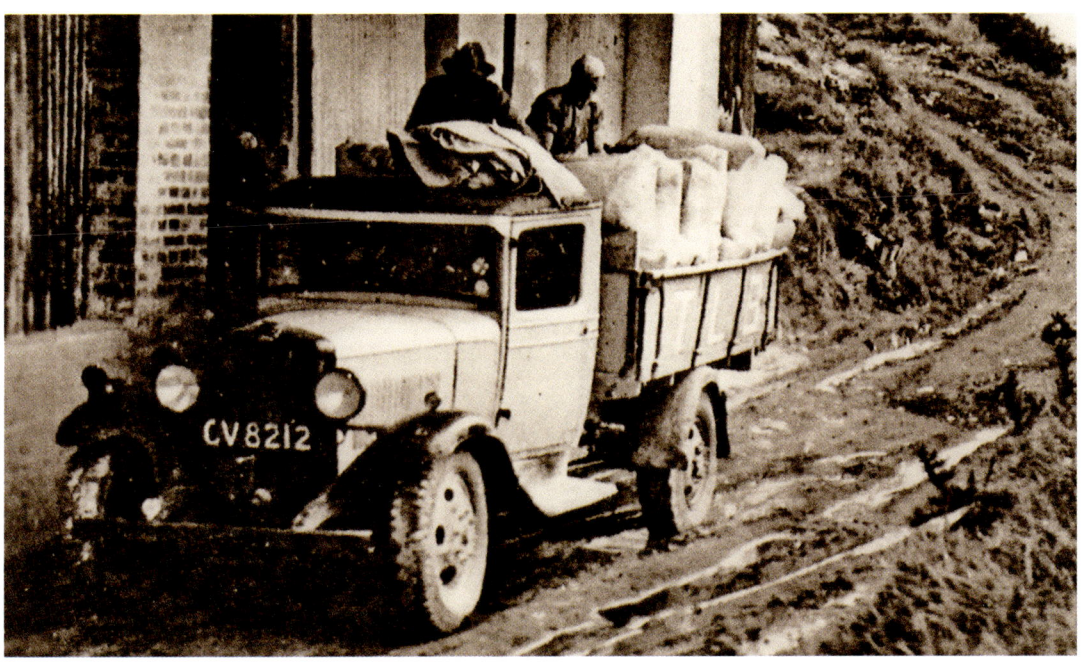

This 2-ton Bedford lorry owned by Taylor & Low Bros of St Austell had seen better days when it was snapped in the mud and ruts loading large bags of China clay bound for Italy. It was given the Cornish registration number CV 8212 in 1932/33.

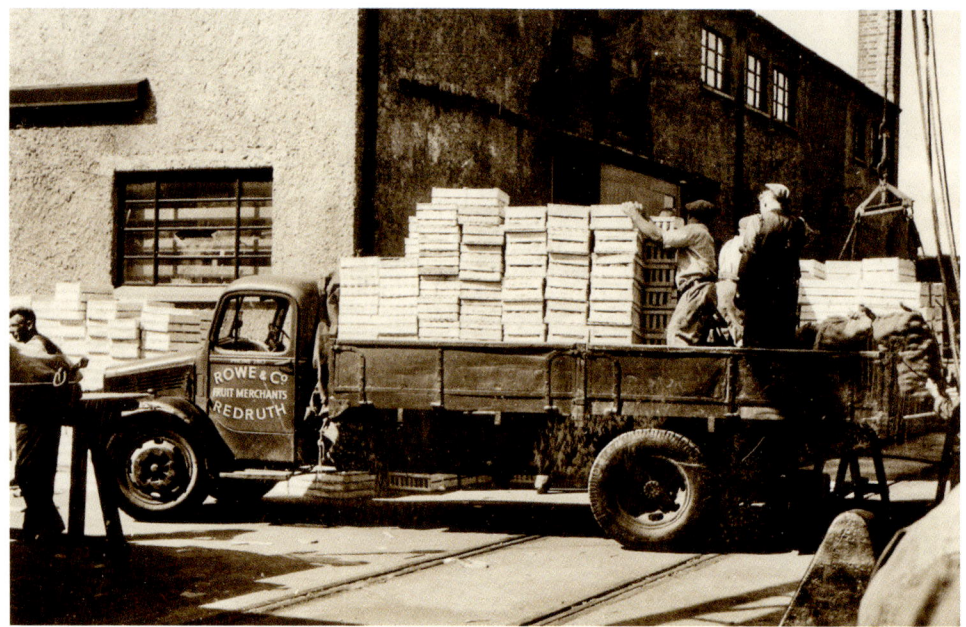

Rowe & Co., fruit merchants from Redruth, are seen here with the first cargo of Italian pears to arrive after the Second World War, being unloaded at Falmouth. Rowe & Co. had been acting as the sole UK representatives of the South Tyrolean growers in their contract with the Ministry of Food.

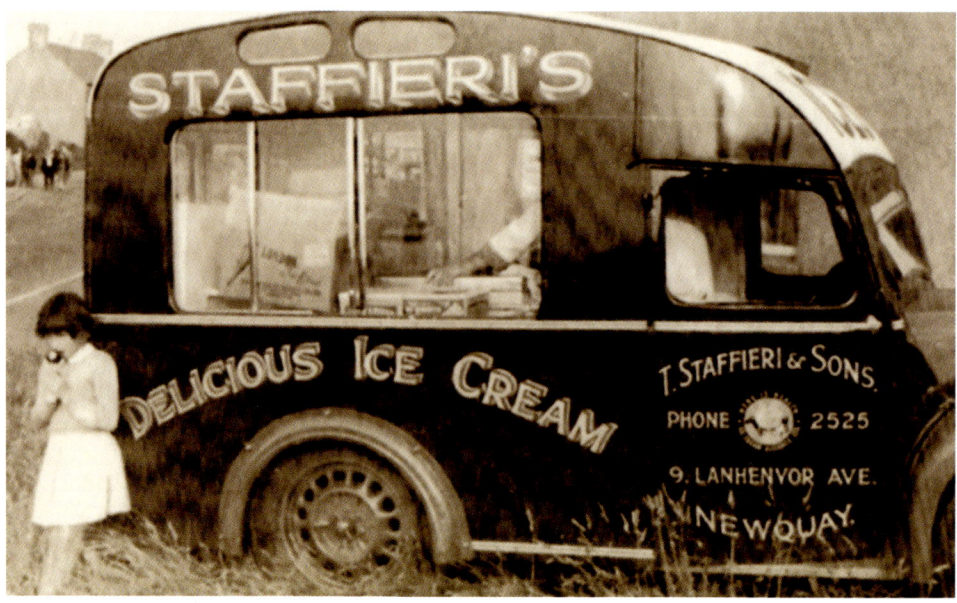

As it says on the side of the van, Staffieri's Delicious Ice Cream, with their phone number as Newquay 2525 and their address as Lanhenvor Avenue; a little girl seems to be enjoying an ice cream. The Staffieri family came from Italy in the early 1900s.

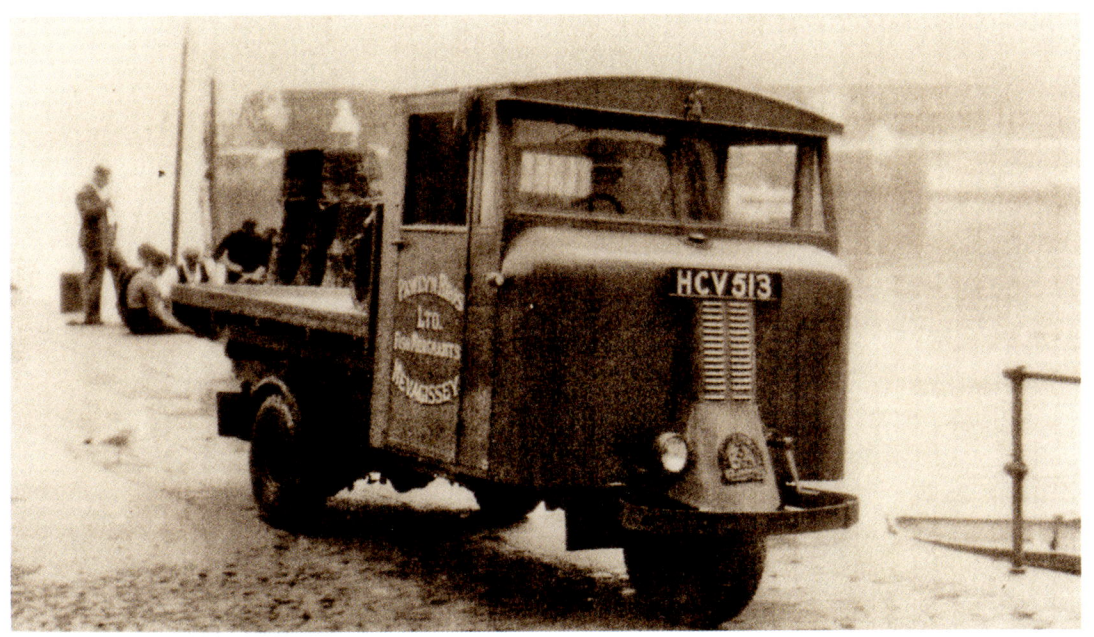

A three-wheel Scammell, HCV 513, from around 1935, belonging to Pawlyn Brothers Ltd, Fish Merchants, Mevagissey, is seen here on the quayside.

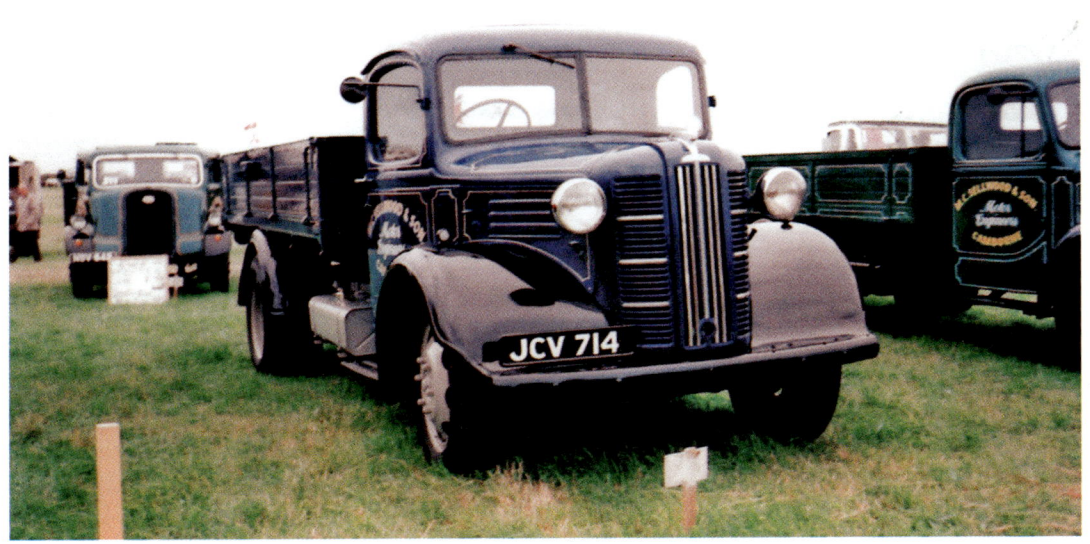

This nicely restored Austin 2-ton lorry, JCV 714, is owned by Malcolm Selwood, Motor Engineer, Camborne. It has a split windscreen, a drop side and a large exposed fuel tank and is ready to take away any dry cargo. Alongside can be seen another Selwood & Son lorry. Both are painted green with a cream lining.

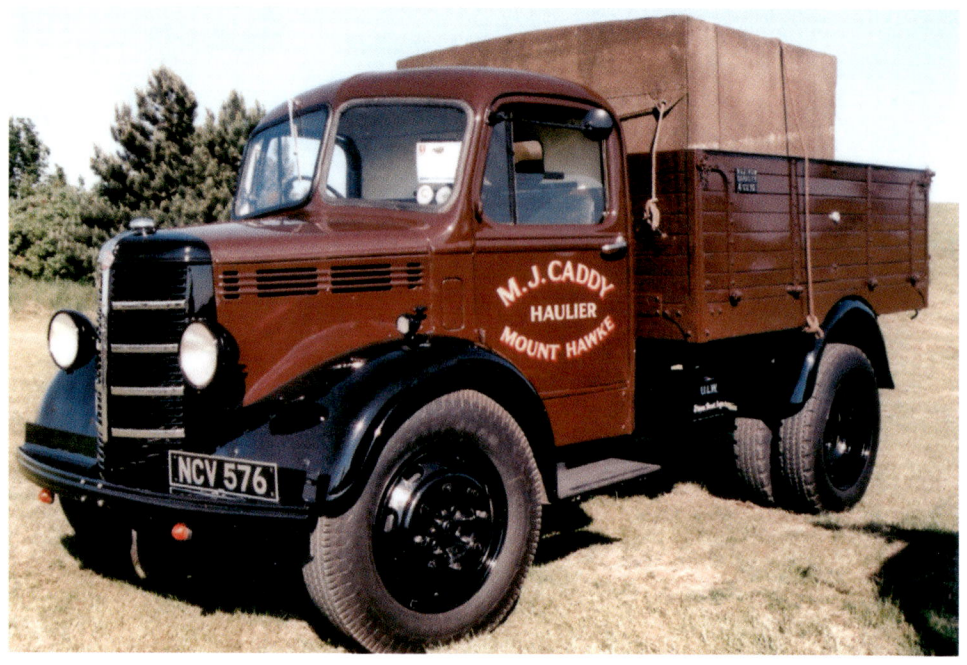

Martin J. Caddy, a haulier from Mount Hawke, owns this absolutely perfect split windscreen O-type Bedford drop-sided lorry, once owned by Williamsons of Camborne and registered NCV 576. It has double wheels to the rear and is almost original, apart from the indicators at the front.

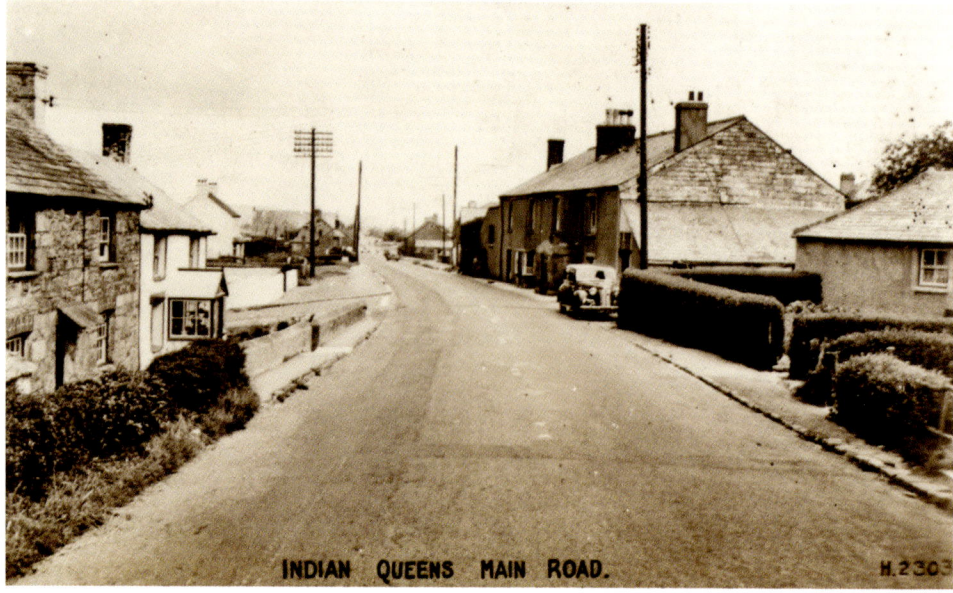

This was the main A30 road through Cornwall, seen here at Indian Queens. Looking at the postcard, it can be seen that not much traffic was using it. After the Second World War a lot of vehicles were exported for a while; later, cars became more plentiful and because of that, traffic built up and several little villages were bypassed, as was Indian Queens.

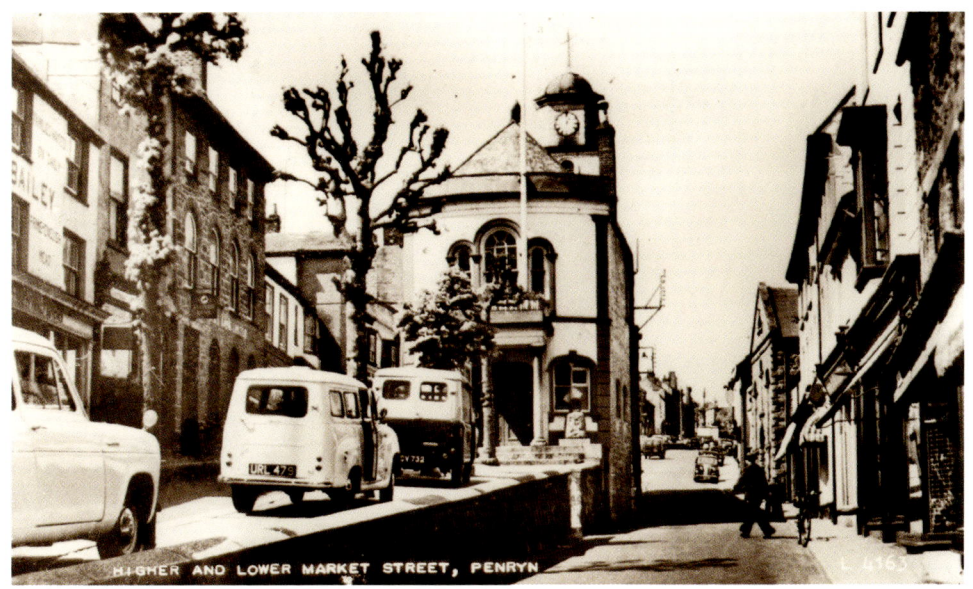

Taken from the lower side of the town clock, this image shows cars and vans parked between the trees. The rounded top of the windows marks the Council Chambers, Penryn. URL 479, with the driver's door opening, is an A35 van showing windows in the side. ?CV 732 is a Ford.

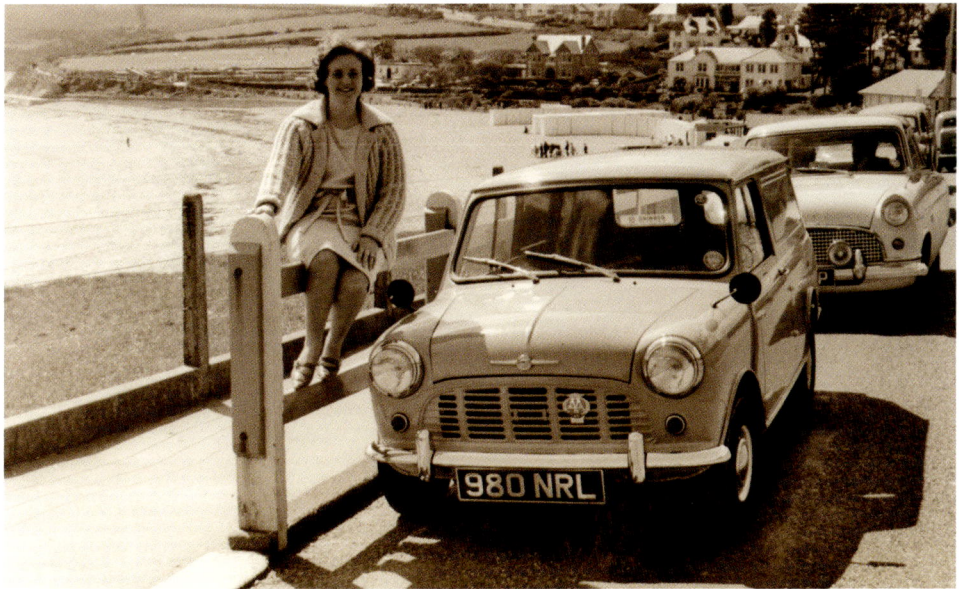

This Morris Mini van, 980 NRL, was bought new from HTP Truro in the early 1960s. The deal was a used Austin plus £120 in exchange for the Mini van with a full tank of petrol, AA membership and 18 months' servicing for free. Behind can be seen a Ford, snapped at Gyllingvase beach, Falmouth, on the day it was bought. Since then, the fencing has been replaced with stainless steel. I know – the lady sitting on the fence is my wife Rosemary and I took the photograph.

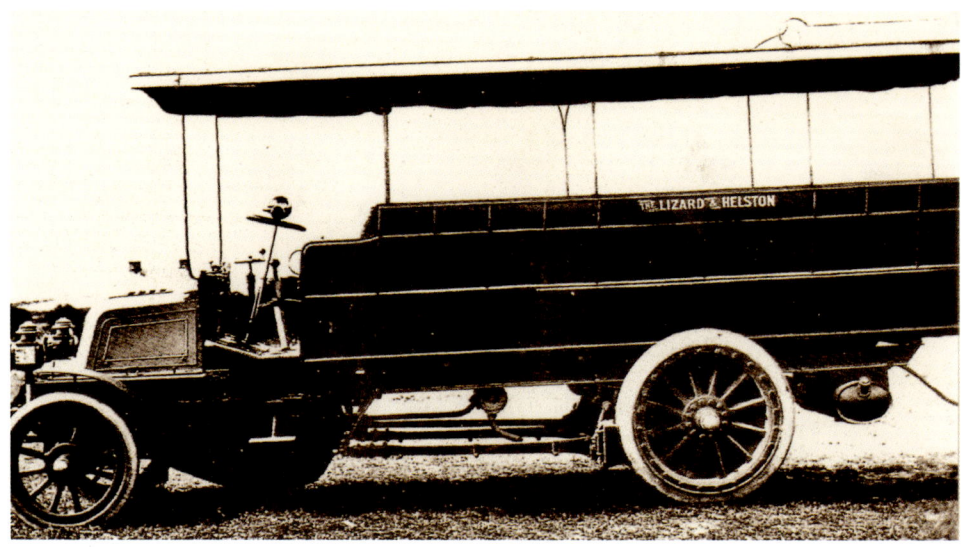

Delivered with candle lamps, this 30 hp Miles Daimler Wagonette, given the number 1, is seen here at the Lizard on its inaugural run from Helston on 15 August 1903 with the Cornish registration number AF 37. Solid rubber tyres costing £200 a set were used on all wheels in those days, and it was common for them to leave the wheel after a few hundred miles. The body was the open type, with no protection for the twenty passengers when fully loaded. The gearbox was arranged to give four speeds forward and one reverse, which meant speeds of between 3 and 14 mph, although petrol was cheap at 4*d* a gallon.

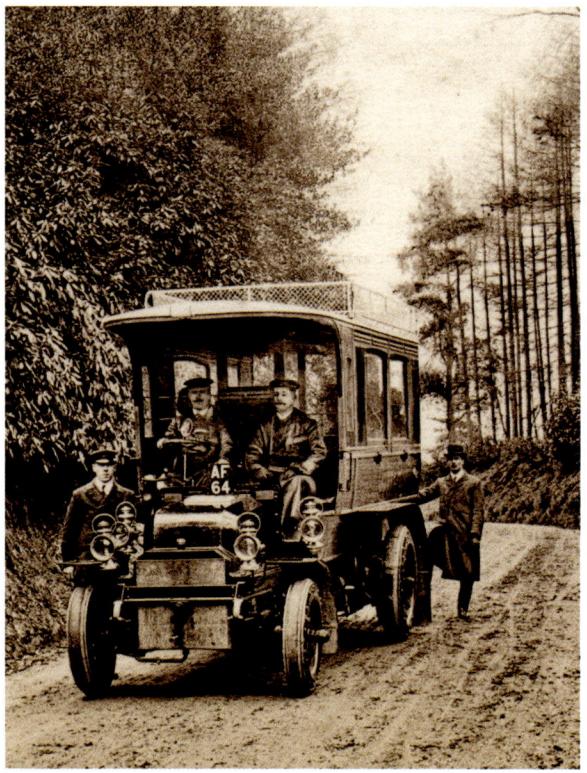

Flossie sent this postcard from Alcester to Birmingham in 1912. It shows a 1904 20 hp Milnes-Daimler, given the Cornish registration AF 64 in 1904. Printed on the bottom, it states that it is on the way to Beaconfield by GWR motor car, running on the solid rubber tyres of the time. I wonder whose job it would be to clean the two sets of brass oil lamps? In all, it looks very well presented.

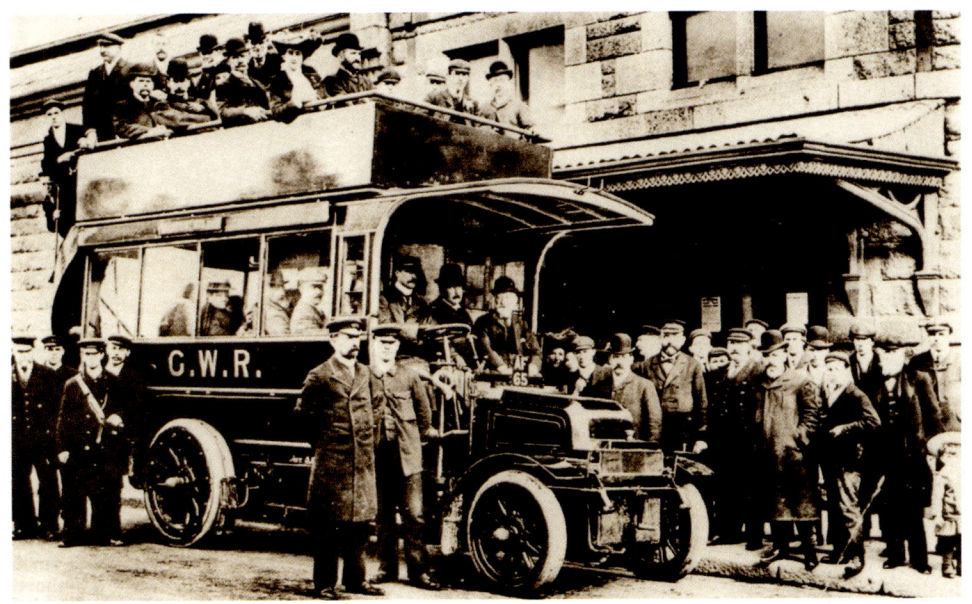

Following on from the last picture of AF 64, this is AF 65, seen on the inaugural run of the Newlyn–Penzance–Marazion route. Again, this is a 20 hp Milnes-Daimler registered in 1904. Seen at Penzance Railway Station, a different design can be seen to the previous image: this vehicle has seating on the top deck instead of luggage, with an outside stair to get there. Take a look at the braking system on the rear wheel of the GWR omnibus. The presence of the station master on this occasion demands some respect, as do the twenty-odd passengers aboard, including the lady on the top deck with a fancy hat.

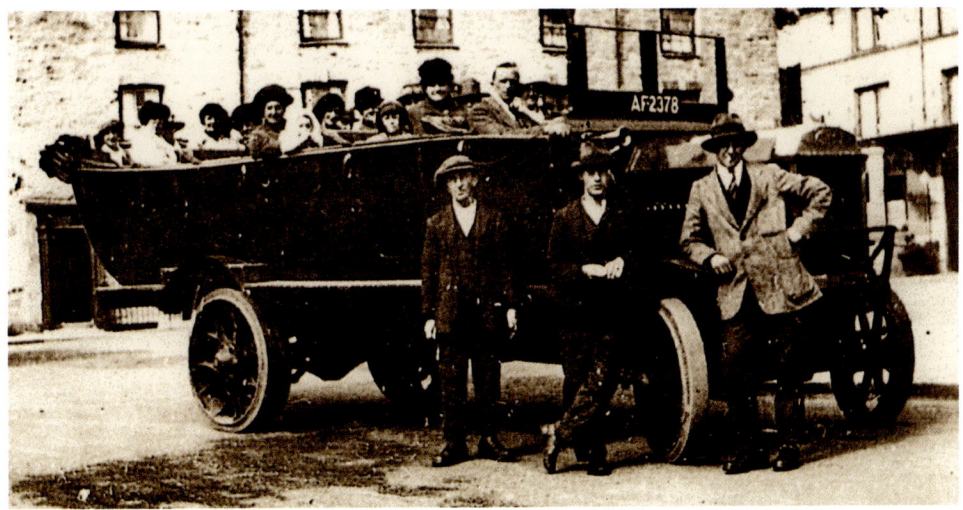

Another vehicle on the Penryn to Falmouth route was this 'Ruby' bus, seen here at Falmouth. The owner, on the right, is Thomas James Rapson of the 15 Balls public house (now closed). The vehicle is a 39 hp Saurer with twenty-eight seats, registered as AF 2378 in 1919, and had dark blue runs on solid rubber tyres. The hood can be seen folded back on this nice day. The Rapson family was involved in coal dealing, the grocery trade and as the Penryn Harbour Master.

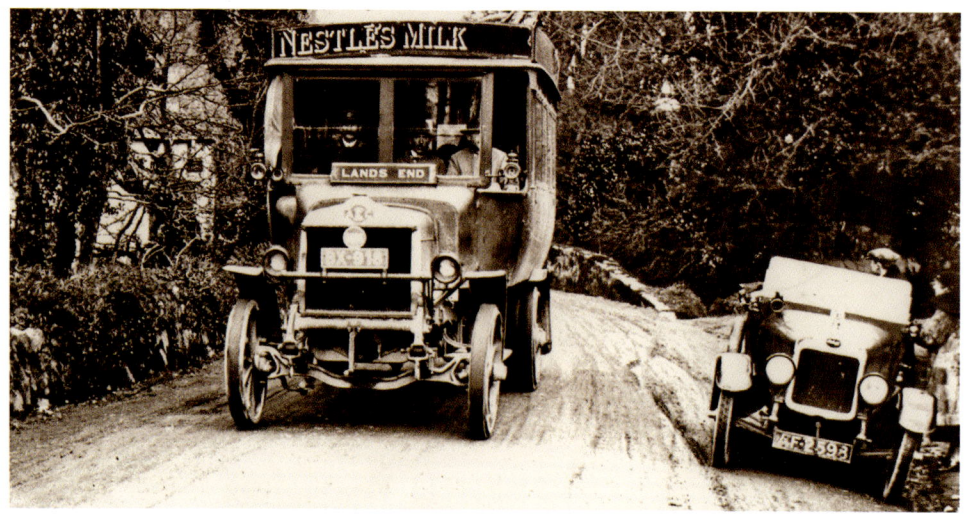

Advertising Nestlé's Milk, this AEC 30 hp bus is on its way to Penzance as the destination board says 'Lands End'. BX 918 (not a Cornish registration) is about to pass on its near side a 10.5 hp Calcott, made in Coventry. AF 2598 (owned by the author) was registered in about 1922; the car was originally bought from Holmans of Penzance, who had an agency for them. The bus is a large one with acetylene head lamps and 'King of the Road' oil lamps and it ran on solid rubber tyres. Two passengers and the driver are visible. Fancy starting this bus by hand in the wet...

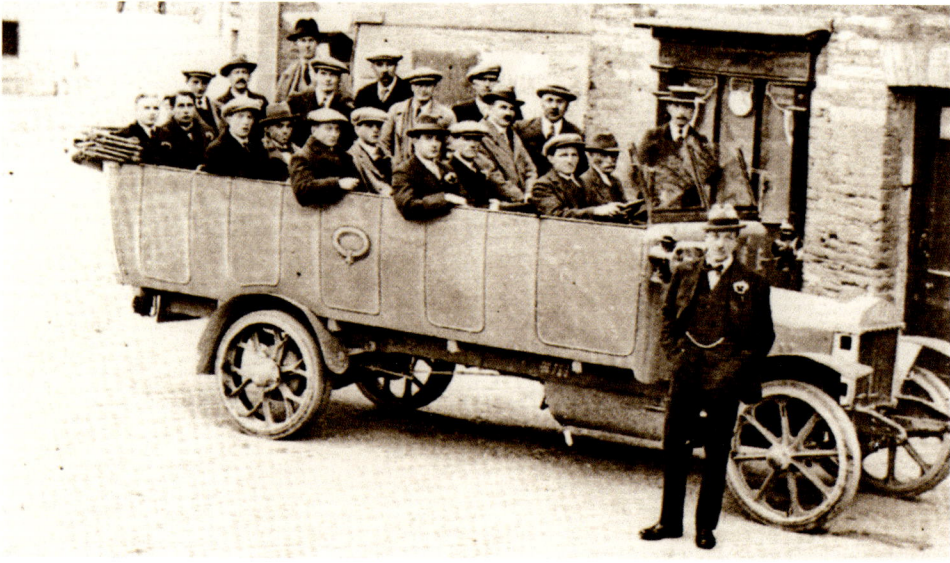

Thomas and William Hawkey of Wadebridge bought a Vulcan 18-seater registered AF 2669 following the death of their father, who founded a business as a coach and carriage builder and saw-miller. This char-á-banc, seen in this picture, was used for excursions from the town and hired out to private parties such as Sunday schools and others. It can be dated to 1920 by the rubber tyres. A small pair of oil lamps can be seen, as can a folded down hood; when in place, it would give a little shelter, but imagine a windy day. The gentleman in the suit and the gold watch chain is believed to be Thomas Hawkey.

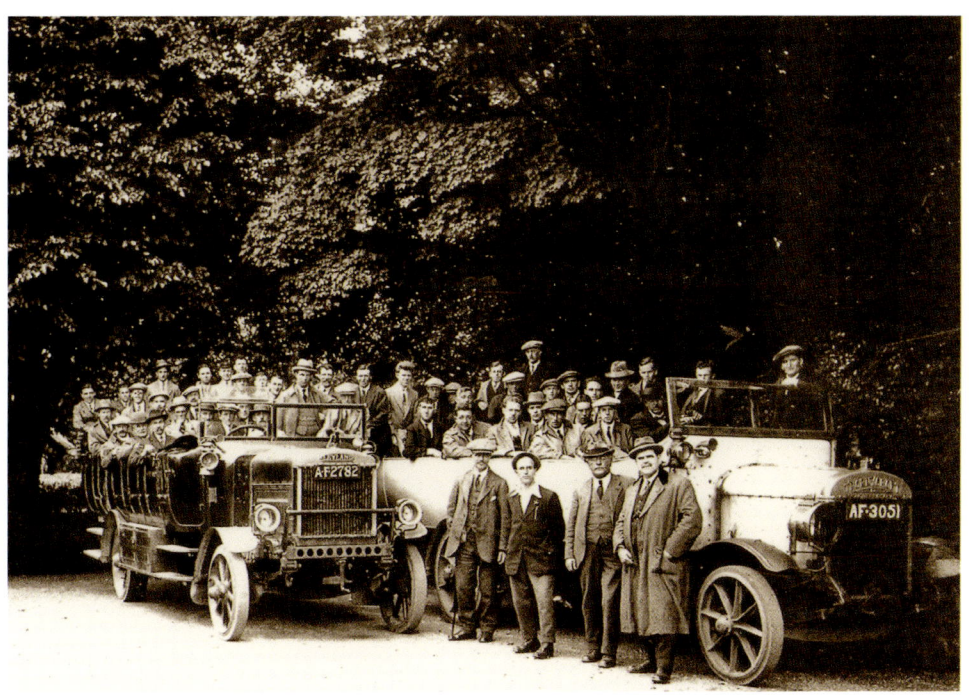

It must have been a bumpy ride in the Thornycroft bus, registered AF 3051, for the Young Man's Bible Class passengers on their outing in 1925, riding on hard rubber tyres. The man standing by the bus with a fur collared coat is believed to be Harry Rich and to his right is Harold Williams.

REDRUTH WESLEY SUNDAY SCHOOL YOUNG MEN'S BIBLE CLASS.

Annual Trip to Restormel, Endsleigh and Launceston. 30th July, 1925

Names of those present arranged alphabetically.

Andrew, H
Angove, J
Blackwell, Fred
Blackwell, F C
Blackwell, J
Butler, Harry
Buddle, W
Curtis, R B
Dunstone, J
Dunstan, Fred
Exelby, R B
Ellis, Alfred
Ellis, Alfred Jr.
Faulkner, H. B. A.R.C.A., Visitor.
Gould, Fred
Hankins, H W

Hooper, J Harry B Sc.
Hall, Charles
Hynes, Peter

Kelly, Sidney
Kemp, William

Lanyon, A
Lanyon, F

Meager, W
Mitchell, Albert M.P.S
Mitchell, Caspar

Newton V. B.

Pellowe, C C

Rich, Harry
Rabey Martin, & son.
Rowe Garfield

Semmens, Sidney
Saundrey, R B

Tregarthen, N
Truscott, Archie
Trevorrow, J
Thomas, R W
Thomas, J
Tregoning, E H
Tregoning, Leslie C
Tresidder, Stanley
Triniman, Leonard
Trevena, W S
Treverton, W
Treverton, B

Wickett, Stanley, J.P.
Williams, J H
Williams, Bryer
Williams, Alfred H
Williams, A J

Wood, R D H
Whindom, C
Whindom, W F

CLASS OFFICERS FOR 1925.

HARRY RICH,
J. H. WILLIAMS, Leaders.
SIDNEY SEMMENS, Sec.
HAROLD HANKINS, Trip Sec.

CLUB
Stanley Wickett, J.P. and W. Trevena, Managers.
R. B. Saundrey, Sec.

ORCHESTRA
H. Dennis, Conductor.
H. Rich, Manager
R. B. Exelby, Secretary.
R. H. James, Librarian

GYMNASIUM
J. H. Richards,
C. C. Pellowe, Instructors.
E. H. Tregoning,

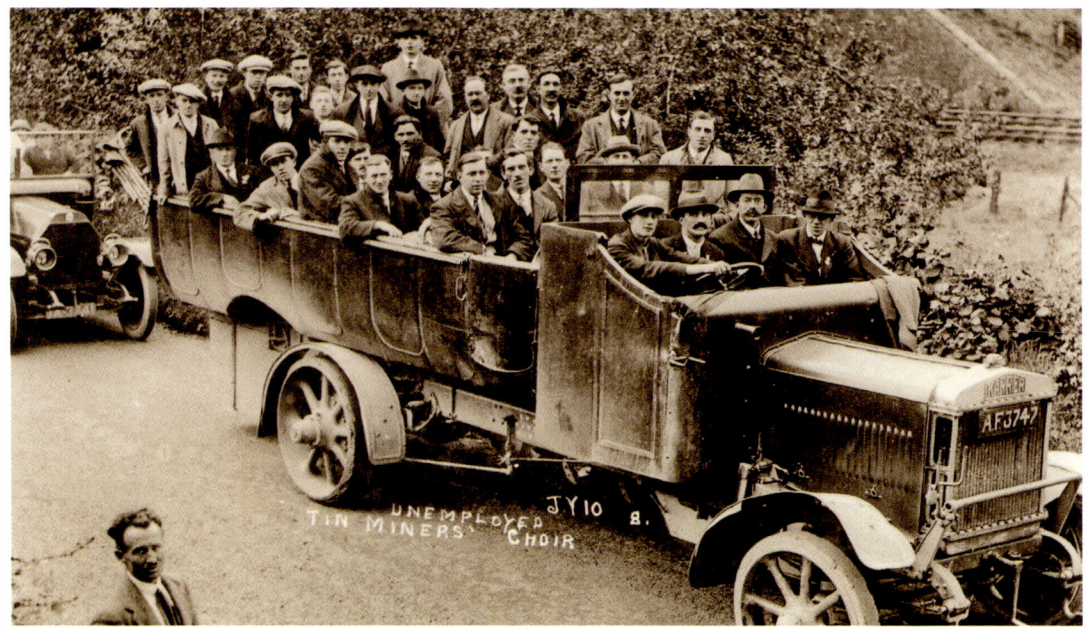

AF 3747, a thirty-seat Karrier from 1921/22, is seen here in July taking a full load – an unemployed tin miners' choir outing. Without lamps, they won't be out after dark. AF 3841, a car of unknown make sporting a large pair of acetylene lamps, can be seen behind the open bus.

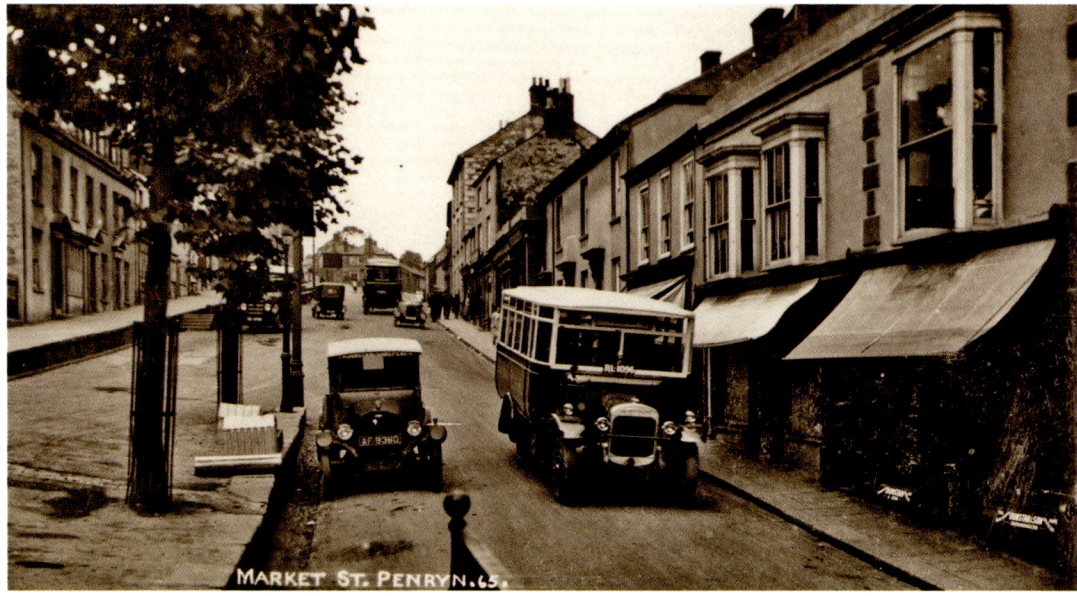

A traffic jam in the main street of Penryn in the mid-1920s. On this unused postcard can be seen RL 1096, a Thornycroft owned by Pendennis Motors; to the left, AF 9360 is a delivery van owned by Mr Dunstan, whose ironmongery shop can be seen on the right with the sun blind extended. In the background, between the trees and the lap post, is another bus, CO 9766, a Reo 20-seater belonging to Hosking & Son of Penryn; the 'Violet' company was later sold to Western National in November 1935 but the sale was not concluded. Both buses were used on the Falmouth route.

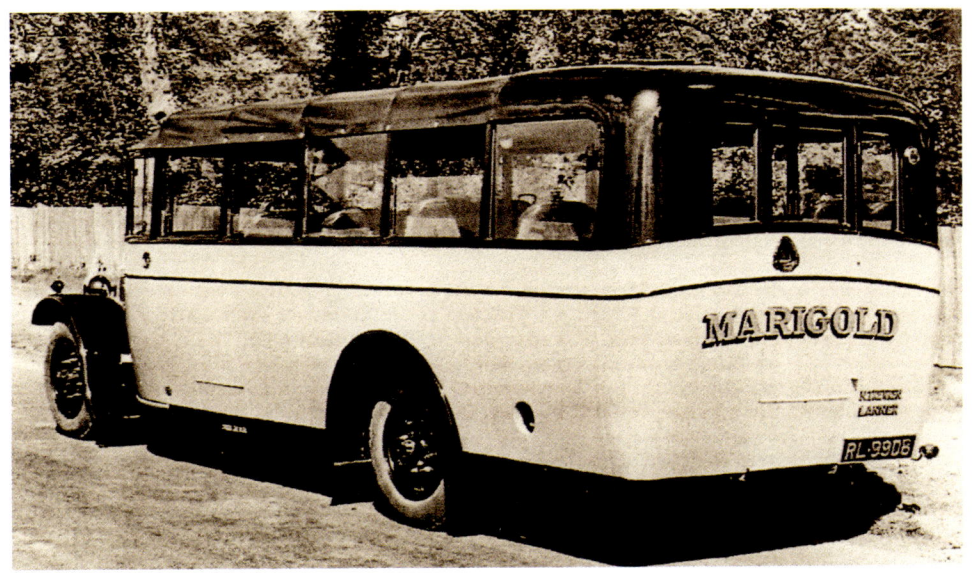

A twenty-seater Thornycroft bus manufactured in 1929 and registered RL 9908 was obtained by Newton Trewren, a carpenter working at Falmouth Docks. In 1926 he saw the need for a service to transport workmen from the Redruth area and thus began a service between Redruth and Falmouth Docks. He maintained a half-hourly service between Lanner and Redruth on Saturdays and competed with the GWR buses on the Redruth to Falmouth service. Traffic on the 'Marigold' company service on Saturdays only was light and it was withdrawn in 1932.

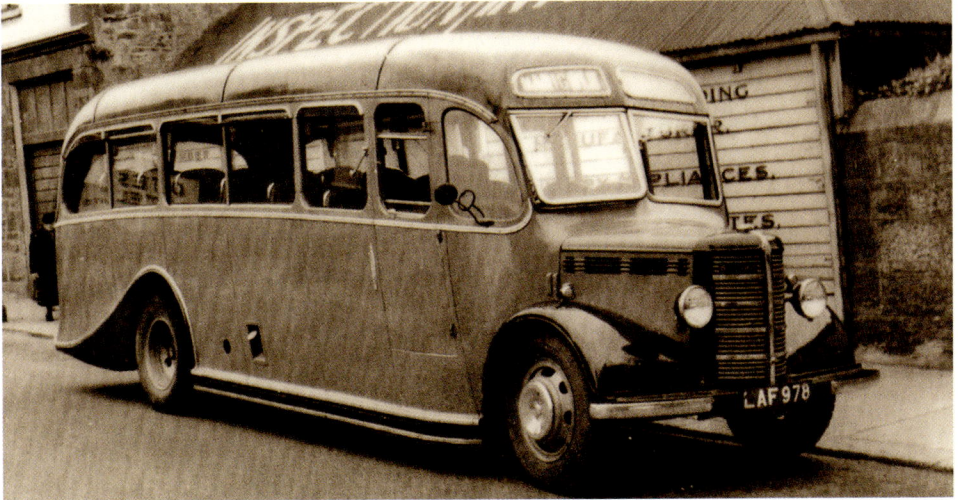

New in 1949, this Bedford Duple twenty-nine-seater, LAF 978, also owned by Marigold, is seen here in Bond Street, Redruth. They also ran a service linking Redruth with Truro on Saturdays. All the Marigold services ran to a regular timetable but pleasure trips were also run on a more informal basis. There were excursions to Plymouth at 7s 6d, and to fairs at Helston, Summercourt and Penzance. By 1931 Trewren's fleet consisted of four vehicles: two Thornycroft twenty-seaters, a Dodge fourteen-seater, and a Reo twenty-seater, all painted in an orange and black livery.

REDRUTH AND TRURO.
SATURDAYS ONLY.

		a.m.	p.m.	p.m.	p.m.	p.m.	p.m.	p.m.
Redruth	dept.	9.0	12.30	3.5	4.30	8.5	9.10	10.30
Lanner	,,	9.5	12.35	3.10	4.35	8 10	9.15	10.35
Sunnycorner	,,	9.18	12.48	3.23	4.48	8.23	9.28	10.48
Frogpool	,,	9.25	1.0	3.35	5 0	8.30	9.40	11.0
Twelveheads	,,	9.40	1.15	3.50	5.15	8 40	9.55	11.15
Bissoe	,,	9.50	1.25	4.0	5.25	8.50	10 5	11.25
Baldhu	,,	10 0	1.35	4.10	5.35	9.5	10.10	
Hugus	,,	10.5	1.40	4.15	5.40	9.10	10.15	
Truro	,,	10.15	1.50	4.25	5.50	9.20	10.25	

		a.m.	p.m.	p.m.	p.m.	p.m.	p.m.
Truro	dept.	10.20	1.55	4.30	5.50	9.20	10.30
Hugus	,,	10.30	2.5	4.40	6.0	9.30	10.40
Baldhu	,,	10.35	2.10	4.45	6.5	9.35	10.45
Bissoe	,,	10.45	2.20	4.55	6 15	9.45	10.55
Twelveheads	,,	10.55	2 30	5 5	6.25	9.55	11.5
Frogpool	,,	11.10	2.45	5.20	6.40	10.10	11.20
Sunnycorner	,,	11.18	2.53	5 28	6.48	10.15	11.28
Lanner	,,	11.25	3.5	5.35	7.0	10.23	11.40
Redruth	,,	11.30	3.10	5.40	7.5	10.28	11.45

A Marigold Bus service notice.

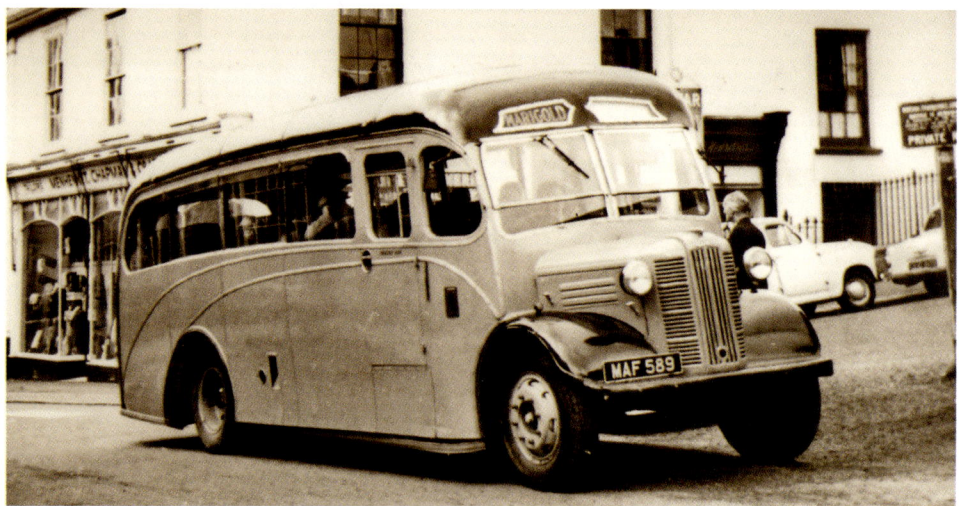

At the bottom of Station Hill, Alma Place, Redruth, this Austin CXB with a Plaxton body and twenty-nine seats was new in 1949. Registered MAF 589, it also belonged to N. Trewren, who a few years after the Second World War purchased a garage at the top of Lanner Hill, extending it to accommodate the coaches. With the increase in the number of men employed at Falmouth Docks, up to seven buses were used daily on the Docks run. In 1954 Noal Coaches Ltd was bought; operations continued until 1955, when Mr Rickard, owner of Penryn & Falmouth Motor Co. secured an option to purchase Noal Coaches. He sold this to Grenville Motors of Camborne for £1,300. During the 1960s operating costs increased alarmingly and passenger numbers fell as private car ownership increased and fares rose sharply. Newton Trewren developed heart problems in 1959 after thirty years of service to the travelling public. The 'Marigold' name finally disappeared in 1974 when the business was acquired by J. C. Pollard (Trelawney Tours, St Ives).

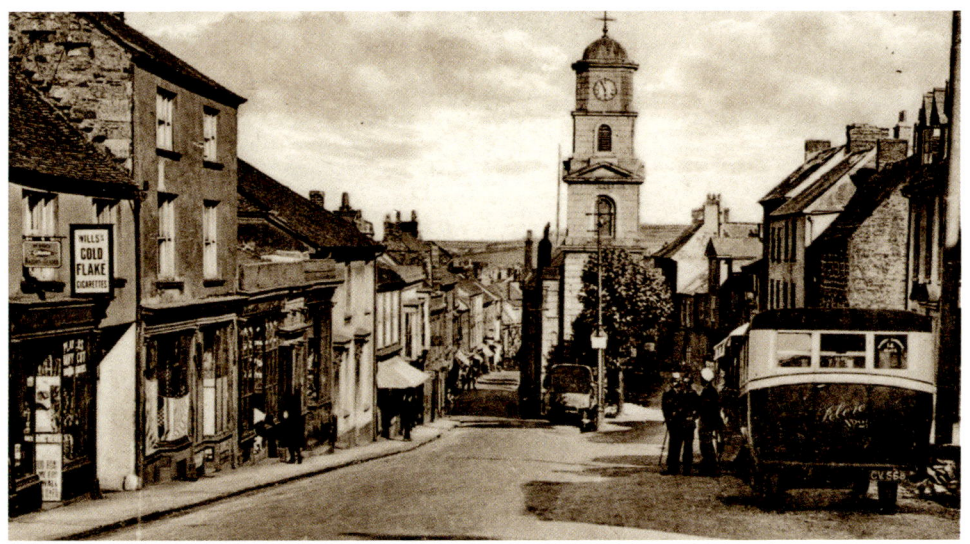

William John George, born 1879, was a blacksmith and farmed West Pelere at Carclew near Penryn. His son Harold learned his trade as a mechanic with Mr Collins, who ran a garage in Falmouth; because of a shortage of work, he was laid off. In 1927 a Chevrolet was bought and kept on the farm while arrangements were discussed with the bank manager, who suggested calling the company 'Pelere Motors'. This postcard shows that bus, CV 568, in the main street of Penryn with driver Harold (in the white cap) waiting for the clock to strike six to depart for Falmouth. On this route there were many competitors, most of whom did not keep a regular timetable; on a busy day they chased up and down to see how many trips they could do while on a quiet day they were conspicuous by their absence.

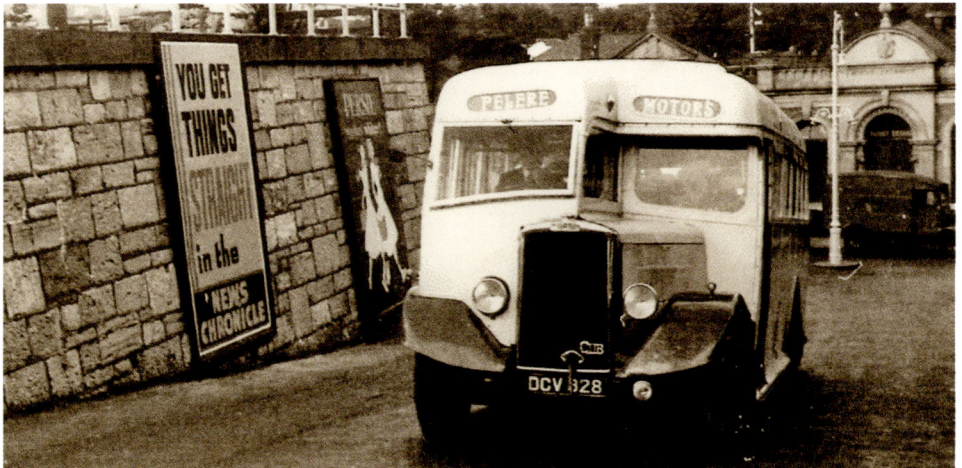

DCV 328, a twenty-seven-seater bus, was new in 1937. This Leyland Cub was bought second hand from Hawkey of Newquay and is seen here with a backdrop of posters and the Mining Exchange, off-route on an evening excursion. Another service for workmen in the Penryn and Old Hill areas was the 'Dinner Basket Bus', where the wives of the dock workers would pay the conductor 2d to take their husbands hot dinner in baskets, to be collected at the dock gates. Fred, another son, drove for his father and wore very thick spectacles; he could not see the town clock and his passengers would tell him when it was time to depart.

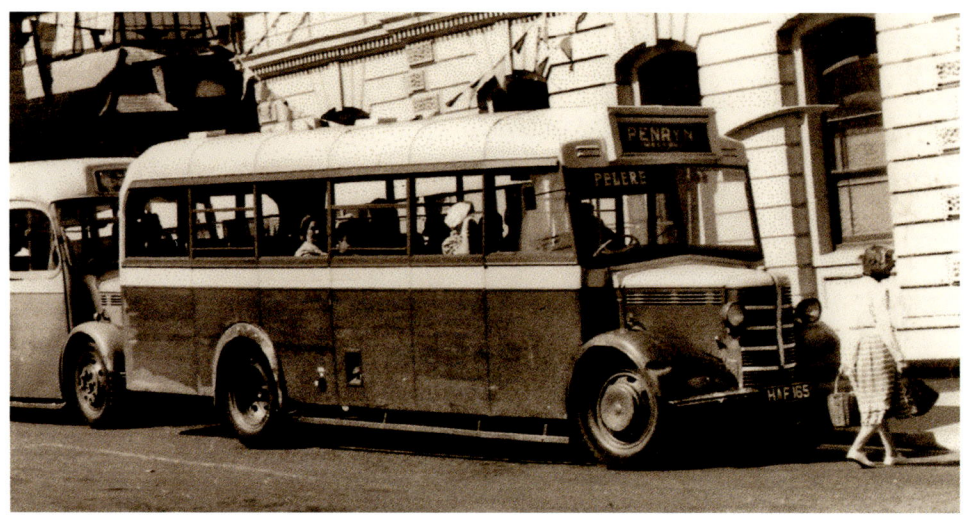

In the early 1930s, Pelere's coaches included Reo, Willys and Thornycroft. They maintained the service during the day with the driver taking the fares (so what's new?) but during peak hours and on Saturday a conductor was carried. Printed bell punch-type tickets were issued on all routes. The vehicles were serviced and repaired at the farm, where the garage was extended to take the bigger fleet of buses; not every vehicle would be housed – in cold weather, the bus was pushed to the top of the hill and rolled it down the slope. The George brothers cajoled their sister into sitting in the driver's seat; as the bus gained momentum, they pushed the door open, leapt in and took over from her. Seen here at Falmouth Moor is a Bedford Duple twenty-two-seater, HAF 165.

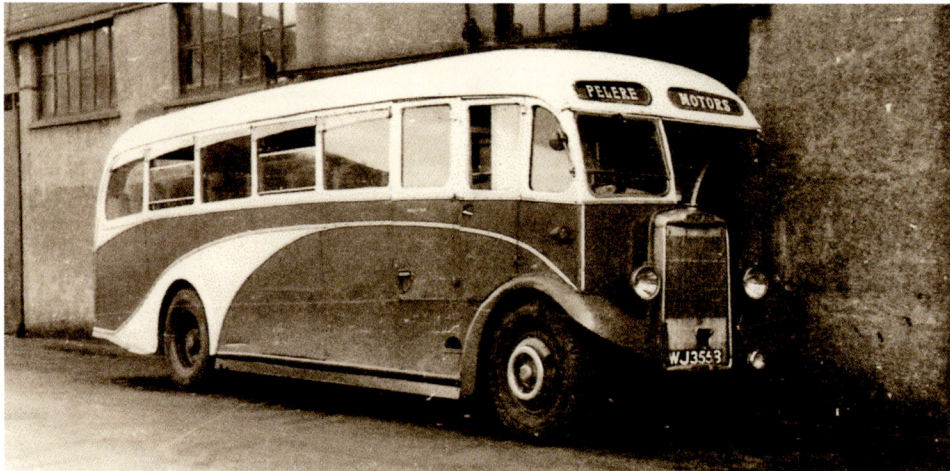

During the Second World War, fuel and spare parts caused much difficulty. Pelere were made to economise; a garage and workshop were established in premises at Commercial Road, Penryn. The farm at Carclew was sold before the end of the war. Mr W. J. George moved to a house in Penryn. The coach hire side of the company expanded in post-war years; as well as traditional outings to St Ives, there were longer trips to London. Pelere coaches were often seen in Plymouth, especially on Saturdays; rugby clubs and chapels were regular hirers and children were taken to school under Council contract. The photograph shows a Leyland from their fleet outside the garage at Penryn.

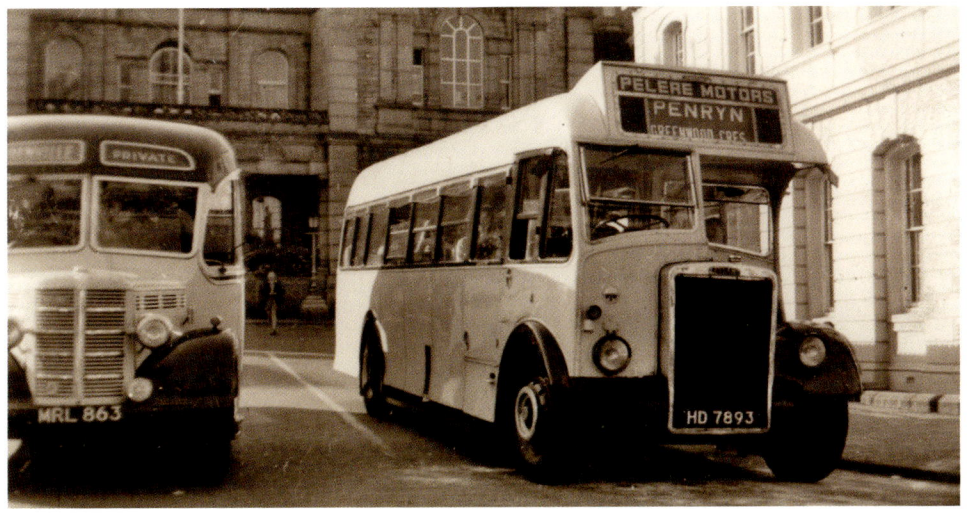

Mr George senior went on a coach trip to Penzance. There were a number of passengers who wanted to stop at a public house on the way home, so his son, who was driving, stopped at a hostelry. Because his father did not drink, he stayed in the coach and they brought out lemonade for him. Nobody knew what happened between the bar and the bus but the father was quite merry when he got home that night. When Mr George senior died in 1967, the remaining family assumed control and ran the business for a short while before putting it on the market. The two buses here were snapped on Falmouth Moor; to the left is MRL 863, a Bedford Duple belonging to Grenville Motors, new in 1950, and to the right is a Leyland 33-seater, new in 1948, owned by Pelere Motors.

Grenville Motors showed interest in Pelere Motors and made an offer of £12,000 which was accepted by the administrators. A figure of £261 6s 7d was agreed for the petrol, diesel and tyres in stock as well. On 4 October 1967 Grenville Motors took over the running of the service and by 5 December the transaction was complete. To the right are some Pelere bell-punched tickets used on their buses and coaches.

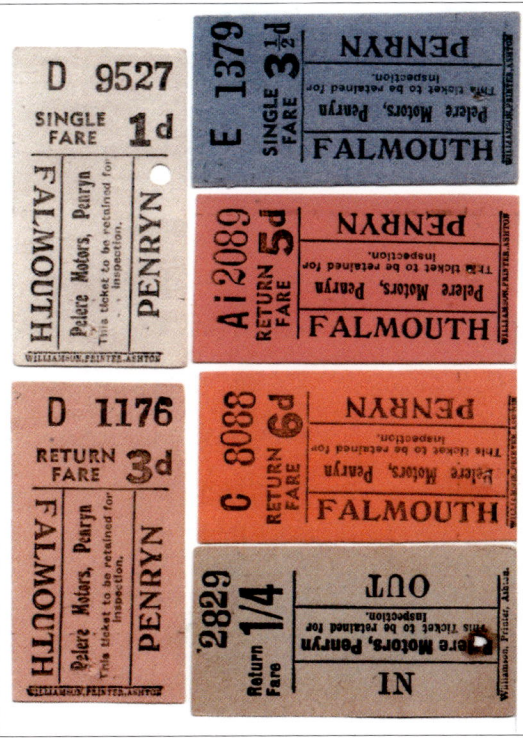

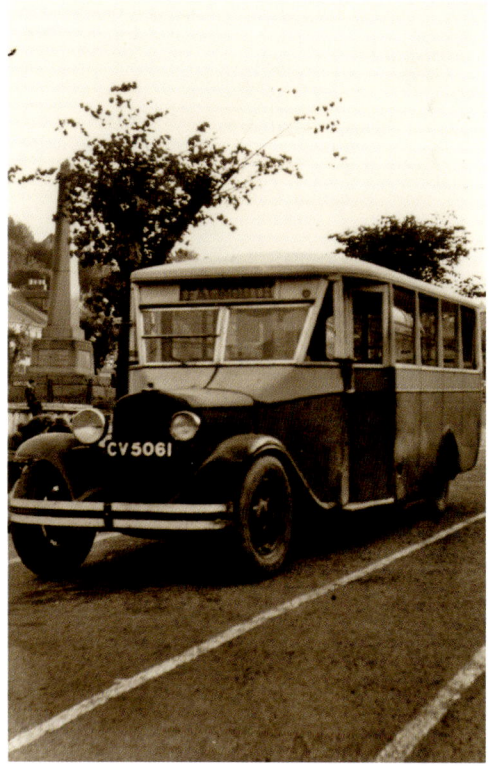

George Banfil, a publican, farmer and proprietor of the Helford River Ferry, assisted by his son Edwin, diversified, running a motor bus from Mawnan Smith to Falmouth four days a week. A Dodge twenty-seater was bought which served them well for twenty years. By the Second World War, though, it was showing its age and was an ancient and rattling vehicle. Mr Banfil drove the 'Selene Bus' with great panache, lurching round corners, tearing down hills at breakneck speed and making dramatic stops. Passengers breathed a sigh of relief when they reached Falmouth. This photograph shows the Dodge, CV 5061, with a Thurgood body, new in 1931, at Falmouth Moor with a pair of odd-sized headlights and a split windscreen.

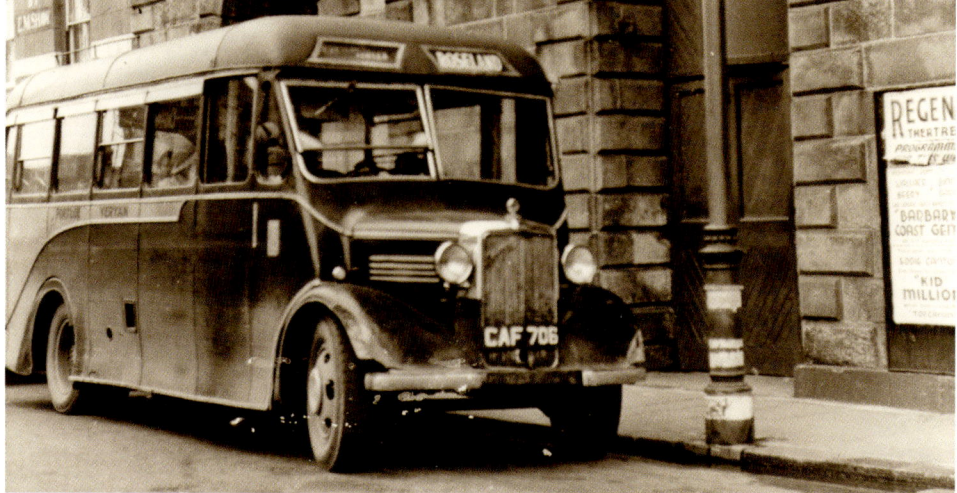

The Morse family moved from the Torpoint area to Portloe, bought a Ford Model T and started a bus service to St Columb. During the 1930s a service to Truro was started on Mondays only; the 'Roseland' ran to and from the Falmouth Ferry at Percuil during the summer, then moved to the next day as well. Another company, 'Pride of Veryan', were granted permission by the Traffic Commissioners to use the same route, each doing alternate weeks. During 1938 the route was extended at both ends, to West Portholland and Truro Railway Station. The photo shows a Bedford twenty-seater, CAF 706, outside City Hall (Hall for Cornwall) when new in 1936, although looking a little tired and dirty.

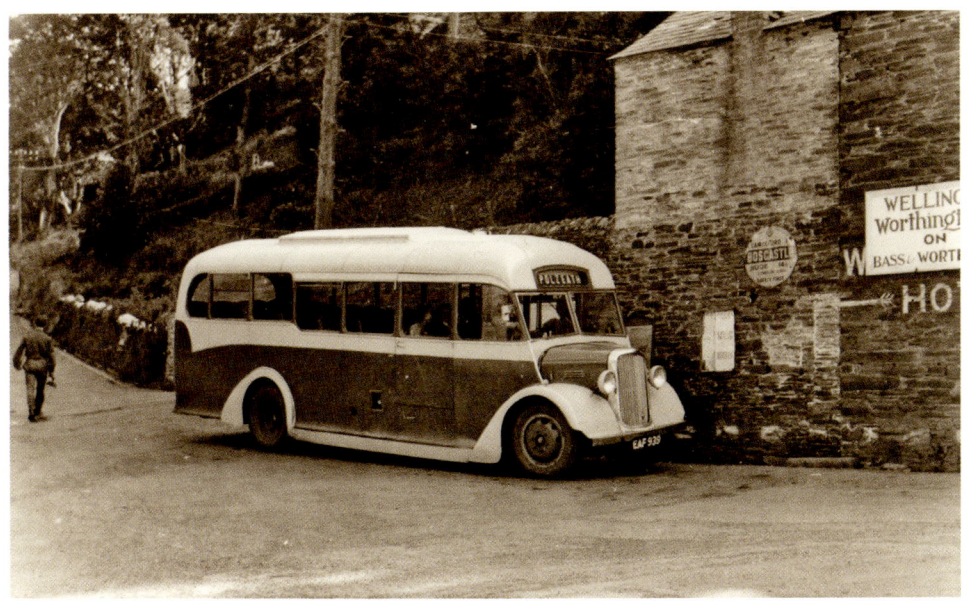

The Blake family, who came from Trelights, near Port Isaac, owned the Central Garage at Delabole. They catered for private motorists until 1928, when a char-á-banc operation began – vehicles were hired out for outings and pleasure trips. By 1931 they owned three coaches and, expanding, eventually the name Blake's Services was known from Boscastle and Polzeath to Plymouth. The upper picture shows a Dodge coach, EAF 939, a twenty-six-seater, at Boscastle. It was new in 1938. Is the driver on the way to the hotel for a Worthington or a Bass? In the lower picture we can see another of Blake's coaches, a Bedford Duple thirty-two-seater with a sliding door which was new in 1945, HAF 540, at Bodmin. Early in 1935, Blake's started their first bus service through the district, between Delabole and Bodmin six days a week.

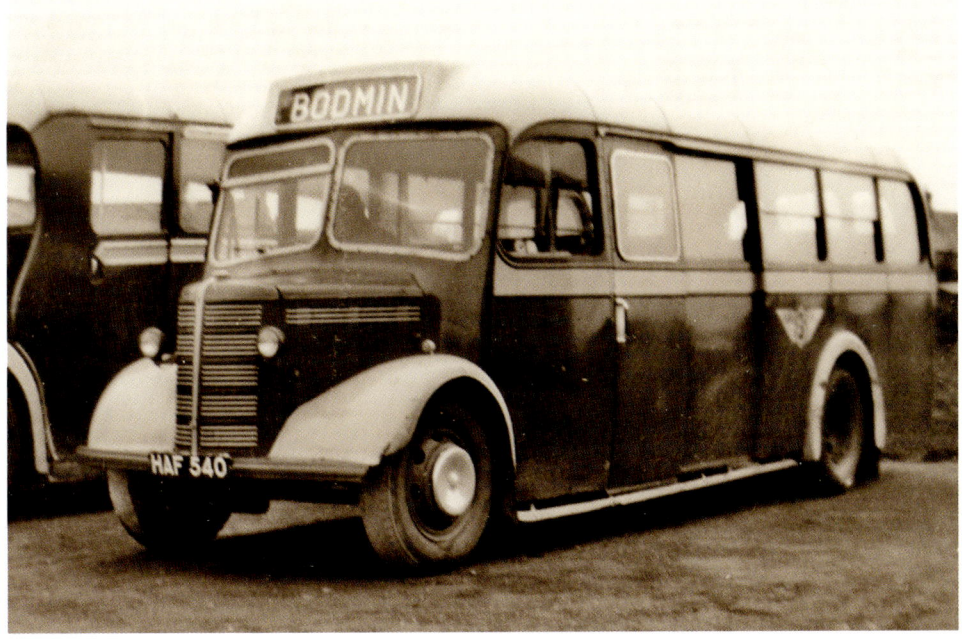

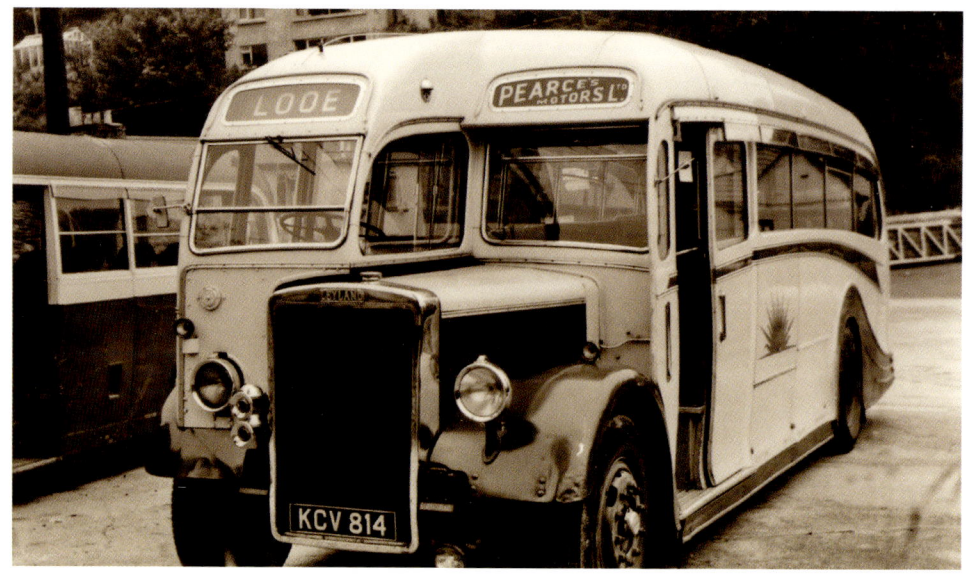

Pearce's Motors Ltd was formed in 1931. The original garage at Big Green in Polperro was amid narrow streets and a turntable was needed to turn the coaches round. After years of this trouble, Pearce Motors bought the site of a burned-down tourist hotel in the mid-1930s, using it as an office, parking for the coaches and a bus terminus. Summer business in the area was so busy that a new service began between Looe and Polruan in 1935. The original premises were flooded and the turntable damaged; the property was sold and later demolished. KCV 814, a Leyland thirty-three-seater, seen above, is from the fleet of Pearce's coaches. Below is another of the Pearce's Tours coaches, parked on the quayside at Looe in 1958. It looks in a beautiful condition, this Bedford OB Duple twenty-nine-seater, almost as good as when it was new in 1950. The business was sold to the Deeble family of Upton Cross in 1974.

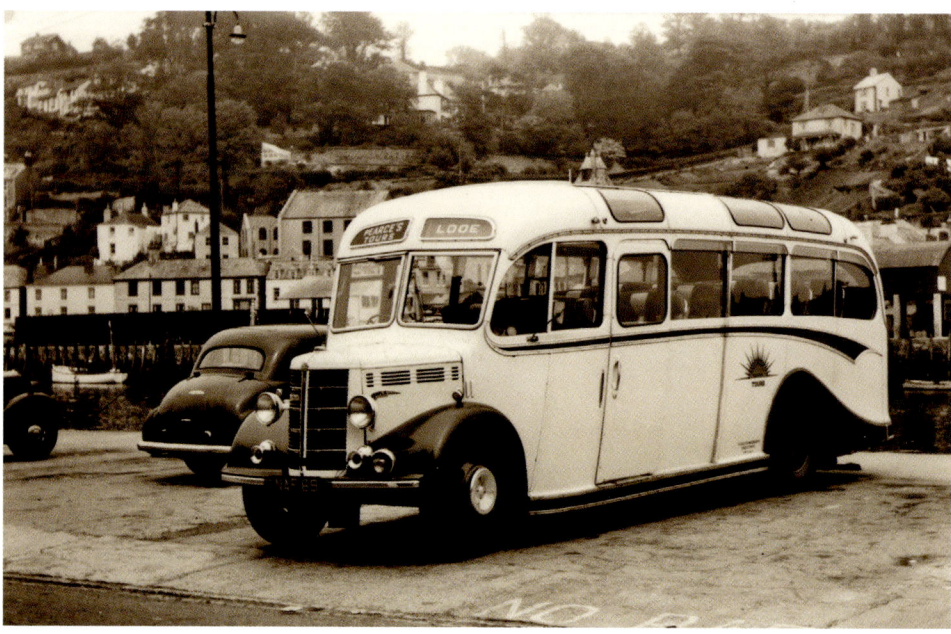

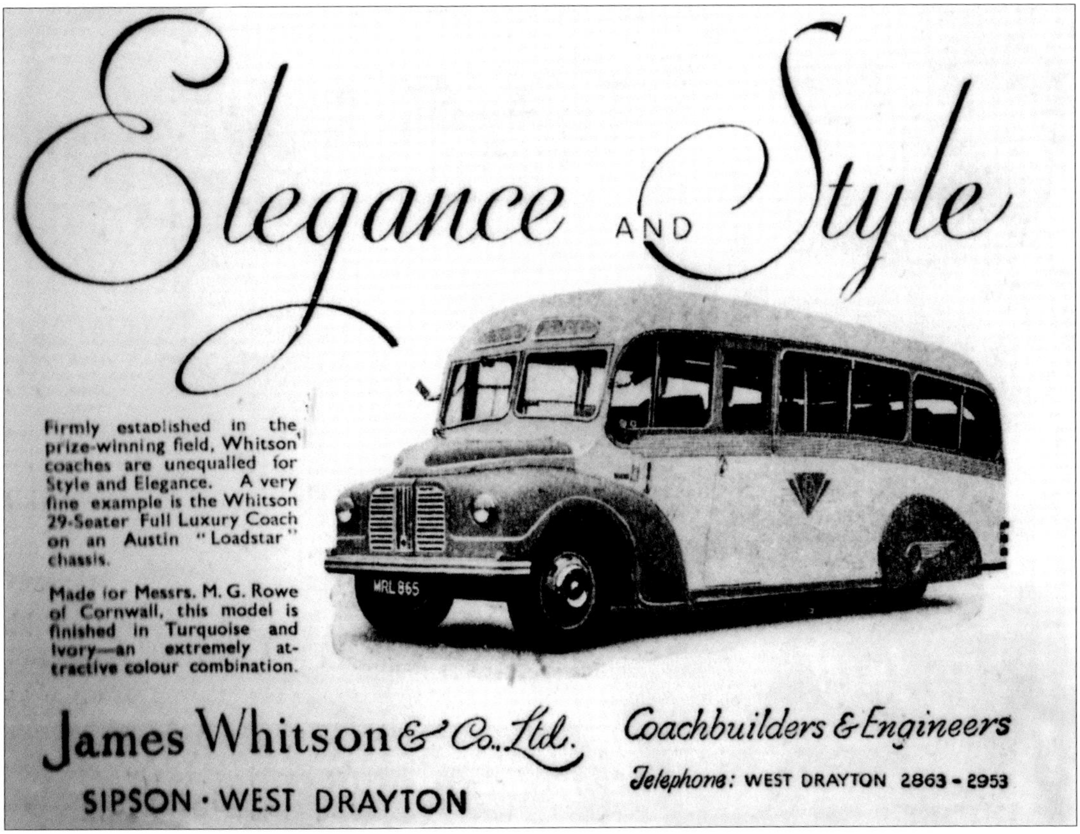

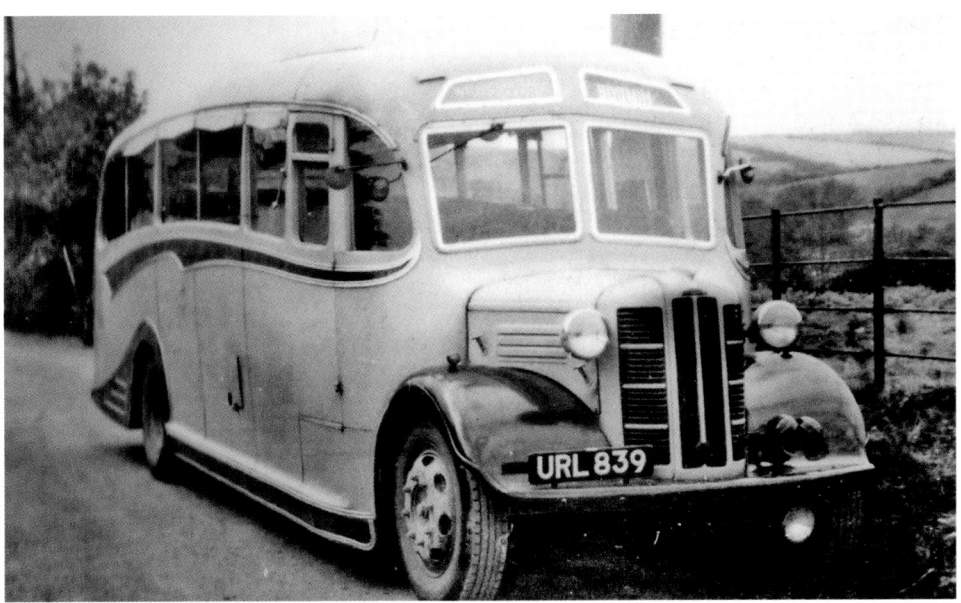

An Austin CXB thirty-seater bus dating from 1947/48 and built shortly after the Second World War, with a 1955 number URL 839, owned by Willis Control Garage, Bodmin, is seen here on a country route.

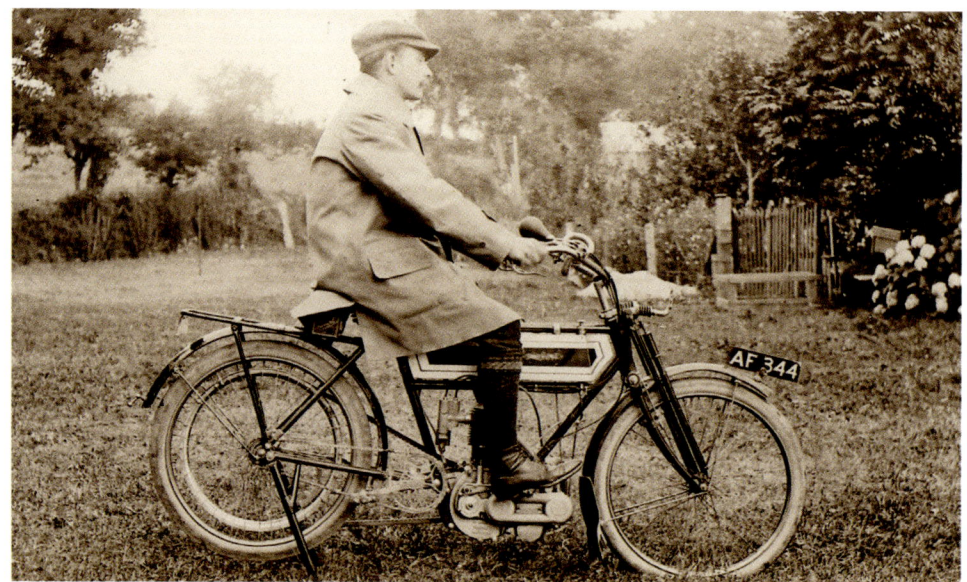

Posing for this snapshot, what could be the first owner of this Triumph motorcycle is dressed in his leather gear with the bike up on a stand. Belt-driven and dating from 1907, AF 344 sports a small leather saddle bag and a tyre inflator attached to the front forks. Without lamps, he didn't intend to do any night driving.

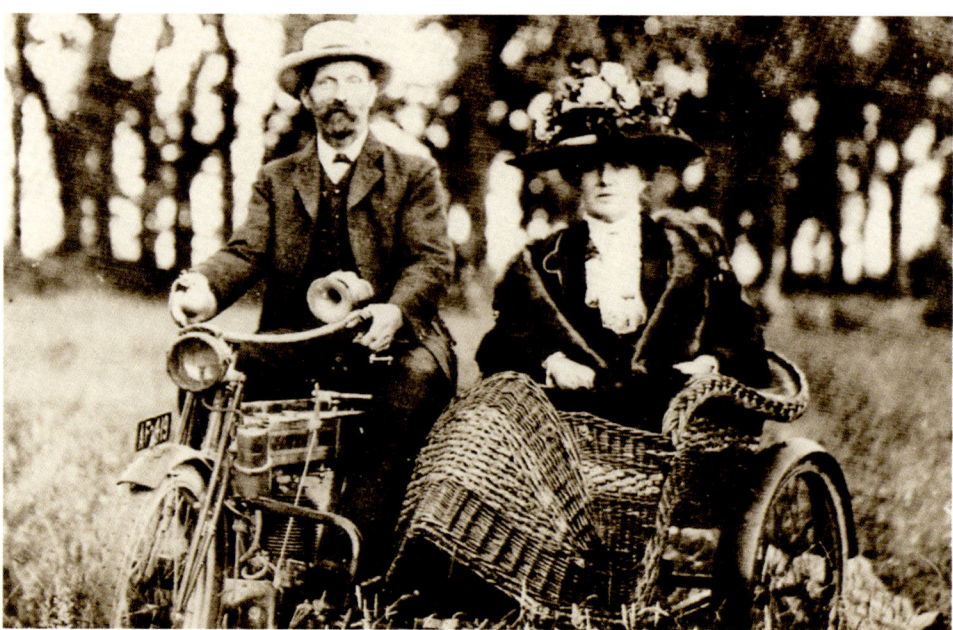

Doctor and Mrs Speigh of Porthleven are seen here sitting on their 1920 Triumph, AF 419, which has the same registration as a Star car of the same year (something which was common in Cornwall). The lady looks very smart in her fur stole and lace, sitting in the wicker sidecar; her enormous hat will blow away if she does not remove it before moving off. Don't forget to retrieve the blanket!

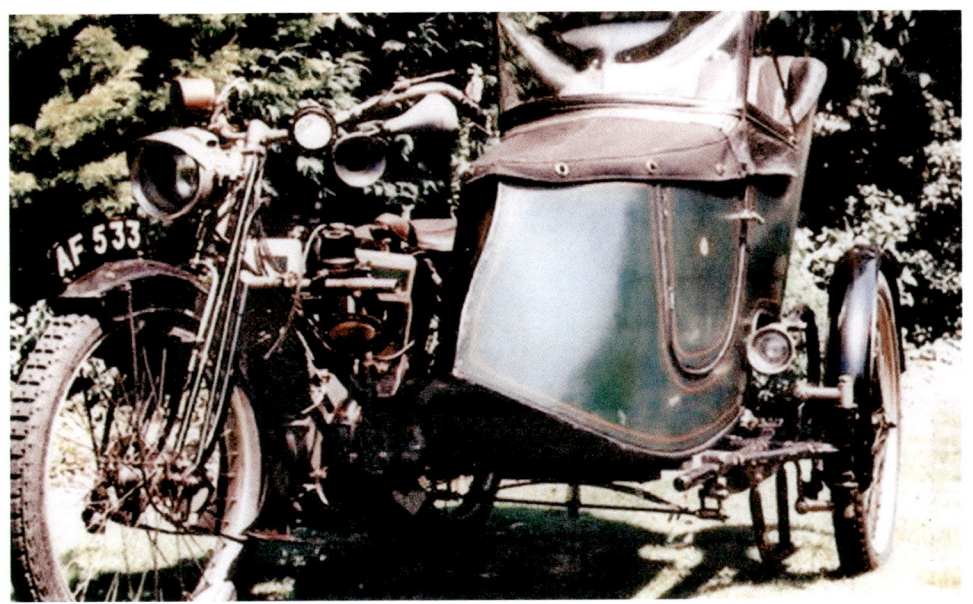

Phelam & Moore, or P&M, is the motorcycle combination seen in this photograph. They later became Panther Motorcycles. The present owner tells me it is original and unrestored. The machine was first owned by a Mr Miller, a large dealer in Surrey. It has done several Pioneer runs (London to Brighton) and also the Scottish six-day trials. Looking at the machine, it has all the mod cons: a speedometer, lamps and a bulb horn. Even the side-car on this 1910 machine, AF 533, has a windscreen and a side light fitted.

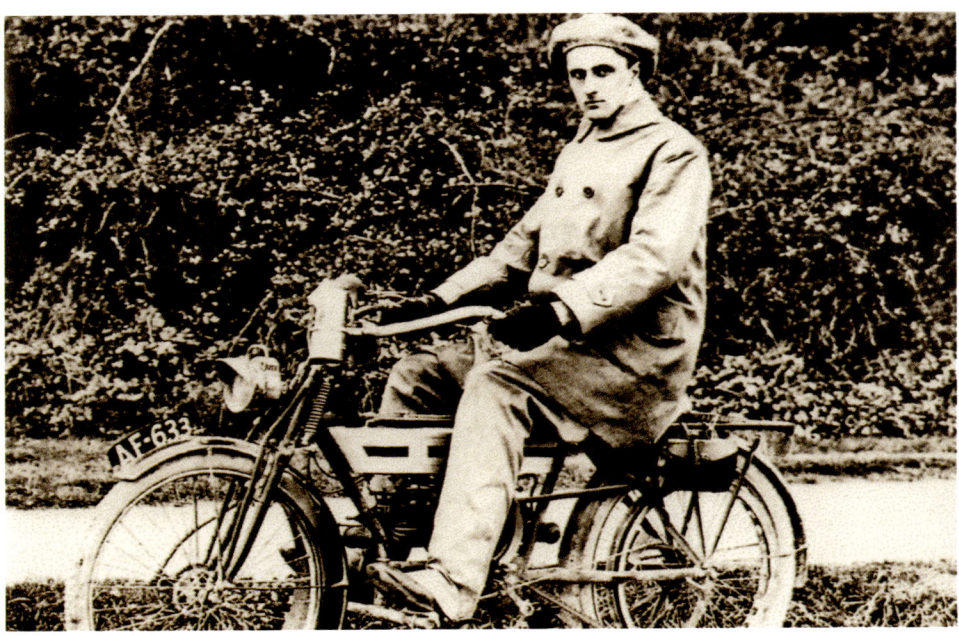

In 1912, this belt-driven Douglas 2½ hp motorcycle was registered as AF 633. It belonged to a Penzance motorcyclist, who is seen here out for a spin, posing with the stand down and his cap on back to front.

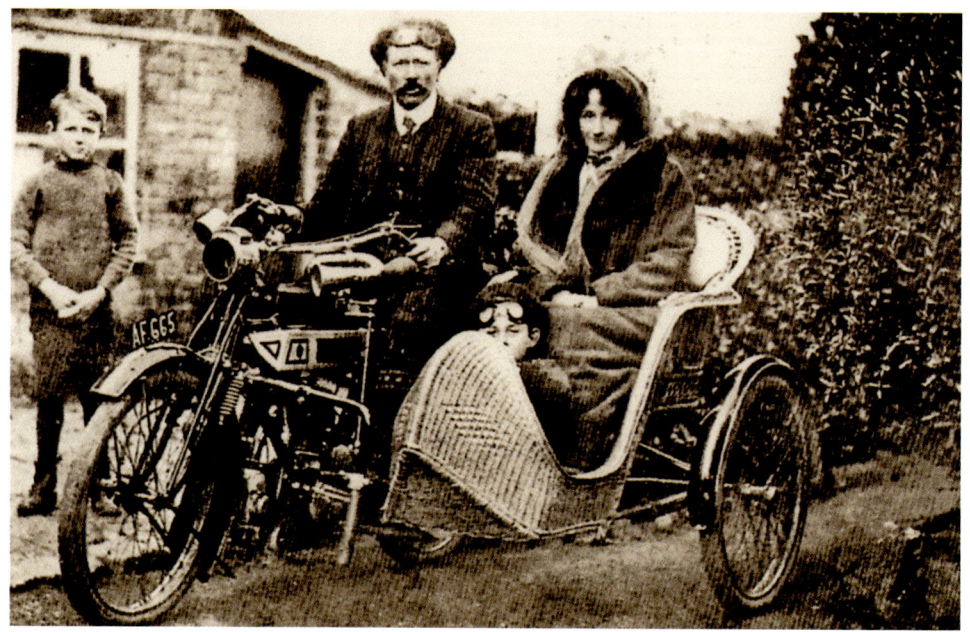

Mr and Mrs Stephens, with their two sons Frederick and Royston, are about to go on a family outing in their 3½ hp Bradbury from Illogan. With the shine on the mudguards, it must be almost brand new. The lady looks comfortable in the wicker sidecar and the driver intends to go at speed, wearing his goggles and with a speedometer to see what speed he is doing. It's a pity about the home-painted number, AF 665.

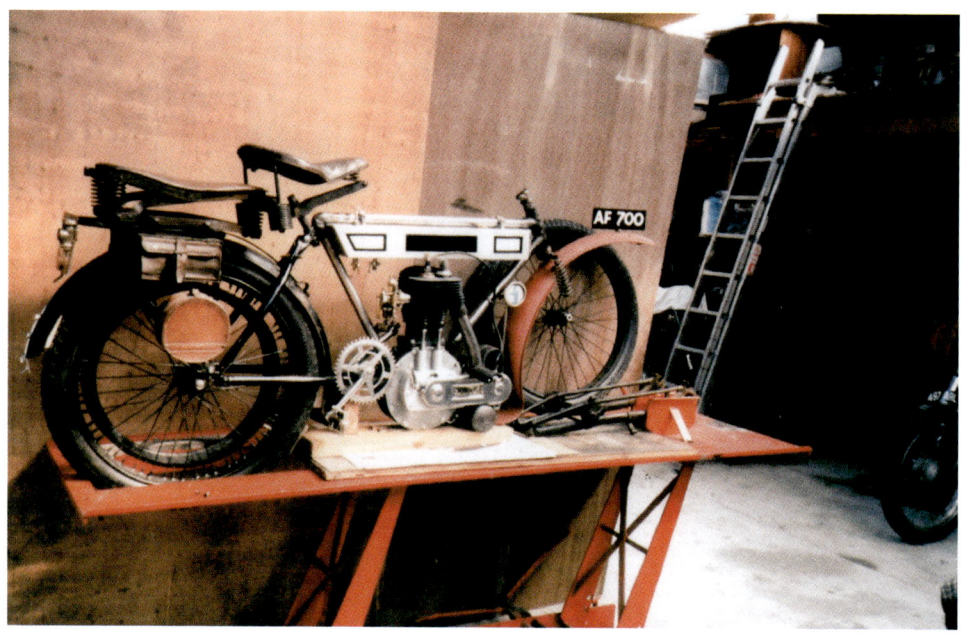

Tom Seward has started to restore his grandfather's twin-seater 500 cc Bradbury from 1908, AF 700, but there's a long way to go – just see the gleaming engine and the air-cooled cylinders. The next picture will show how it will look when it is fully restored.

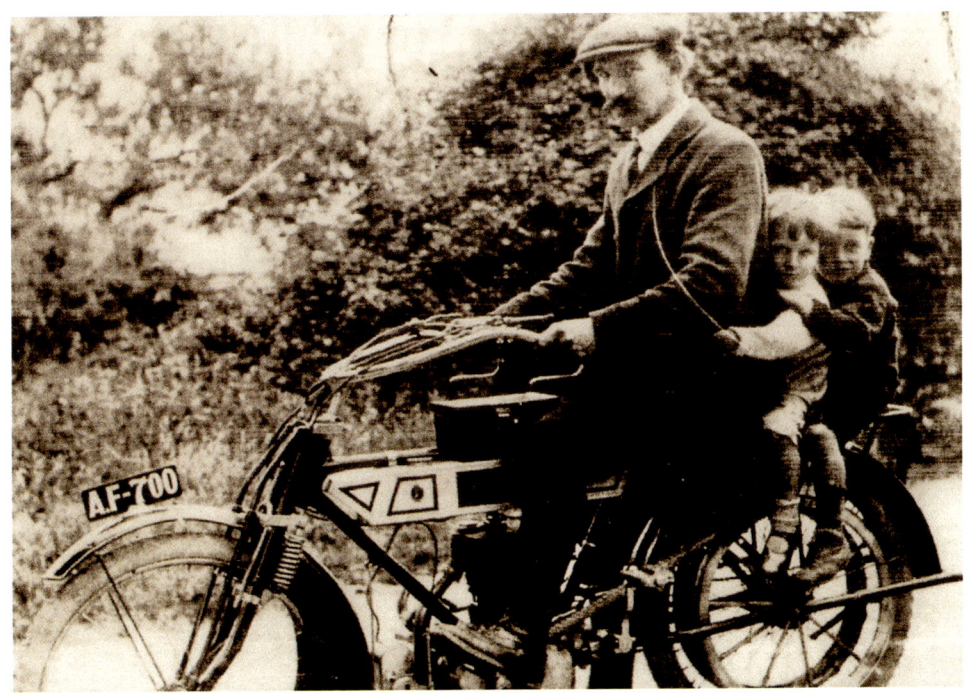

This is the machine Tom Seward is restoring, when it was owned and used by Joshua Jenkin, his grandfather, a motor engineer from Mount Charles, St Austell. The boys riding on the single saddle are his sons, Jack and Bill. Belt-driven with cow-horn handle bars, he looks like he is balancing a box on the petrol tank. What a beauty – keep it in the family, Tom.

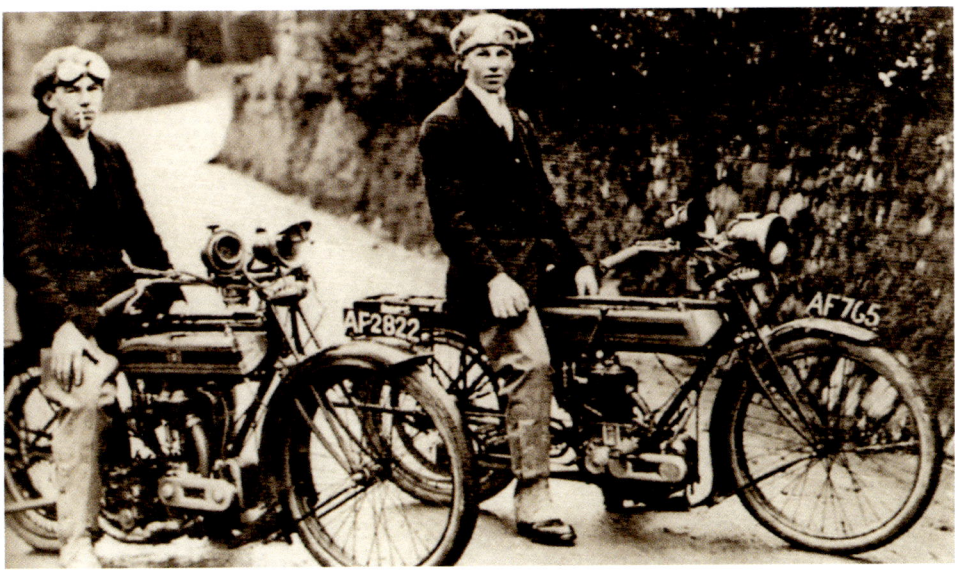

A pair of Triumphs: AF 2822 is a 1920 4 hp; the other, AF 765, is a 3½ hp of 1912. It is almost a spot the difference puzzle; apart from the date, one man is smoking and the other isn't. What is noticeable is that they both have a plunger-type of hooter, seen here in a Cornish lane.

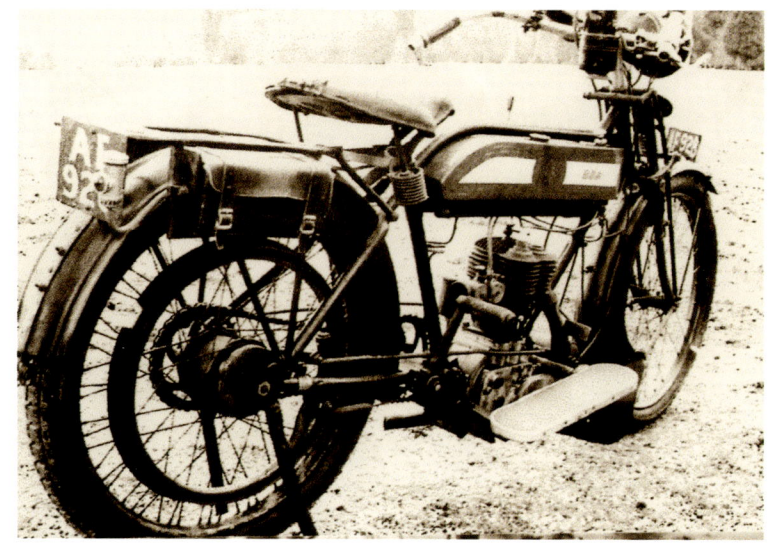

Pausing for a rest while on the Pioneer Run in 2004, this is a 1912 BSA (Birmingham Small Arms), AF 928, now owned by a Scottish gentleman. It is well turned out with an air-cooled 3½ hp engine, chain-driven and lamps front and rear, and even a little leather pouch to keep tools in. This bike is believed to have come from a garage near Penzance.

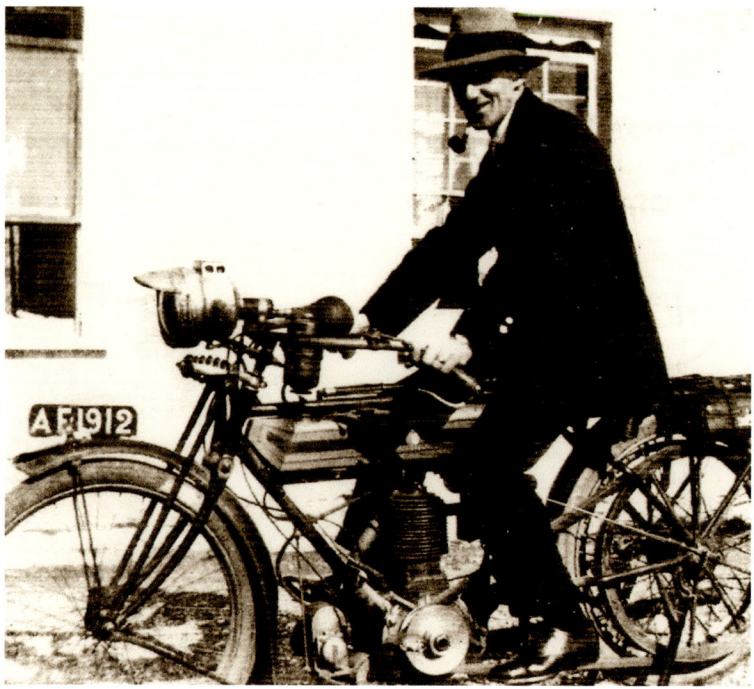

AF 1912, dating it as registered in 1919, this 1915 Triumph 3½ hp model is seen here at Allet near Truro. William Vincent is sitting astride his motorcycle with the stand in a parking position. This type had a Sturmey Archer clutch and gear box in the rear hub.

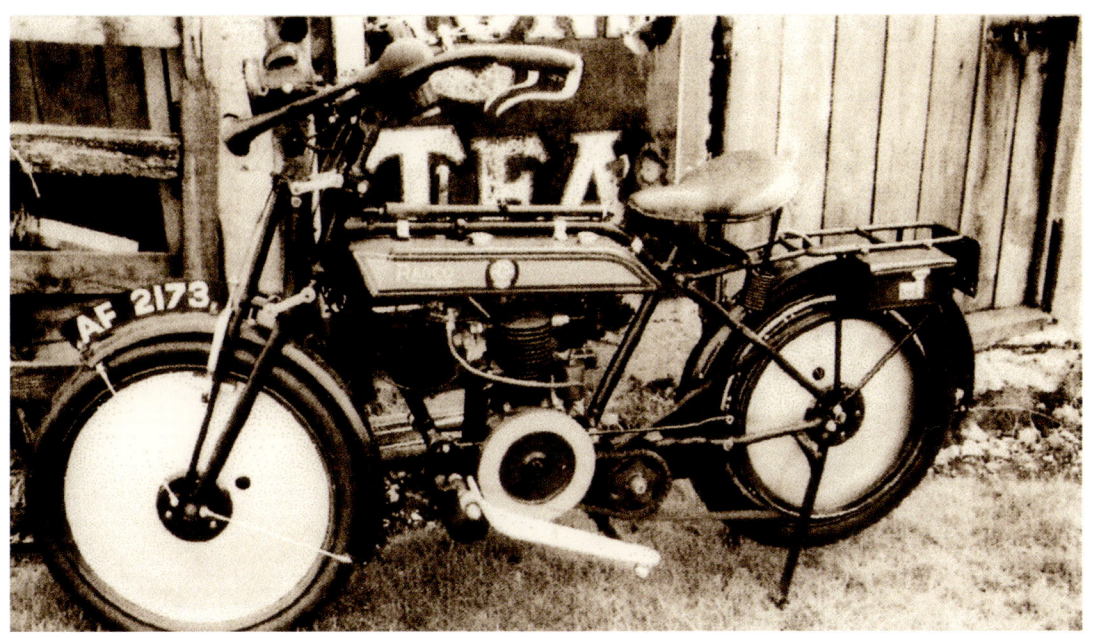

This 1916 Radco, AF 2173, was made in Birmingham; with a 2-stroke engine, they were popular as a cheap and reliable means of transport. I wonder if the discs on the wire wheels make it go faster? It looks nice and clean and well turned out.

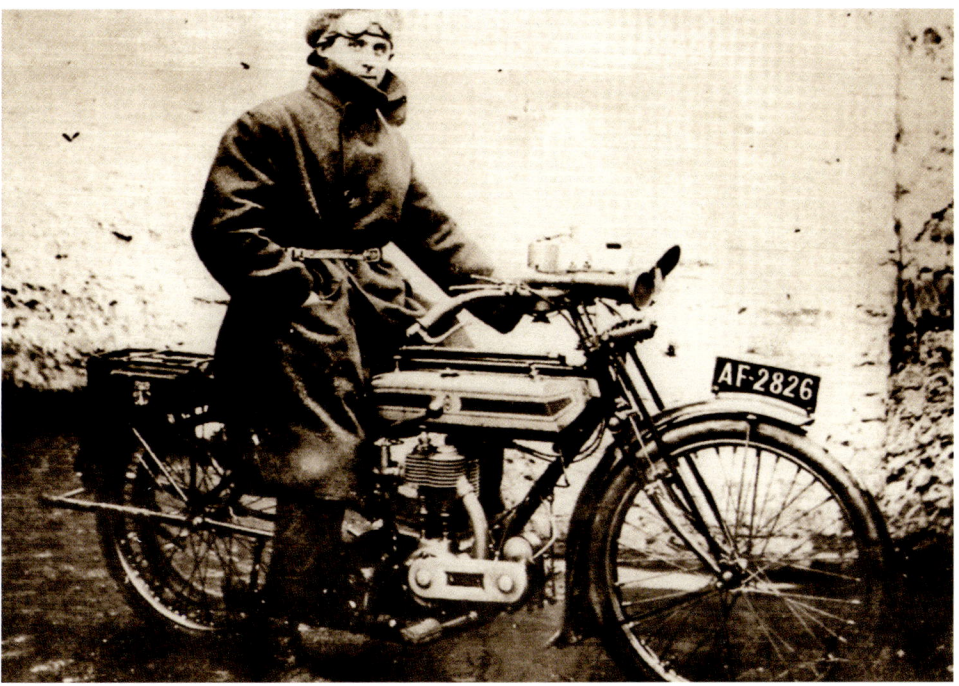

This 500 cc Triumph, AF 2826, looks almost new, and has probably just come from the motorcycle dealer in Truro, either Argall & Solomon, S. Hicks or perhaps Louis Lavanchy – all were motorcycle dealers.

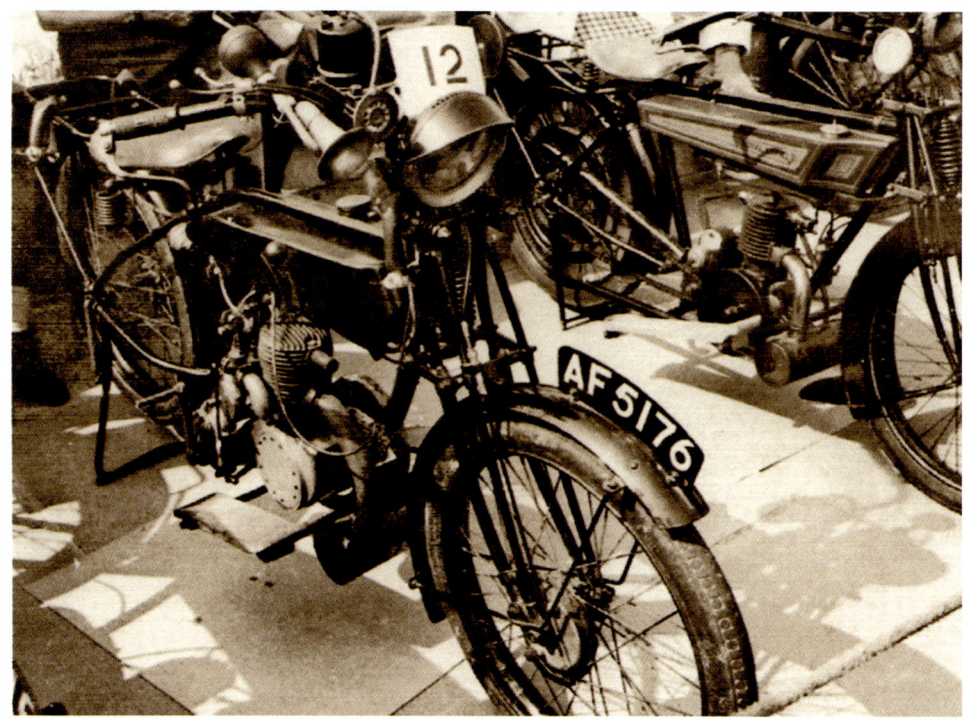

It looks like a kickstart for this 1922 Velocette, a lightweight motorcycle in a used condition with a bulky horn and acetylene lights. AF 5176 could do with a tidy up and a repaint.

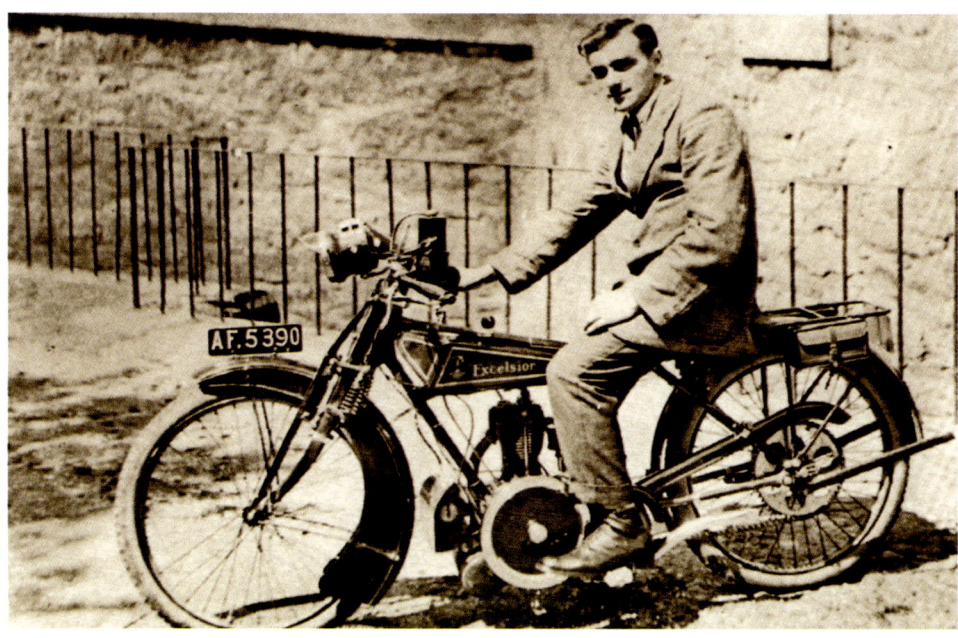

G. Kneebone, a motorcycle agent from Helston, sits astride this 350 cc Excelsior from 1922, AF 5390. Excelsior were another company that started by making and selling bicycles and went on to make automobiles.

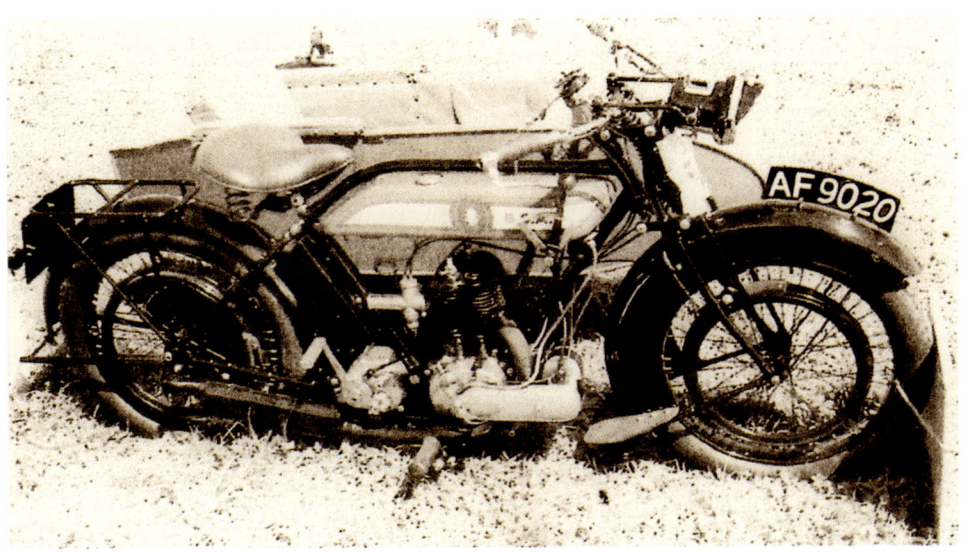

This 1924 3½ hp BSA, AF 9020, was first owned by James Ball and bought from William Foster's of Polbathic. After several owners, it at last found its way back to the family of the original owner and is seen here after an extensive restoration and looking very smart with a sidecar at a show in the West Country.

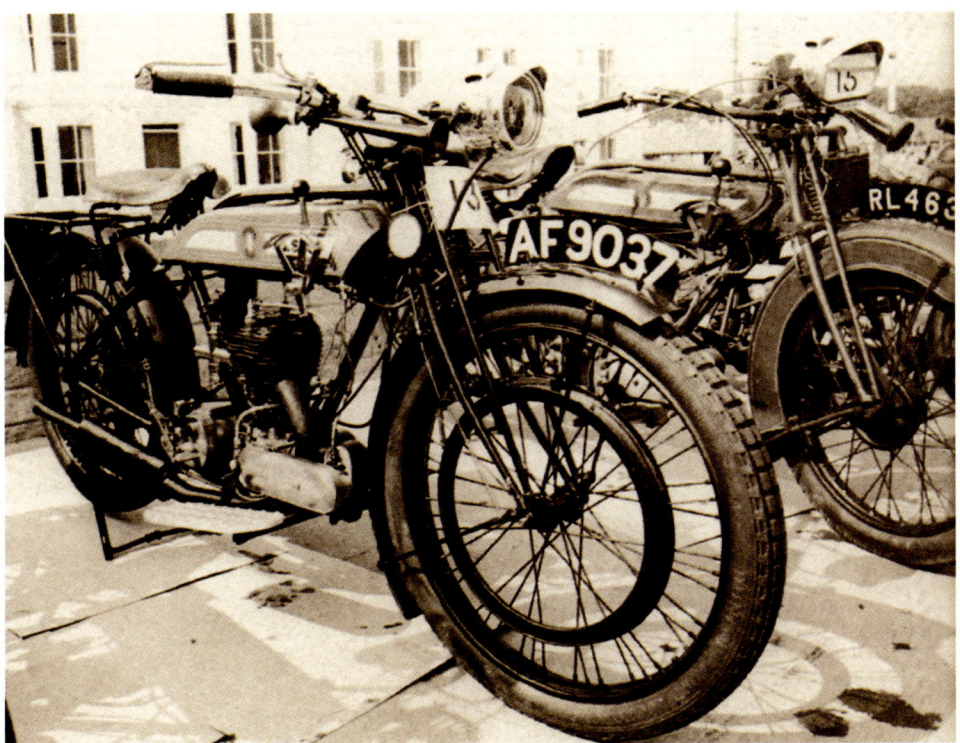

With a registration number of AF 9037, this very well restored BSA 3½hp motorcycle is dated as 1924 and belongs to Elywn Jose. It took quite some time to restore it to this lovely condition, using as much of the original parts as possible (except tyres).

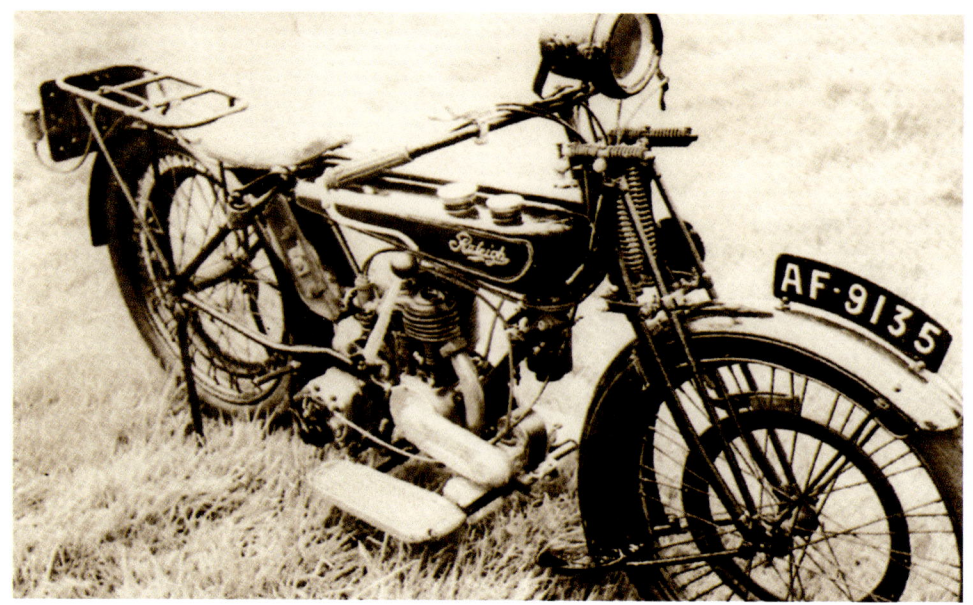

AF 9135 is a 1924 Raleigh 3 hp motorcycle. The company started life making bicycles and progressed to motorcycles, then went on to manufacture a small number of automobiles. The first was made in 1905; it must have been a busy factory then, turning out bicycles of all descriptions, motorcycles, etc. In 1922 an experimental flat twin was built to rival the Rover 8, but never marketed. In 1933 a three-wheeler, the Safety Seven; a 742 cc 'V' twin engine with a three-speed gearbox, it sold well, a full four-seater body costing £110.

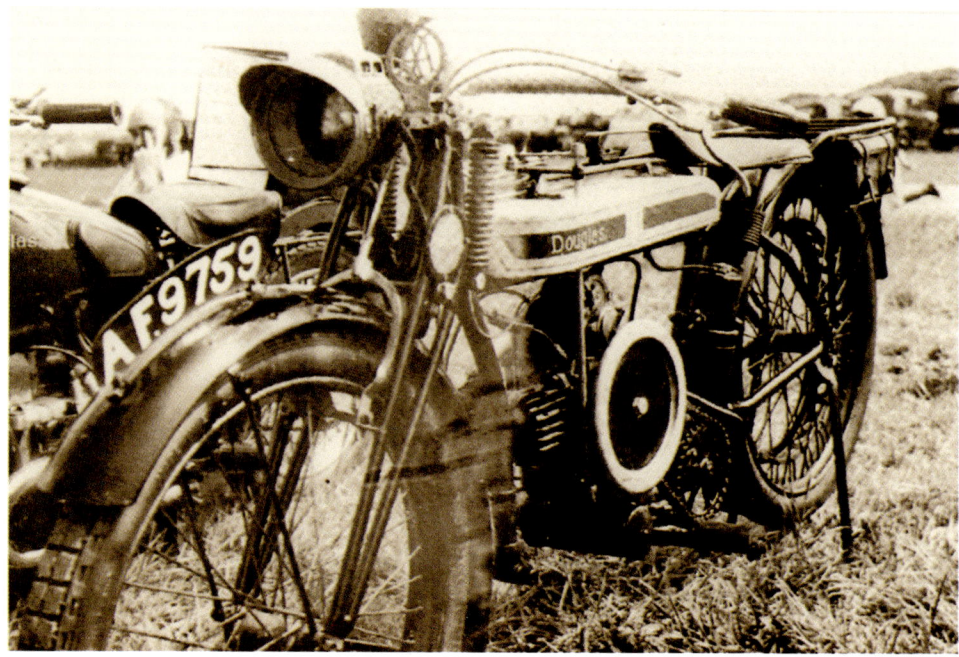

This 2¾ hp Douglas of 1924, registered AF 9759, is seen here at a rally. The rather oversize AA badge looks out from behind the hooded acetylene gas headlight.

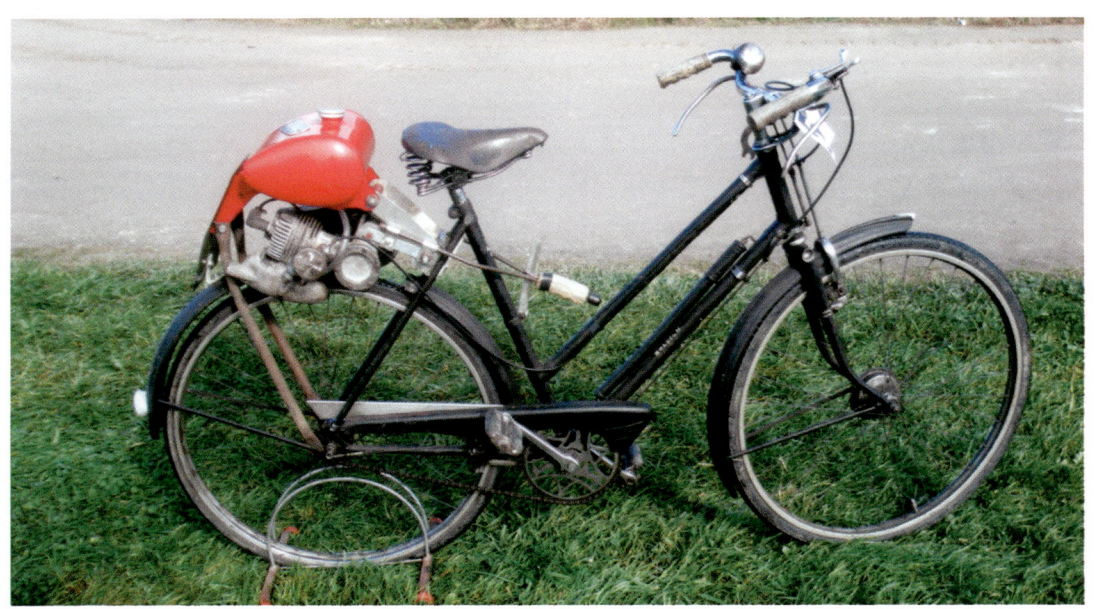

This lovely restored machine belongs to Bobby Smith of Perranporth, which is not far from where it was made by Teagle. It is a bicycle with a bolt-on power unit of 10 cc; the drive was from a friction roller on the rear wheel tyre. The red fuel tank would only hold 5½ pints going through to an Amal carburettor. The handle beneath the saddle was used to ratchet the engine into position. This 1953 model was priced at £18 or, with 12 volt lighting, £20 15s.

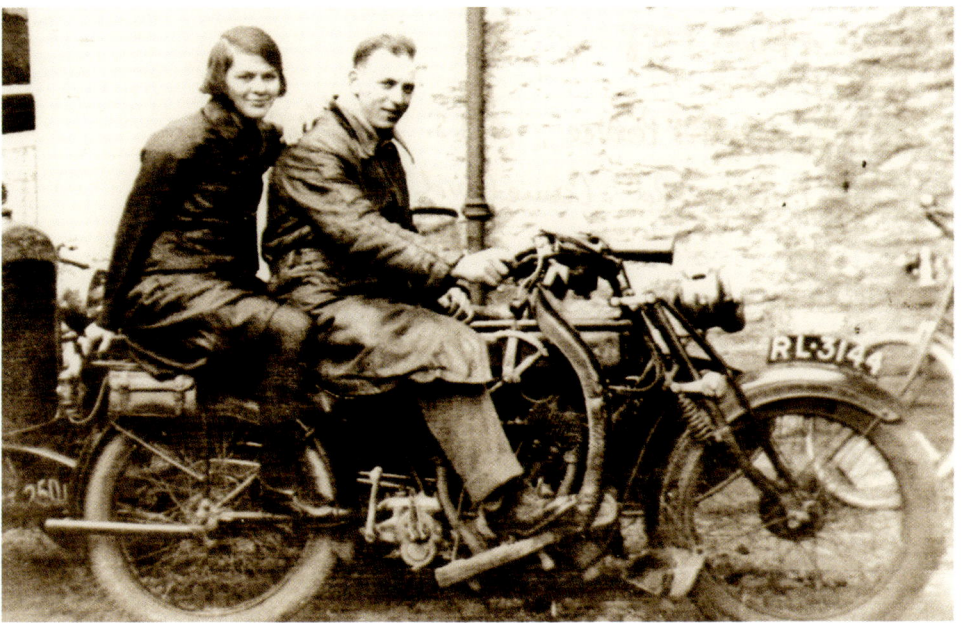

RL 3144 was a 1925 AJS (A. J. Stevens Ltd) motorcycle and sidecar made in Wolverhampton. It was owned by William Pearce, who is shown here with his wife riding on the pillion seat wearing wet weather gear but with no head protection. A sidecar is just visible on the near side. It must have been quite a job to kickstart this machine.

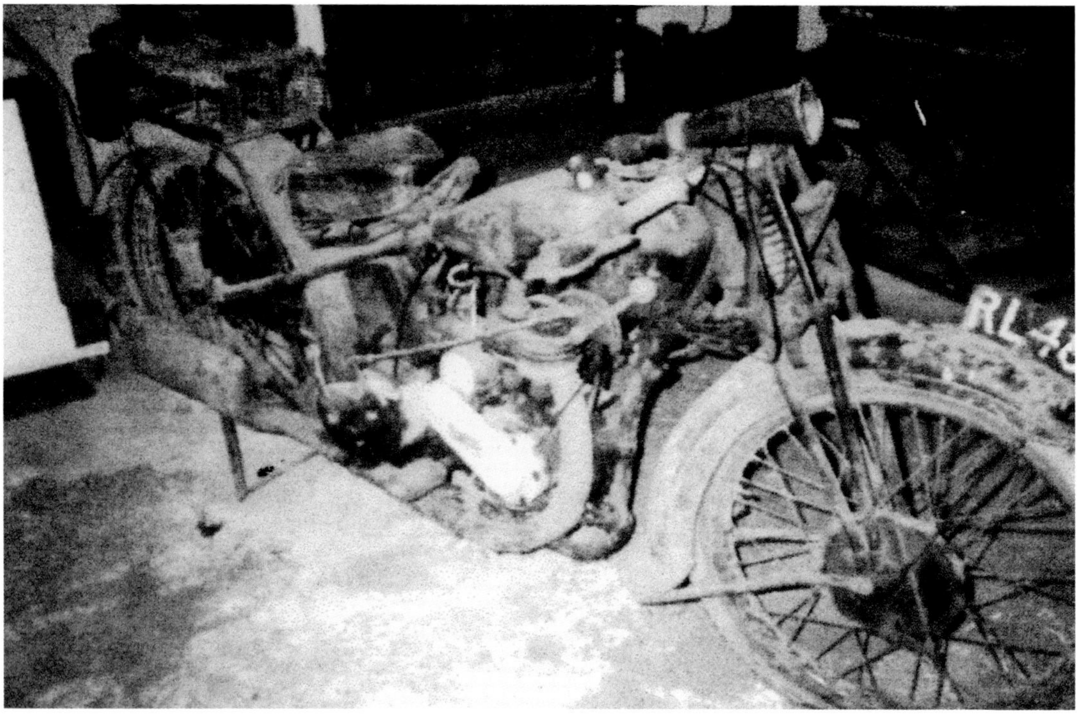

Before and after pictures snapped by Les Willis showing his hours and hours of painstaking hard work restoring this 1931 Ariel, RL 4843, almost to perfection. He tells me it runs better than it looks; the only thing missing is the bulb horn from the handle bars.

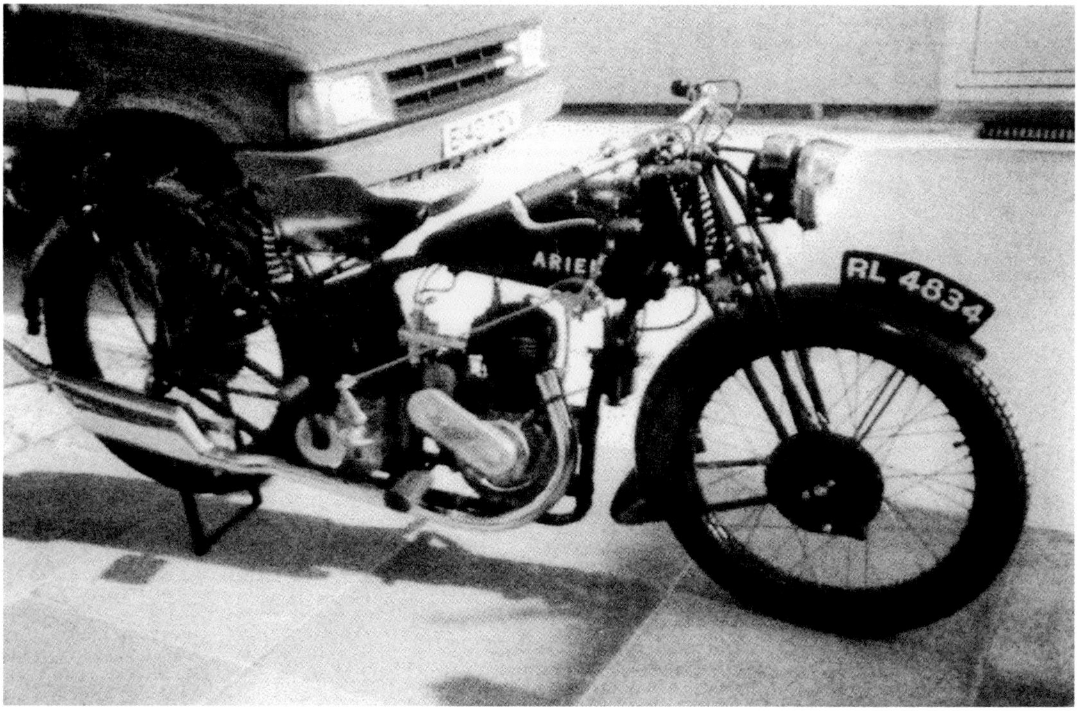

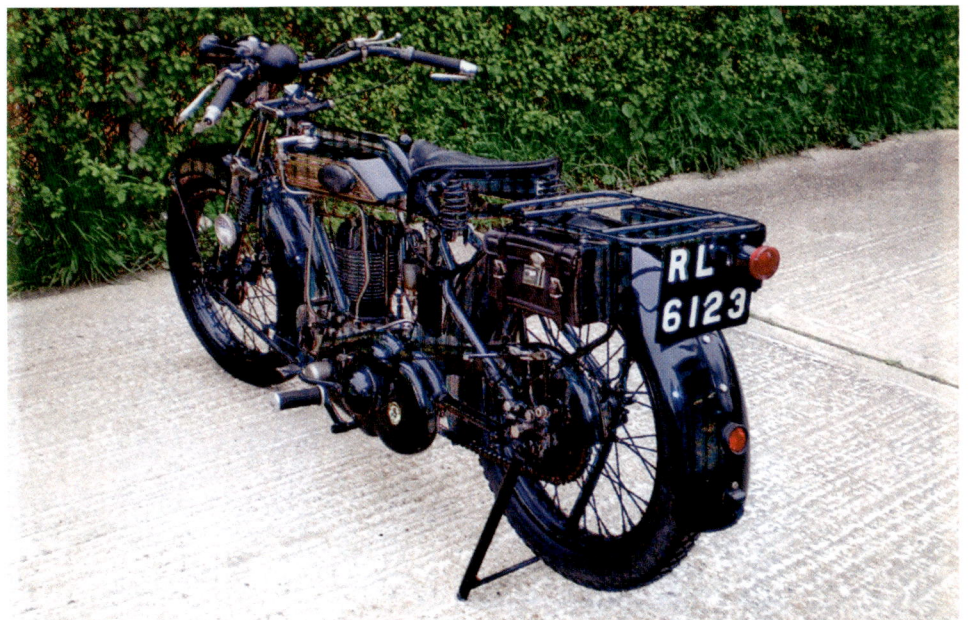

J. B. Wilton owns this 1927 AJS side valve single 500 cc motorcycle. Beautifully restored and used regularly, RL 6123 was in a bit of a state and it took quite some time to get it in the condition seen here. The AJS firm went on to make commercial vehicles and also a car. Prices for the cars ranged from £210 to £240, which was expensive. The parent firm collapsed in 1931 and the design was taken over by Willys-Overland-Crossley Ltd.

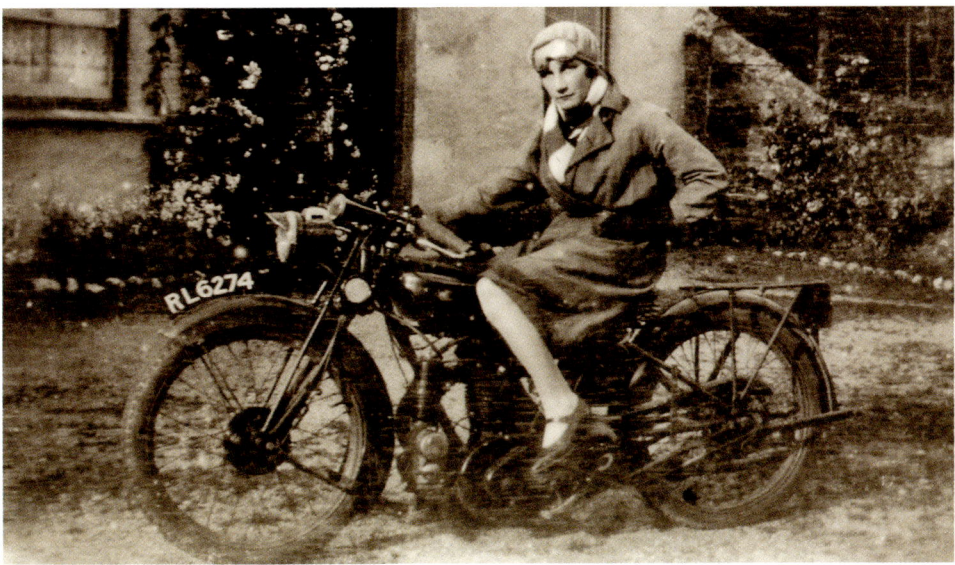

This eighteen-year-old lady, Doris George, is seen here about to go for a quick spin on her James motorcycle, RL 6274, first registered in 1927, at Tehidy. With a scarf around her neck and goggles to protect her eyes, she really looks the part. It appears that she used it quite a lot, going all over Cornwall. She went on to drive an Austin 7 Nippy car and a larger car, an Austin 10 (see the top of page 36).

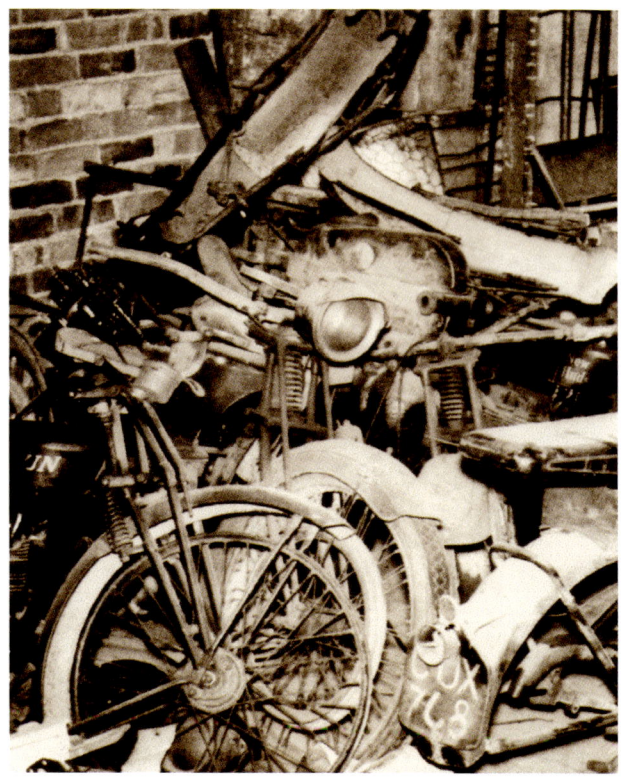

This is the way to find old motorcycles. They belonged to an old dealer named Prowse, living at New Mills, Penzance. At one time they were three or more high when I saw them in the 1960s, but the roof on the shed collapsed and several were stolen. A lot of them were bought as one lot and went 'up-country'. Some of the motorcycles were interesting; indeed, as you can see, one is a 'Sun' and another is a 'New Hudson'.

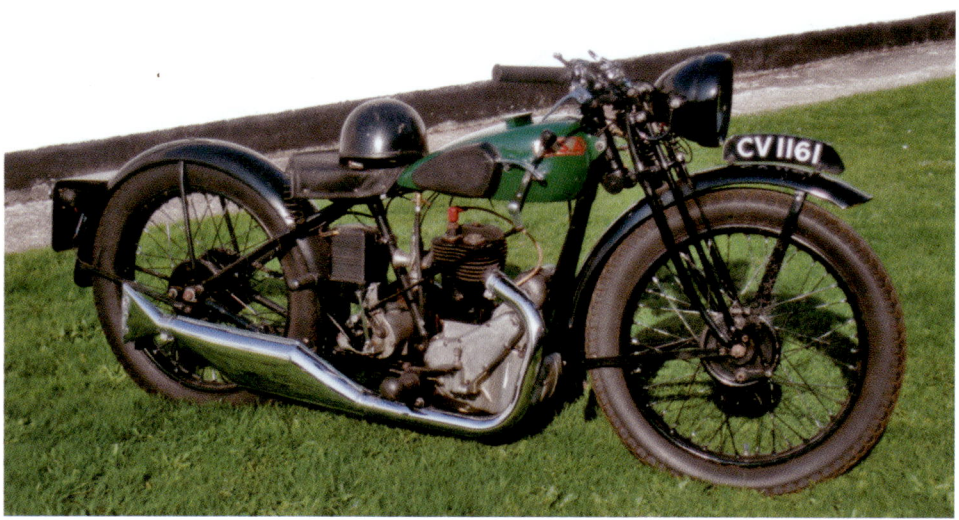

CV 1161, a really lovely restored 350 cc BSA, was made and registered in 1931. It was purchased in the 1990s in pieces in a very poor condition. Almost complete and in numerous small boxes, a lot of painstaking time was spent restoring the motorcycle over a period of time to its wonderful condition. The present owner John Stovell tells me that he enjoyed the project in 2002/3, with the help of his employees, using all original parts where possible. When new, it cost £38.50 and £1.50 road tax; the lump on the saddle is a period helmet!

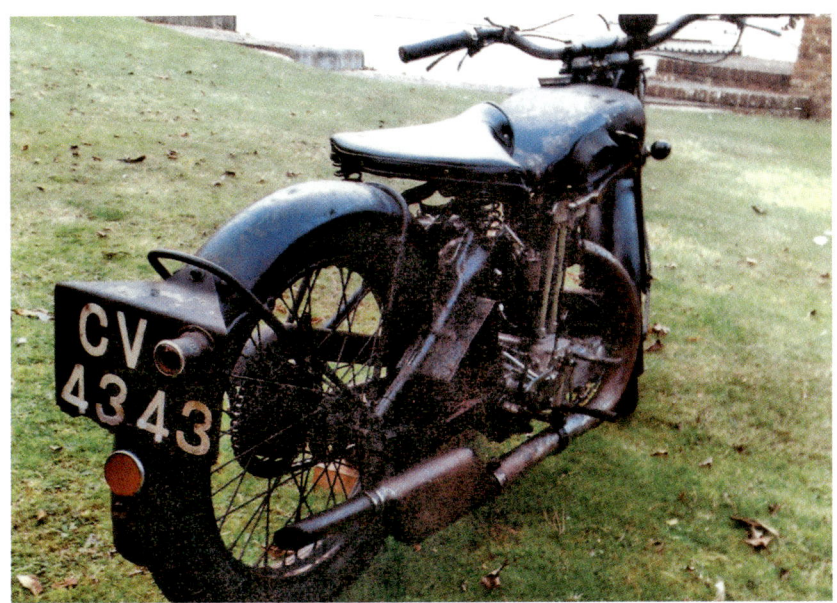

CV 4343 was first registered on 25 March 1931 and last used in 1949. It never left Cornwall until it was bought from Helston and now lives in West Sussex. It is seen here in its totally original condition, including what is left of the paint. The owner has renewed the crankshaft and intends leaving it as it is, a hand-change BSA.

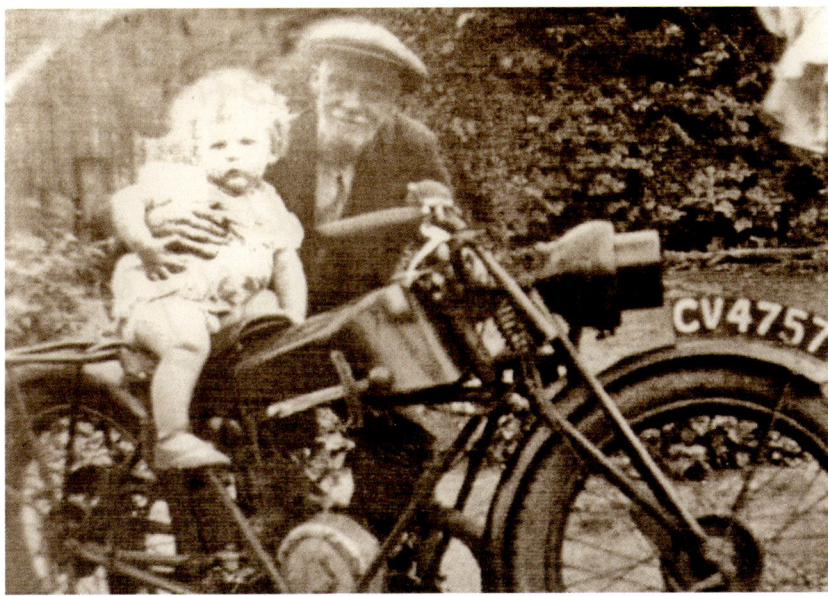

Ned Moyle is seen here in 1941, holding his grandchild Morcom Moyle on the saddle of his Francis Barnett. CV 4757 would be 1930/31. The bike is sporting a headlamp mask to deflect the headlight beam during the Blackout if you were lucky enough to be able to use the machine and had any petrol, because it was rationed.

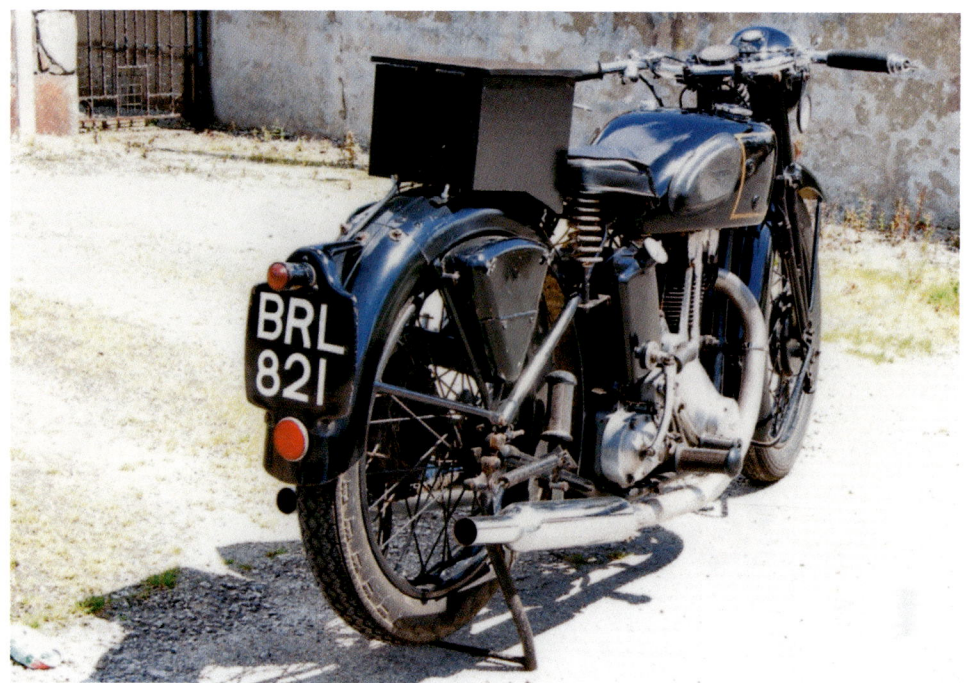

The Triumph in the picture, BRL 821, belongs to Ken Warren. The registration dates it to April 1936, when it was new to Ken's father. The 500 cc twin port single cylinder came into the present owner's hands 40 years ago; he restored it and it still goes very well.

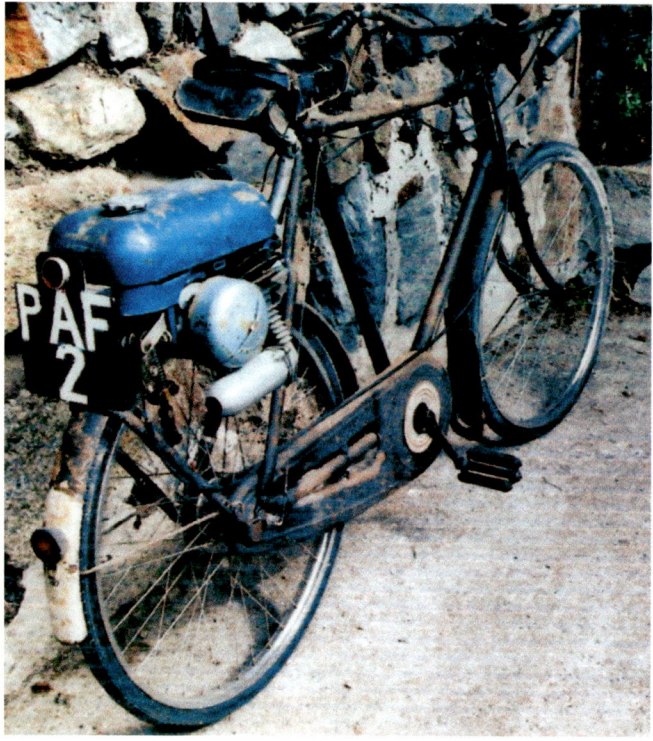

A most unusual little 45 cc Trojan model made by the Mini Motor Co. of Croydon in 1952. Purchased more than 50 years ago, it was kept in boxes for that entire time. It was the first motorised machine the present owner, Peter Ford, owned and assembled – a friction roller driven from the rear tyre. It has a lovely old Cornish number, PAF 2, and a fuel capacity of ¾ gallon, giving 144 mpg. Looking at the photograph, it needs another restoration.

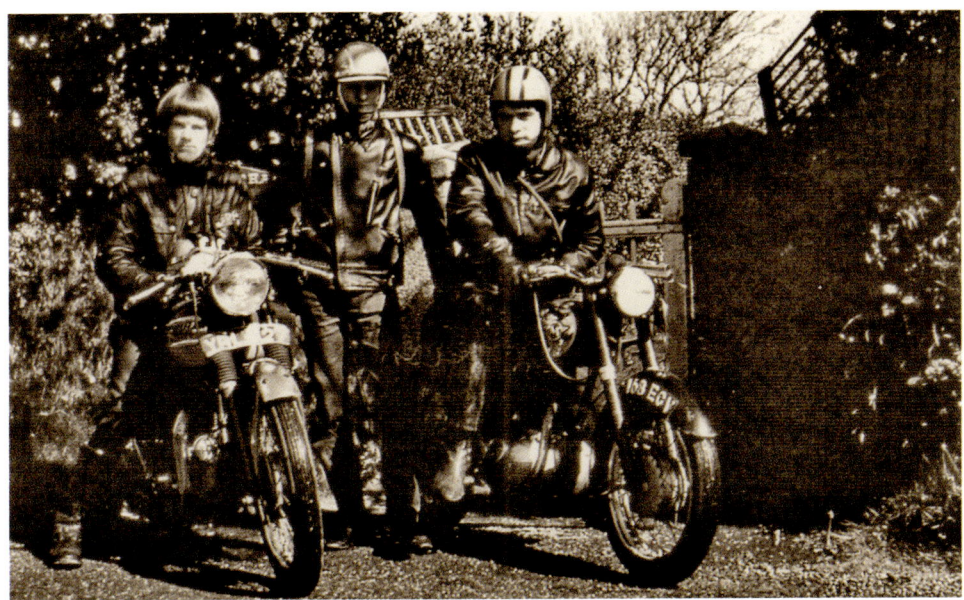

Taken at Tehiddy. From left to right, see Trevor George sitting on his 1957 Triumph twin-speed YRL ?27; Ivan Pockinghorne standing; Keith Phaby astride a Matchless G2, also 1957, 158 ECV. The last two are still wearing their space helmets – with shiny tyres, they must have just driven through some puddles.

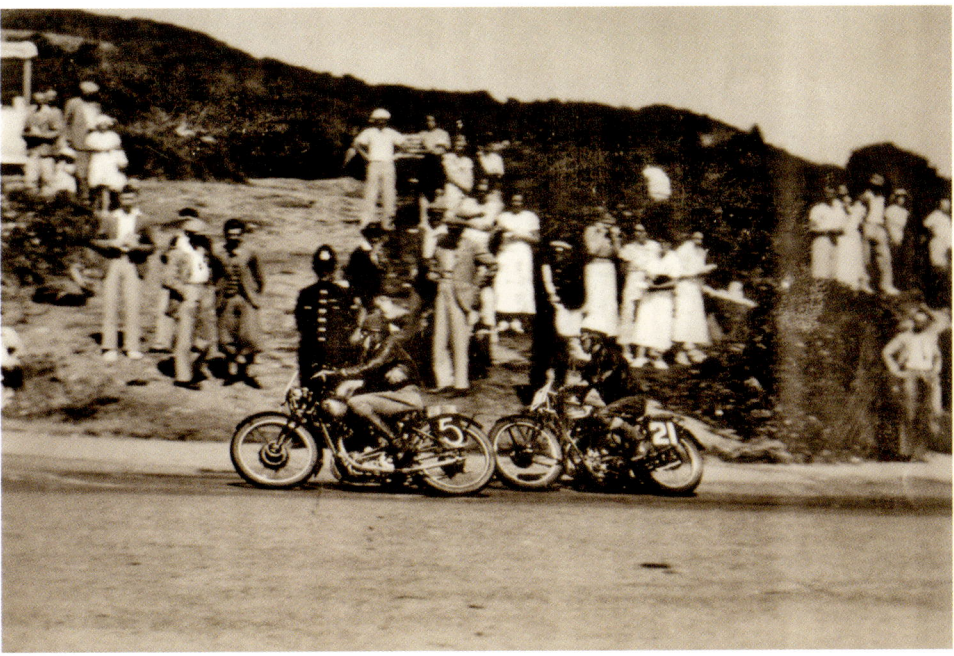

Motorcycle racing around Castle Drive, Falmouth, on the August Bank Holiday, 1935. In the morning 350 cc event, R. Greatbatch on a New Imperial endeavours to pass T. H. Foster astride a Rudge. These races were very popular for many years.

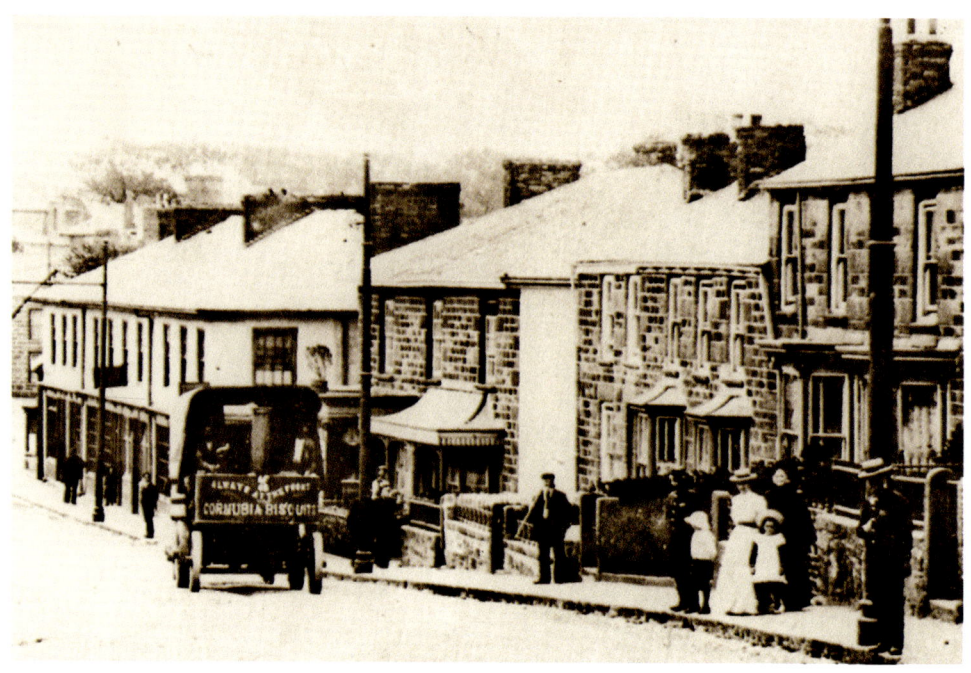

'Always at the Front, Cornubia Biscuits' is painted on the front of this Thornycroft steam lorry, AF 45, of Hayle Flour Millers, ascending Fore Street, Pool.

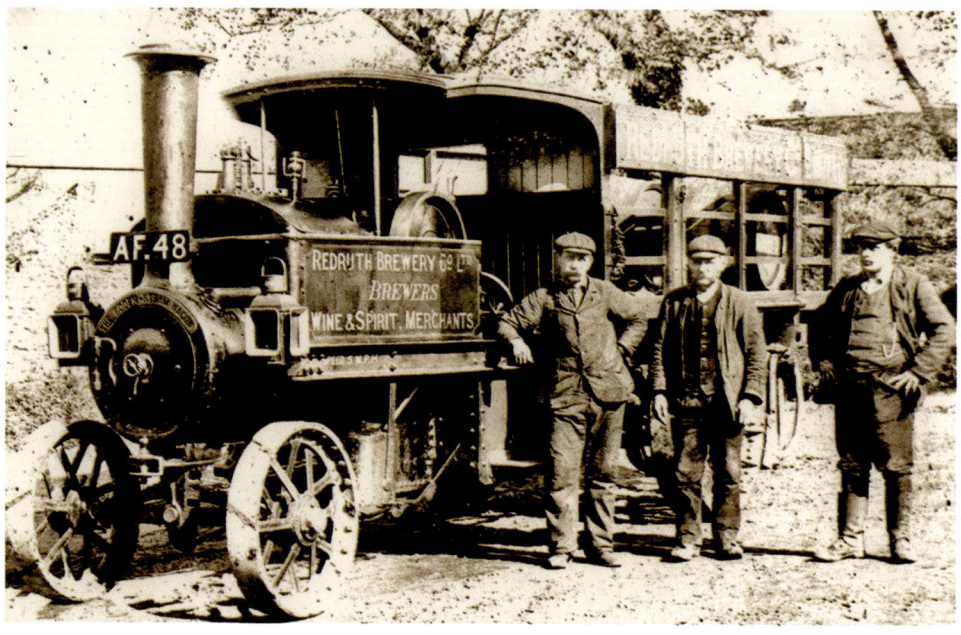

At a speed limit of 5 mph, this 'FODEN STEAM WAGON' (marked below the base of the chimney) belongs to, as it says on the name plate, 'REDRUTH BREWERY CO. LTD BREWERS, WINE AND SPIRIT MERCHANTS.' AF 48 dates it to 1904. Running on iron wheels, it must have made a lot of noise, but what a lovely pair of oil lamps. The three men posing are Billy Dunn; -?-; and Harry Yeo, waiting for this photograph to be taken.

Tehidy House is the name of this horse-drawn fire engine. The Merryweather, built between 1891 and 1893, was bought new by the Bassett family of Camborne. Although records show they bought one earlier in 1865, costing £432 8s ½d, that one could pump 250 gallons a minute. This fire engine is thought to have been taken to Truro following a disastrous fire in the city, taking part in a demonstration and jetting water over the spire of St Mary's church. It is now owned and maintained by the West of England Steam Engine Society – who cleans all that brass?

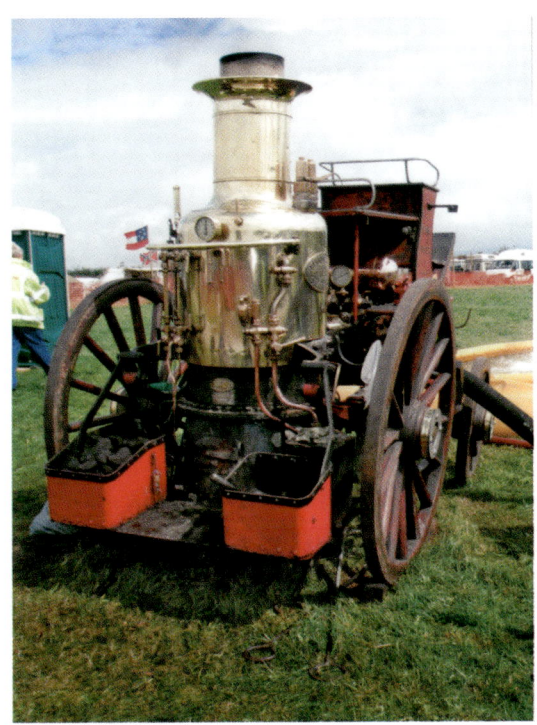

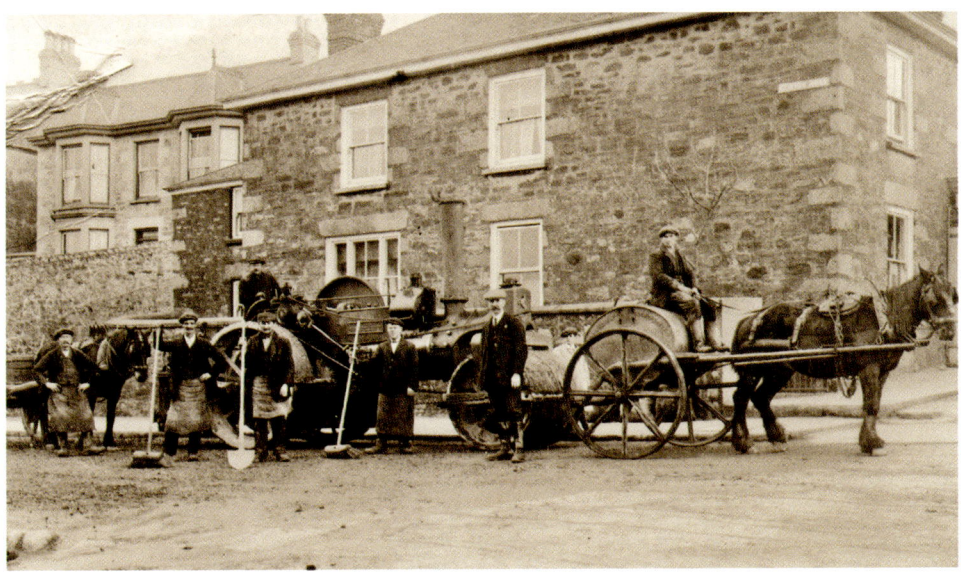

Clinton Road, South Downs, Redruth is the scene of this photograph. The Trefusis Arms public house is behind the horse's head. The horse is pulling a water tank to cool the tar and stop it sticking to the roller of the steam engine behind it, which could be a Fowler. This area is notorious for old tin mine shafts. Recently the house on the extreme left collapsed; the shaft was capped and now a new house stands there, almost the same shape as the original. The workmen have stopped work, including the foreman with the tie. There is one more Cornish connection, which is the shovel one man is holding. See the shape of it? – 'Tis a real Cornish shovel, me handsome.'

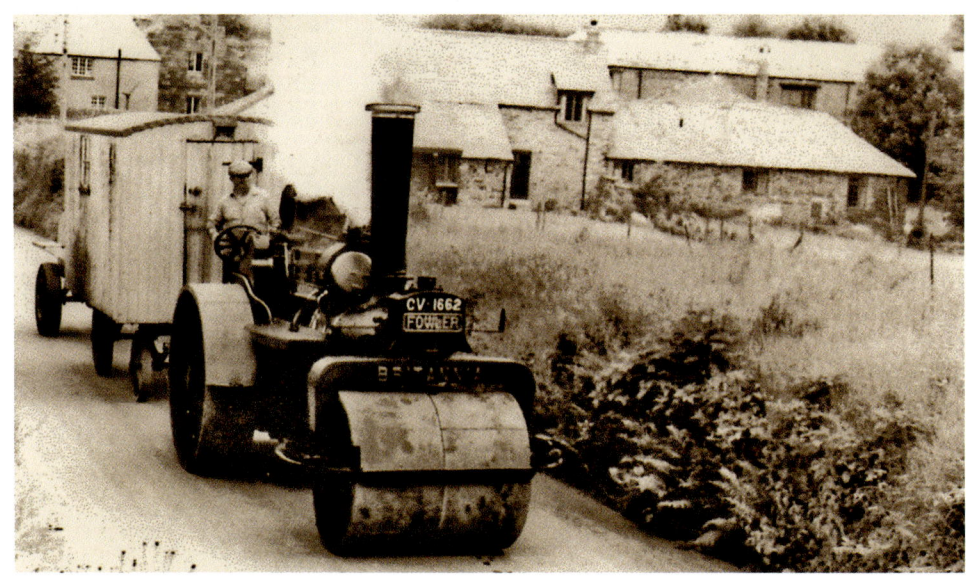

CV 1662, from about 1930, a Fowler 20-ton Britannia steam roller, is seen here towing a workman's caravan and a water cart. This was one of the first steam rollers to be preserved by Dingles of Stoke Climsland after a lifetime of use by them all over Cornwall.

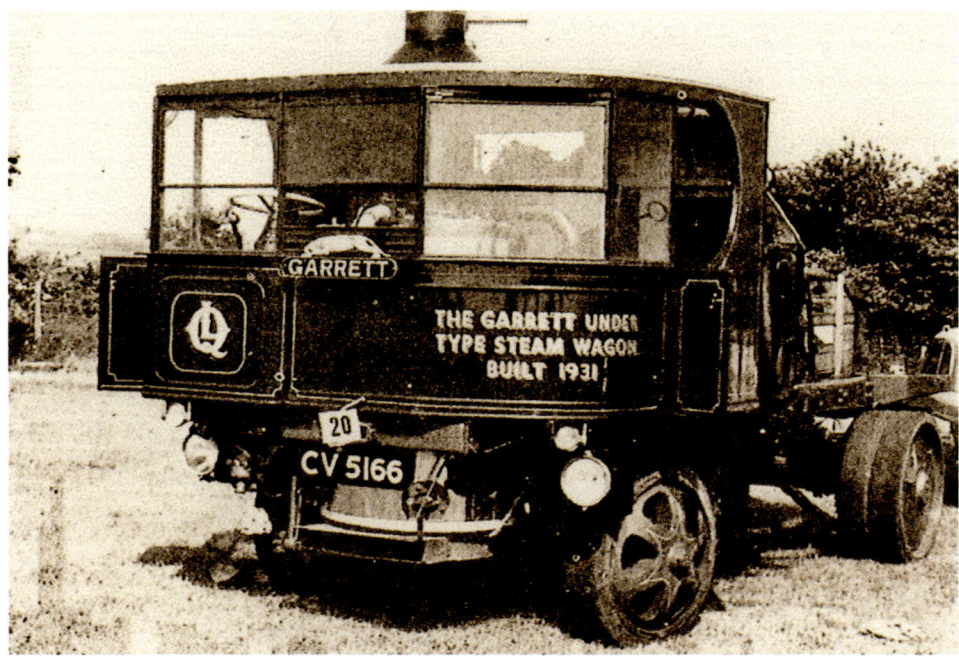

This Garrett QL End Tipper, weight 8 tons, was built in 1931 with a registration number of CV 5166, bought new by Glover & Uglow of Callington. Later sold to Cornwall County Council in 1949, it was used until 1954. This vehicle was completely restored and rebuilt by the Goold brothers of Camerton. It is the last Garrett with solid tyres ever built. Chain driven to the rear wheels and with modern driving lights and a number 20 showing, it must have been at a static display when this photograph was taken.

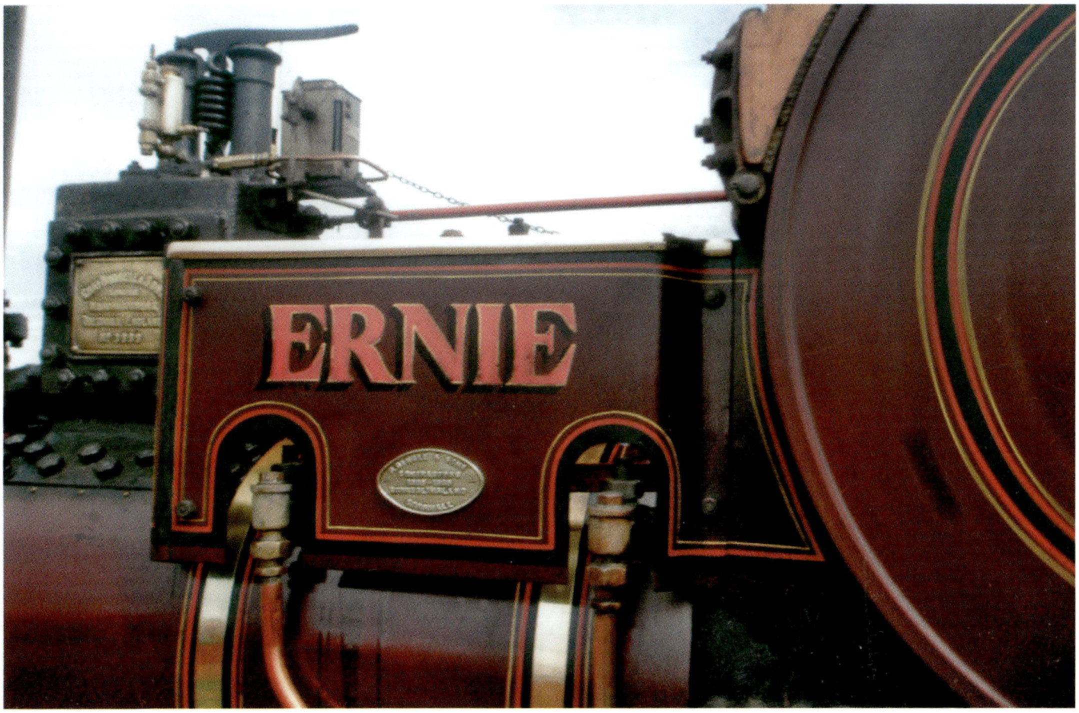

Ernie, a 5 hp, 12 ton Burrell Class A single cylinder steam roller, was built in 1924 and registered RL 74. Supplied new to Messrs R. Dingle & Sons, Stoke Crimsland, it spent most of its working life in the Penryn area. Acquired by the present owners in a partly dismantled condition and completely rebuilt to its present state, it lives with the Sanders at Herniss near Penryn.

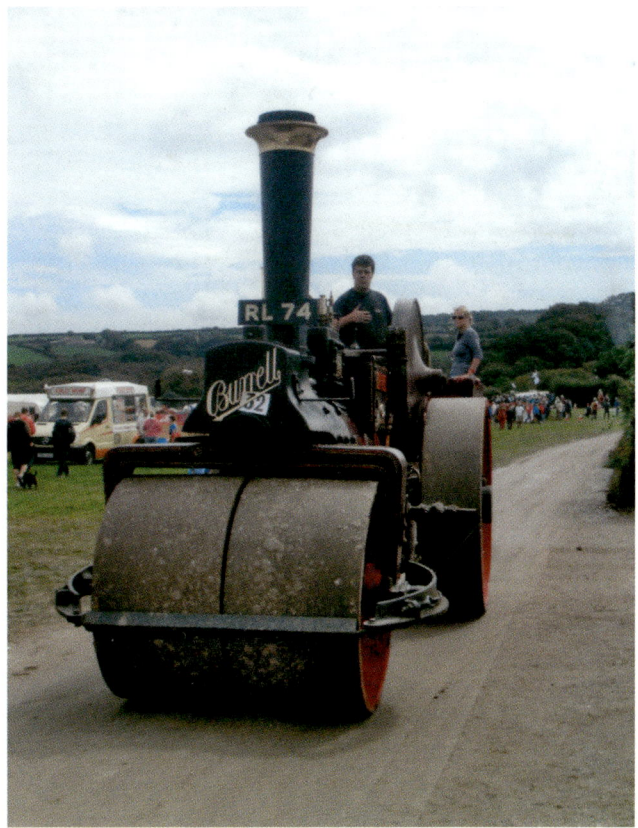

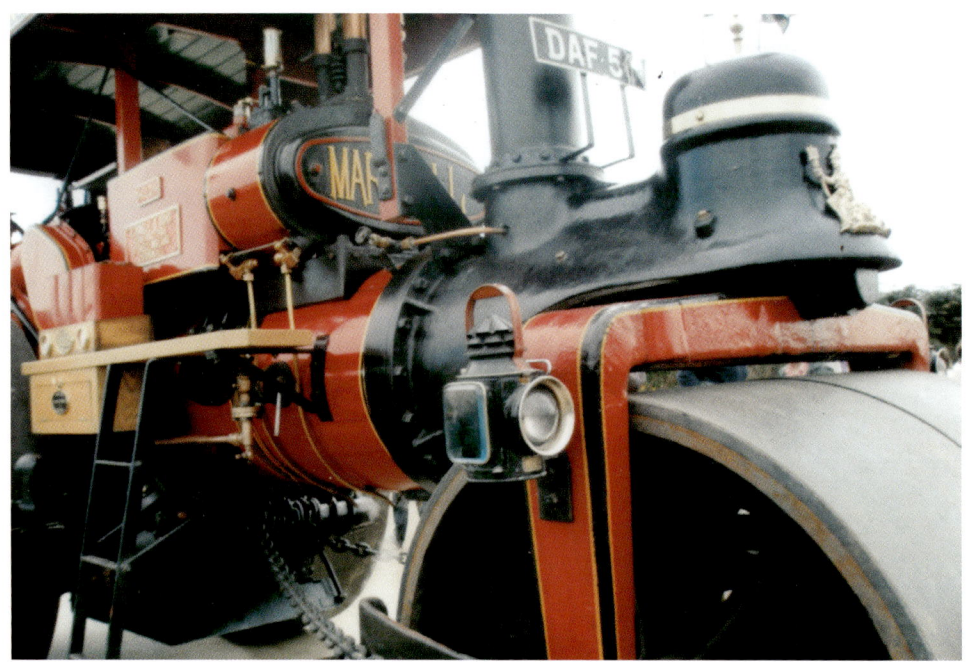

DAF 560, a Marshall built in 1937, has been named *Hilda*. A 12-ton, 6 hp S type compound piston valve roller, it was new to R. Dingle & Sons and was used up until the 1960s. Once owned by John Pengelly of Penryn, who fully rebuilt it in 1969, it is now owned by Cyril Thomas, who acquired the vehicle in 2003 and carried out further extensive work.

The end of another perfect weekend at the West of England Steam Engine Society rally. *Toby*, DAF 499, and its owners say goodbye with young Peter Heal, a keen enthusiast, looking behind.

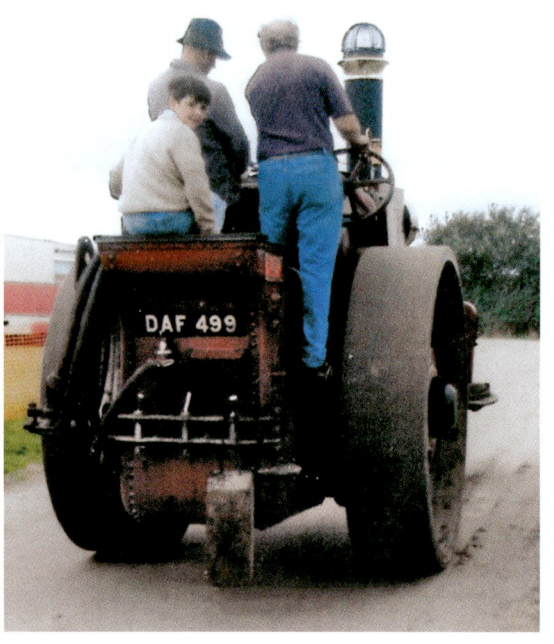

I sincerely hope you have enjoyed this book, my first attempt at writing about Cornish transport. My next will include cycling, flying, ballooning, car and passenger ferries and trains as well as more of what you have just read. Do you have any postcards, photographs similar that I may borrow to copy? I will be happy to hear from you.